人际投射小句与主体间性的语篇建构

Interpersonal Projection Clauses and the Discursive Construction of Intersubjectivity

辛志英 ◎ 著

厦门大学出版社 国家一级出版社
XIAMEN UNIVERSITY PRESS 全国百佳图书出版单位

图书在版编目(CIP)数据

人际投射小句与主体间性的语篇建构/辛志英著.—厦门:厦门大学出版社,2012.10
ISBN 978-7-5615-4448-8

Ⅰ.①人… Ⅱ.①辛… Ⅲ.①英语-语言学-研究 Ⅳ.①H31

中国版本图书馆 CIP 数据核字(2012)第 251504 号

厦门大学出版社出版发行

(地址:厦门市软件园二期望海路 39 号 邮编:361008)
http://www.xmupress.com
xmup @ xmupress.com

厦门市金凯龙印刷有限公司印刷

2012 年 10 月第 1 版 2012 年 10 月第 1 次印刷
开本:889×1194 1/32 印张:12.5 插页:2
字数:339 千字 印数:1~1 500 册
定价:37.00 元
本书如有印装质量问题请直接寄承印厂调换

本书获厦门大学外文学院外国语言文学博士一级学科授权点建设经费资助

序 一

　　学位论文是获取博士学位的一项必备条件，但也充满了挑战。辛志英在厦门大学攻读博士学位期间给我留下了深刻的印象。她充分利用时间，广泛阅读语言学的有关书刊，潜心开展研究工作，积极参加各种学术活动，在国内外本学科学术刊物上发表了多篇文章，表现出很好的科研潜力。记得辛志英在撰写博士学位论文时，认真搜集有关投射小句和主体间性的资料，并联系国内外有关学者，讨论有关问题，全身心地投入研究工作。在完成了学位论文的初稿之后，辛志英能精益求精，认真进行了数次的修改，不断完善，完成了博士学位论文的研究和写作工作，并获得了省优秀博士学位论文一等奖。

　　辛志英博士在博士学位论文的基础上，完成了《人际投射小句与主体间性的语篇建构》一书。我们知道，人际投射小句是系统功能语言学的一种重要概念，也是人们表达意义的一种重要资源，因此得到了许多学者的研究和探讨，但大多涉及投射小句的内部句法关系或其主体的情态评价。辛志英在书中回顾了不同学者对人际投射小句的研究，并进行分析归纳，指出以前研究的不足之处，在此基础上运用系统功能语言学的理论，提出人际投射小句的概念，把人际投射小句看作加强主体间性的有效资源。该书强调投射小句的人际功能，区分出了四类人际投射小句。为了说明人际投射小句的语篇行为，该书搜集英语语言学书评和语言学刊物编者按作为语料，考察了英语语言学书评中人际投射小句的运作机制，充分结合量化分析方法，详细统计和比较了人际投射小句的分布，说明各类人际投射小句的使用差异，讨论人际投射小句的主体间加强功能，指出人际投射小句的使用受制于语篇的语类属性和社会交际功能。可见，辛志英博士的研究做到了理论和实际分析相结合，很好地把功能语言学理论与英语语言学书评和编者按的分析结合起来,不仅提供了研究人际功能的新视角,而且加深了读者对人际投射小句的认识和理解。

几年来,辛志英博士在学术道路上埋头苦干,刻苦钻研。我相信她在今后的岁月中能再接再厉,产生更多的科研成果,取得更大的成绩。

杨信彰

2012 年 5 月

于厦门大学

序 二

记得是2007年7月，我应信彰兄邀请到厦门大学参加他的三个博士生的论文答辩；到机场来接我的博士生中就有辛志英。当知道她姓辛时，我马上想起了南宋词人辛弃疾和他的《丑奴儿·书博山道中壁》。这首词的关键词是"愁"，这是众所周知的，但如果把"愁"这个核心词换成"学术论文写作"，应该也是可以说上几句的：人年轻的时候不知道怎样写论文，当然也不知道做学问的苦滋味，不懂怎么写又不得不写（因为有这样的考核和那样的评估），因此也就硬着头皮写，这就是"为赋新词强说愁"；等到你成熟了，懂得游刃有余地在学术圈圈里自由行走了，尝到了做学问的酸甜苦辣了，对很多问题有体会、有主见了，想写出来了，但却最终没有说（因为这样的考核和那样的评估与我无关了），这就是"欲说还休"，所以就干脆谈论天气了。通过对辛弃疾的这首词的"新解"，我想说明这样一个人生的道理：当你有时间有精力的时候你没有钱，当你有精力有钱的时候你没有时间，当你有时间有钱时却没有精力，这就是人生的几个不同的阶段。因此，生活总是有缺陷和遗憾，这样大家才不断有新的追求，人间才有悲欢离合。也正因为人生是这样充满矛盾，所以我们更应该珍惜已经拥有的，用好属于自己的分分秒秒，过好生活的每一天。

辛志英给我的第一印象是很好的，最深的一点是对学问的执着。从与她的交谈中得知，她曾想来中山大学读书，但由于种种原因本科硕士博士都没有来到中山大学。凑巧的是，2008年中山大学开始实行国内博士生访学项目，专门招收名牌大学在读的博士生到学校访学一年。因此，志英就来参加这个项目，她攻读博士学位的第三年是在中山大学度过的。2009年7月，志英博士毕业后到中山大学做了两年博士后研究，我也第二次当了她的合作导师。屈指一算，她在中山大学整整度过了三年,比本科少一年,比硕士多一年(中山大学的硕士是二年制)。

辛志英在中山大学的三年里,我们一起做了很多事情,除了研讨学术问题和谈论人生外,还合作发表多篇论文,一起合编合著了三本书:《功能语言学通论》(北京:外语教学与研究出版社,2011)、《系统功能语言学研究现状和发展趋势》(北京:外语教学与研究出版社,2012)、《什么是功能语法?》(上海:上海外语教育出版社,2012)。志英的理论基础特别扎实,学术写作也训练有素;与她一起探讨学术问题常常能够得到启发,和她一起做研究和写作是一件非常愉快的事。

辛志英是同龄人中的佼佼者,这是不言而喻的。志英是一位勤奋的学者,也是一个多产的作者。她的博士论文在厦门大学(后来还在福建省)获得优秀博士论文的称号,她在中山大学的博士后研究也获得优秀。凭着许多的"优秀"和在国际国内的重要期刊发表的学术论文以及所申请到的科研项目,辛志英博士后一出站又回到厦门大学,从"讲师"一步晋升到了"教授"。对此我特别高兴,仿佛在茫茫学海中找到了"同伴",因为我当年从英国学成回国时也是从"讲师"直接升为"教授"的。

辛志英的博士论文研究的是人际投射小句。这是个较为新颖的领域。大家知道,在系统功能语言学里,投射通常是在概念功能的范围内讨论的。志英能够跳出窠臼,选取从人际功能的视角审视投射现象,实属难得。罗丹说过,美是无处不在的,缺少的是发现美的眼睛。诗人顾城也曾说过:"黑夜给了我黑色的眼睛,我却用它来寻找光明。"把这两句话用在做学问上,就是要善于发现新问题,善于选取独到的角度,善于用新的方法解决问题。从志英的专著看,她注意到了学界对主观性的研究,并顺势把主观性往前推进了一大步,直接研究主体间性。这在国内国际都是很前沿的。可以说,志英的研究在语法、功能和语篇之间找到了一个上佳的契合点。她能够围绕着"人际投射小句"这个现象写出洋洋洒洒数十万字,是颇需要些训练和功夫的。我曾说过,做文章,要么做大,要么做小。说做大,是做理论建构或研究综述，好处是可以做得大气，纵揽全局，为所在学科或领域的发展把脉。说做小，是围绕一个具体问题具体现象深入研究，如志英的这部专著。好处是可以做得很深入、透彻，需要研究者拥有深厚的学术素养、观察问题的独到眼光和进行系统分析的能力。

辛志英这部专著的另一个意义所在是，做学问写文章要有主线、有框架、有条理。这个主线就是"气"，是不能散的，不然文章就没有了精气神。框架是"气"的外在构型，如同人的五官体型一样，要匀称养眼，要"体现""气"，有什么样的"气"，就要有什么样的外型来匹配体现。条理是组织网络，内接主线，外连框架。这些都处理好了，才算搭配停当，可以拿出去见人了。从这三点看，志英的专著算是符合标准的。其实，做学问和演戏拍电影一样，都讲戏里戏外：戏里，你有要扮演的角色；但是如何演好，更多是戏外的功夫。就是说，要"入戏"，要用心，要上心。做学问也是如此。据我所知，志英一直在做人际意义方面的研究，2011 年还以人际投射为题申请到了博士后基金特别资助项目。这样专心做事情，当然一定会有收获的。

很高兴看到志英在学术领域的茁壮成长；我相信，她的学术潜力还会更好地发挥出来。我们期待阅读她的下一本书，期待她更上一层楼。

是为序。

黄国文

2012 年 5 月 11 日

于中山大学康乐园

前　言

　　历经几番修改，倾注了我三年心血的博士论文终于破茧而出，以专著的形式面世了。付梓之际，回想起读书时的点点滴滴。记忆像放映机，瞬间仿佛时光倒流，那些苦乐参半的日子历历在目。重现在脑海里的那个自己，奔波于图书馆—饭堂—宿舍三点一线，磕绊在"山重水复疑无路"和"柳暗花明又一村"之间，又忽而沉浮于无涯苦作舟的书海里，或在思考中忽然听到晨起鸟儿的欢叫，亦或是在厦大博士楼那一方斗室来回踱步。在写作的日子里，常常苦苦思考无果，不洗不漱和衣而卧，昏昏含恨睡去。

　　这个让我欢喜让我忧日思夜想难舍弃的东西就是人际投射小句。我要用功能语言学和语篇分析的知识，捕捉它飘忽不定的行踪，揭开它神秘的面纱。用学术术语讲，我的研究就是试图在系统功能语言学的框架下，从人际意义出发研究投射现象。具体说，就是通过考察人际投射小句在英语语言学书评这一特定语类中的语篇行为特征，论证人际投射小句是语言使用者用来加强主体间性的有效资源。本书采用定性和定量结合的研究方法。

　　本书的研究首先涉及两个重要概念，即人际投射小句和主体间性。前者指通过投射识解人际意义的小句。后者指语言使用者对交际双方的参与程度、关注程度以及适合特定社会义化语境的社会规约这三者的间接调控。

　　以往的研究或者从单纯的句法关系考察人际投射小句同被投射句之间的关系，或者从语义上探讨人际投射小句如何体现说话人的主体情态评价等，但都缺乏对该语言现象的系统研究，尤其是对主体间性语篇建构的考察。本书提出人际投射小句的概念，并通过对真实语料的观察和分析，识别人际投射小句的种类，建立了较为完善的分析框架。我们认为，人际投射小句特有的句法特征和语义特征使其成为有效的主体间性加强语。我们同时认为，人际投射小句的语篇行为特征受制于特定语篇的语类属性。

本研究识别了四种人际投射小句。由于人际投射涉及交际双方，因此识别和划分人际投射小句的标准是依据作者/读者在语篇中的"可见程度"以及与投射者之间的关系。具体而言，第一种人际投射小句，即 I 类人际投射小句，通过 I/you 将作者/读者直接识解为投射者。第二种人际投射小句，即 we 类人际投射小句，通过 we/one/reader 等资源将作者/读者识解为投射者中的一员。第三种人际投射小句，即无交互方类人际投射小句，不出现投射者。第四种人际投射小句，即非交互方类人际投射小句，投射者识解的是非作者/读者的"第三方"。本研究旨在揭示人际投射小句的实质是语言使用者用以加强主体间性而实施的有效手段。因此，贯穿本书整体结构的主线有两条：一条是对人际投射小句的系统及其词汇语法体现资源系统的描写，一条是语篇中的主体间性如何通过人际投射小句系统得以建立和突显。

本书由七个篇章组成。第一章"导论"介绍了本研究的理论背景、研究意义、研究方法、语料的收集处理和全书的结构框架。

第二章"文献综述"，分别从传统的描写、语块研究、认知语言学、修辞学、文体学和结构功能语言学等领域对人际投射现象的研究，指出以往研究的不足和存在的问题，从而为本书的研究寻找突破点和研究路径。被尊为"西太后"的英国著名服装设计师 Vivienne Westwood 曾说过，"寻觅想法的唯一途径是回顾人们过去做过些什么。这才是令你产生创作的方法。你无法光凭想象创作，因为空盒子不会变出任何东西。"这适用于任何领域。

第三章"理论框架"首先提出了人际投射小句的分析框架，然后在系统功能语言学框架内将元功能的互补性、投射的跨元功能体现、语类和主体间性等主要概念纳入本研究的分析框架。这里面一个非常重要的理念就是把概念投射和人际投射看作互为补充的关系，它们共同协作对经验作不同的识解。

本书第四、五、六章是本研究的核心部分。第四章分析描写英语语言学书评的语类属性和语类结构潜势,并对英语语言学书评和英语语言学杂志编者按两种语篇进行了语类对比分析,着重指出两者在社会功能属性和社会服务目的方面的异同。本章是为接下来的两章对人际投射小句的分析做铺垫。要描写人际投射小句对主体间性在语篇中的建构作用,首先要确定所在语篇的社会属性,语篇参与者的社会身份,等等。这些都是本章要解决的问题。

第五章和第六章实证研究各类人际投射小句的词汇语法体现资源。同时,还对人际投射小句进行英语语言学书评和英语语言学杂志编者按的语类对比研究。通过这两种不同语类的对比,本研究指出,作为主体间性加强语的人际投射小句的语篇行为受制于特定语类的语类属性和社会交际功能。此外,第五第六章还着重探讨了投射小句的作者读者联盟,读者取位和人际衔接等主体间性加强功能。

本研究的主要发现包括:

(1) 文献回顾表明,尽管人际投射现象不乏关注,但存在以下几点不足:很少从投射角度分析此类现象;较少从它的主体间性建构角度考察;更缺少从语篇层面上描写分析人际投射;较少把此类现象的分析同不同的或特定的语篇类型相结合。这些也是本研究试图解决的问题。

(2) 通过考察两个平行语料库中的语料,依据人际投射小句中的投射者是否识解交际双方,本研究发现了四类人际投射小句,分别是 I 类人际投射小句、WE 类人际投射小句、无交际方类人际投射小句和非交际方类人际投射小句。这四类人际投射小句形成一个连续统,从 I 类到非交际方类依据交际方在小句中的"可见程度"依次减弱。

(3) 研究发现,人际投射小句的语篇行为与语篇类型有密切关系。在英语语言学书评这一语类中,作者一方面要告知读者所评论作品的内容,同时还要作出客观有说服力的评价。人际投射小句与语类之间的关系体现在,书评作者常常使用人际投射小句资源来实施与读者的联盟,引导读者的注意力和兴趣取向。这是因为,在此类语篇中的人际风险要比其他语篇中的高(参见 Hyland,2000)。

(4)通过对两种语篇类型的对比分析,研究发现它们所具有的语类属性是不同的。英语语言学杂志编者按本质上是积极评价的,更接近于广告类型的语篇。在此类语篇中,作者通过使用人际投射小句来说服读者接受所宣传的学术产品。对比分析表明,人际投射小句的语篇行为主要受制于社会赋予不同语篇的不同交际功能和属性。大致说来,在英语语言学书评中,人际投射小句主要用以加强主体间性,尤其是当作者预见到可能的人际冲突时。而在英语语言学杂志编者按中,人际投射小句则主要用来引起和维系读者对所推荐文章的兴趣,从而给读者留下正面的良好印象,达到宣传的目的。

从具体的分析来看,作为主体间性加强资源的人际投射小句,在使用频次、词汇语法体现资源(主要体现在过程类型、时态和情态化)、与语类结构潜势要素的配置等方面都体现出语类内的和语类际的差异。同时,在加强主体间性时,人际投射小句还体现出多功能性的特质。

本研究的意义主要包括:

(1)系统回顾了以往对人际投射小句的研究。在总结前人研究的基础上,指出不足,并构建了在系统功能语言学框架下分析人际投射小句的理论架构。

(2)本研究从语类结构潜势等方面详细分析了两类语篇类型(英语语言学书评和英语语言学杂志编者按),以及它们与人际投射小句之间的关系。本研究对人际投射小句的跨语类分析采取学科内的视角,这样与当下流行的学科际视角形成互补。同时,本研究采取的视角也将对如何对类似的语言现象进行跨语类分析提供了参照。

(3)本研究的发现具有教学指导意义,尤其是对语言教学、外语教学以及学术写作具有具体的指导意义。

本书得以出版,我要感谢很多人。首先我要感谢恩师杨信彰先生。杨先生是个极其认真、极讲原则的人。他看学生的论文,是小到定冠词、不定冠词都要改的。他批注用的红笔都不知道用掉多少支。不夸张地说,他带的学生,都是他一笔一笔批改调教出来的。除了做事认真的态度,我还从杨先生那里学到很多做学问的"秘诀"。他曾说过,"博士是做出来的,不是读出来的。"我深深体会到这一点。写博士论文是一项浩大的工程。从设计到具体操作都马虎不得,不然就会前功尽弃。同时最重要的是,要有自己的想法,并把它合理论证出来。我跟杨先生学到的另一个秘诀是:时时刻刻问自己"你到底要做什么?"。我写博士论文时把这句话贴在我抬眼所及的地方,时刻提醒自己保持思路清晰、言之有物、有的放矢。所以说,一个好的导师,不仅仅给他的学生进入高深的学术殿堂的机会,更重要的是引导学生最终练得点石成金的"金手指"。这是我对"拜师学艺"的理解。

  我还要特别感谢黄国文先生。我用了一年时间在他那里做国内博士生访学项目,后来又跟从黄先生做博士后研究工作。我喜欢听他讲"功能语言学",通俗易懂,又从不枯燥乏味。我还喜欢听他分析点评学生的论文,每每有豁然开朗的通透和喜悦之感。如果说做学问是把简单的问题复杂化,而讲课是把复杂的问题简单化,黄先生在这两方面都做得游刃有余。黄先生善待学生,从不忍心拒绝学生提出的要求。我还记得,论文初稿完成之后,我请黄先生提意见。得知我很急迫,他马上放下手头的工作,甚至都没有午休,逐字句地看我的论文,看得眼睛酸痛,并提出修改建议,非常中肯。我还记得,我曾把 Hasan 的名字 Ruqaiya 错写成 Ruquaiya,黄先生一眼看出,并耐心给我指出来。我还记得,为了回答一个硕士研究生提出的问题,他专门写了一篇论文,后来发表在《外语教学与研究》上("英语'John is easy/eager to please'的系统功能语法分析",《外语教学与研究》,2010 年第 4 期)。悉闻黄先生近来对研究《论语》很感兴趣,在此我想斗胆借其中的一段话来写照黄先生:"子夏曰:'君子有三变:望之俨然,即之也温,听其言也厉'"(《论语·子张篇第十九》)。

  我还要表达对师母洪梅英女士的深深谢意。她的善良和爱心就像冬日的暖阳一样。她很关心我们的学习和生活,常常挤出时间犒劳我们这些苦学生。偶尔有哪个心情不佳,她还会耐心安慰和开导,直至破涕为笑为止。背后我们都亲切地称她是我们的"二导师"。她和杨先生真是"慈母严父"的黄金组合。

我要感谢 Halliday 和 Hasan 两位大师。我曾跟他们讨论我的博士论文,谈到我对人际投射的看法。他们很认真,甚至把话题延续到饭桌上。

我要感谢西南大学的刘承宇教授和陕西师范大学的孙坚教授。他们工作科研任务繁忙,仍热心帮我采集语料。

我还要感谢读博期间的同窗杨林秀博士、张曼博士和潘宁博士,感谢她们对我的关心和帮助,和她们的谈话常常碰撞出写作的灵感和火花。

最后,我要感谢我的亲人。感谢我的父母双亲、妹妹和弟弟,他们总是以他们独特的方式表达对我不变的支持;感谢我的先生永涛,他毫无怨言地承担着照顾家里老幼的重担,还要安慰鼓励我;感谢我们的女儿骎骎,她小小年纪,但很懂事,从来没有拿"要我还是要论文"之类的问题让她的妈妈愧疚难当,也从来没流露出要换一个妈妈的想法。这么多年来,我深深感受到,我的亲人们就是我坚强的后盾和坚定的支持者。有他们一如既往的爱、信任和支持,我有过疲惫,但不曾孤单过;我有过失败,但不曾胆怯过;我有过哭泣,但不曾放弃过。谢谢你们,爱我的人和我爱的人!

尽管几经修改,但由于本人能力、水平有限,书中肯定还有纰漏、不足甚至错误之处,恳请各位专家学者批评指正。

在此特别感谢厦门大学出版社的王扬帆编辑,感谢她认真辛苦的工作。也特别感谢厦门大学外文学院对本书出版的资助。

辛志英

2012 年 7 月 27 日

于澳大利亚黄金海岸

目录
Contents

Chapter 1
Introduction ··· 1
  1.1 Background of the Study and Definition of IPC ············ 2
  1.2 Rationale for the Study ·· 10
  1.3 Objectives of the Study ·· 14
  1.4 Data and Methodology ··· 15
  1.5 Organization of the Book ··· 18

Chapter 2
Literature Review ·· 20
  2.1 Traditional Descriptive Approaches ····························· 21
    2.1.1 Jespersen (1933) ··· 21
    2.1.2 Quirk *et al.* (1972; 1985) and Quirk & Greenbaum (1973) ·· 22
  2.2 Phraseological Approaches ·· 25
    2.2.1 Hunston & Francis (1999) and Charles (2006a) ············ 26
    2.2.2 Siepmann (2005) ·· 30
  2.3 Frequency-Driven Register-Oriented Approaches ········· 33
    2.3.1 Biber *et al.* (1998) ··· 33
    2.3.2 Biber *et al.* (1999) ··· 35
  2.4 Cognitive Linguistic Approaches ································· 39
    2.4.1 Langacker (1991/2004) ······································· 39
    2.4.2 Diessel & Tomasello (2001), Thompson (2002) and Verhagen (2005) ··· 41
  2.5 Rhetoric and Stylistic Approaches ······························· 48

- 2.5.1 Simpson (1993) ······ 49
- 2.5.2 Werth (1999b) and Gavins (2007) ······ 52
- 2.6 Pragmatic Approaches ······ 54
  - 2.6.1 Prince et al. (1982), Holmes (1984), Myers (1989) and Skelton (1997) ······ 55
  - 2.6.2 Stubbs (1986), Meyers (1997), Namsaraev (1997) and Givón (1995) ······ 59
  - 2.6.3 Vande Kopple (1985), Crismore et al. (1993) and Hyland (2005a) ······ 62
- 2.7 Structural-Functional Linguistic Approaches ······ 64
  - 2.7.1 Dik (1997) ······ 64
  - 2.7.2 Nuyts (2000) ······ 66
- 2.8 SFL Studies ······ 69
  - 2.8.1 Hudson (1972) ······ 69
  - 2.8.2 Halliday & Matthiessen (2004) ······ 71
- 2.9 Approaches to ABR ······ 75
  - 2.9.1 Hyland (2000) and Tse & Hyland (2006) ······ 76
  - 2.9.2 Belcher (1995) and Motta-Roth (1998) ······ 78
- 2.10 Comments on Previous Studies ······ 81
- 2.11 Summary ······ 87

Chapter 3
Theoretical Framework ······ 89
- 3.1 The Framework for IPC Analysis ······ 89
  - 3.1.1 IPC as an Intersubjectivity Booster ······ 90
  - 3.1.2 Categories of IPC and the Analysis Framework ······ 95
- 3.2 Metafunctions and Metafunctional Complementarity ······ 98
  - 3.2.1 Metafunctions of Language ······ 98
  - 3.2.2 Metafunctional Complementarity ······ 113
- 3.3 Projection Manifestation Across Metafunctions ······ 118

3.3.1 Ideational Projection ················· 118
3.3.2 Interpersonal Projection ··············· 127
3.4 Genre ································· 138
3.4.1 Genre, Register, and Metafunctions ········ 139
3.4.2 The GSP of a Genre ···················· 142
3.4.3 Genre of Academic Discourse ············· 146
3.5 Intersubjectivity ························· 149
3.5.1 From Subjectivity to Intersubjectivity ······· 150
3.5.2 Intersubjectivity in ABR ················· 153
3.6 Summary ······························ 156

Chapter 4
Genre of ELBR ································ 160
4.1 Genre of ABR ··························· 161
4.1.1 Significance of ABR ···················· 161
4.1.2 Functions of ABR ······················ 163
4.1.3 Generic Identities of ABR ················ 164
4.1.4 Identities of the ABR Writer ·············· 169
4.2 The GSP of ELBR ······················· 173
4.2.1 Requirement/Criteria for ABR Writing ······· 173
4.2.2 The GSP of ELBR ····················· 177
4.3 Genres of ELBR and ELJE: A Comparison ······ 185
4.3.1 Rationale for Comparing ELBR and ELJE ···· 185
4.3.2 Definition of ELJE ····················· 187
4.3.3 Generic Identities of ELJE ··············· 188
4.3.4 The GSP of ELJE ····················· 191
4.4 Summary ······························ 194

Chapter 5
I-IPCs and *we*-IPCs in ELBR ··················· 196
5.1 *I*-IPCs ································ 197

  5.1.1 The Social-Interactional Approach to *I* 197
  5.1.2 Metafunctional Features of *I*-IPCs 199
  5.1.3 A Cross-Genre Analysis of *I*-IPCs 208
  5.1.4 *I*-IPCs as Intersubjectivity Boosters 217
 5.2 *We*-IPCs 230
  5.2.1 The Concept of Generality 230
  5.2.2 Metafunctional Features of *we*-IPCs 232
  5.2.3 A Cross-Genre Analysis of *we*-IPCs 240
  5.2.4 *We*-IPCs as Intersubjectivity Boosters 247
 5.3 Summary 255

Chapter 6
No-interactant and Non-interactant IPCs in ELBR 258
 6.1 No-interactant IPCs 259
  6.1.1 Justification and Classification of No-interactant IPCs 259
  6.1.2 Metafunctional Features of No-interactant IPCs 263
  6.1.3 A Cross-Genre Analysis of No-interactant IPCs 272
  6.1.4 No-interactant IPCs as Intersubjectivity Boosters 282
 6.2 Non-interactant IPCs 296
  6.2.1 Justification of Non-interactant IPCs 296
  6.2.2 Metafunctional Features of Non-interactant IPCs 299
  6.2.3 A Cross-Genre Analysis of Non-interactant IPCs 305
  6.2.4 Non-interactant IPCs as Intersubjectivity Boosters 313
 6.3 Summary 321

Chapter 7
Conclusion 323
 7.1 Overview of the Current Study 323
 7.2 Main Findings of the Current Study 325
 7.3 Significance of the Current Study 328

7.4 Limitations and Remaining Issues for Further Research
.... 329
Bibliography 332
Appendix 1 Data sources 359
Appendix 2 Data samples 361
Appendix 3 A list of some IPCs in ELBR and ELJE 364
Appendix 4 Concordance of IPCs (part) in ELBR and ELJE
.... 367

List of Figures

Figure 1.1　The System of Modal Assessment ………… 4
Figure 1.2　Types of Orientation ………………………… 5
Figure 1.3　The Prosodic Domain in English …………… 12
Figure 2.1　The Classification of Disjuncts …………… 23
Figure 2.2　The Construal Configuration and Its Basic Elements ……………………………………………… 44
Figure 2.3　Construal Configuration for First-Person Perspective ………………………………………… 46
Figure 2.4　Construal Configuration of Impersonal Complementation Constructions ……………… 47
Figure 2.5　Functions and Interrelations of Modal Systems of English ……………………………………… 49
Figure 2.6　Modal of Point of View …………………… 51
Figure 3.1　The Framework for IPC Analysis ………… 97
Figure 3.2　Basic Systems for Clause Complexing …… 102
Figure 3.3　The Modality System in English ………… 106
Figure 3.4　Textual Waves of Prominence and Non-prominence in the Clause ……………………………… 108
Figure 3.5　Thematic Systems in English ……………… 109
Figure 3.6　Clause as a Tri-functional Construct ……… 112
Figure 3.7　Ideational Construal Standing for Interpersonal Enactment …………………………………… 115

Figure 3. 8	From Ideational Projection to Interpersonal Projection 130
Figure 3. 9	Register Recontextualized by Genre 140
Figure 4. 1	Colony of Promotional Genres 167
Figure 4. 2	Colonization of Academic, Professional and Other Institutionalized Genres 190
Figure 5. 1	*I*-IPCs in ELBR by Process Type 199
Figure 5. 2	*I*-IPCs in ELBR by Tense and Modalization 204
Figure 5. 3	Cross-Genre Comparison of *I*-IPCs by Cognitive and Desiderative Processes 210
Figure 5. 4	Cross-Genre Comparison of *I*-IPCs by Tense and Modalization 213
Figure 5. 5	Generic Structural Distribution of *I*-IPCs in ELBR 215
Figure 5. 6	Generic Structural Distribution of *I*-IPCs in ELJE 215
Figure 5. 7	*We*-IPCs in ELBR by Process Type 237
Figure 5. 8	Cross-Genre Comparison of *we*-IPCs by Projector Realization 241
Figure 5. 9	Cross-Genre Comparison of *we*-IPCs by Process Type 243
Figure 5. 10	Generic Structural Distribution of *we*-IPCs in ELBR 246
Figure 5. 11	Generic Structural Distribution of *we*-IPCs in ELJE 246
Figure 6. 1	Cross-Genre Comparison of No-interactant IPCs by Tense, Modalization, and Passivity 276
Figure 6. 2	Generic Structural Distribution of No-interactant IPCs

	in ELBR ………………………………… 280
Figure 6.3	Generic Structural Distribution of No-interactant IPCs in ELJE ……………………………… 280
Figure 6.4	Cross-Genre Comparison of Non-interactant IPCs by Theme-Rheme Distribution …………… 309
Figure 6.5	Generic Structural Distribution of Non-interactant IPCs in ELBR ……………………………… 311
Figure 6.6	Generic Structural Distribution of Non-interactant IPCs in ELJE ……………………………… 311

List of Tables

Table 1. 1	Options in the System of ORIENTATION	6
Table 2. 1	Overview of Lexicogrammatical Realizations of SLDMs in English with a Specialization of Sentence Fragments	31
Table 2. 2	Comparison of Frequencies of Stance Complement Constructions Across Genres	38
Table 2. 3	Properties of Various Epistemic Modal Constructions	67
Table 2. 4	Interpersonal Model of Metadiscourse	77
Table 2. 5	Categories of Evaluation in ABR	78
Table 2. 6	Rhetorical Moves in ABR	80
Table 3. 1	Process Types and Nuclear Participants	99
Table 3. 2	The System of MOOD Realized on the Clause Structure	105
Table 3. 3	Multiple Themes and the Ordering of the Elements	110
Table 3. 4	Thematized Comment	117
Table 3. 5	Contrast Between Ranking and Downranked Clauses in Projection	124
Table 3. 6	Projection of Ideas vs. Pre-projection of Facts Across Process Types	126
Table 3. 7	Textual Distribution of IPCs and the Projected Clauses in a Text	135

Table 3.8	Symbols Used to Describe Generic Structure	144
Table 4.1	The Academic Genre System	168
Table 4.2	ELBR Texts by Generic Structure	183
Table 4.3	ELJE Texts by Generic Structure	193
Table 5.1	*I*-IPCs in ELBR by Process Type and Subtype	201
Table 5.2	*I*-IPCs in ELBR by Tense and Modalization	204
Table 5.3	Cross-Genre Comparison of *I*-IPCs by Frequency	209
Table 5.4	*We*-IPCs in ELBR by Projector Realization	233
Table 5.5	*We*-IPCs in ELBR by Process Type	236
Table 5.6	*We*-IPCs in ELBR by Tense and Modalization	238
Table 5.7	Cross-Genre Comparison of *we*-IPCs by Frequency	240
Table 6.1	No-interactant IPCs in ELBR by Process Type	264
Table 6.2	No-interactant IPCs in ELBR by Tense and Modalization	268
Table 6.3	Cross-Genre Comparison of No-interactant IPCs by Frequency	272
Table 6.4	Cross-Genre Comparison of No-interactant IPCs by Process	273
Table 6.5	Non-interactant IPCs in ELBR by Projector Type	300
Table 6.6	Non-interactant IPCs in ELBR by Theme-Rheme Distribution	304
Table 6.7	Cross-Genre Comparison of Non-interactant IPCs by Projector Type	306

Abstract

This book attempts to explore projection from the interpersonal perspective, within the theoretical framework of Systemic Functional Linguistics. The objective of the study is to justify interpersonal projecting clauses as an effective resource to facilitate the language user to augment intersubjectivity. The study scrutinizes the discursive behavior of interpersonal projecting clauses in the particular genre of English linguistics book reviews. The research methodology adopted by the project is a combination of qualitative and quantitative approaches.

The study therefore primarily focuses on two concepts, namely, interpersonal projecting clauses and intersubjectivity. The former categorizes those clauses which construe interpersonal meaning through projection. The study interprets ideational projection and interpersonal projection as a complementary pair co-opting to construe human experience of the world. The latter concerns the language user's indirect regulation of participation, joint attention, and social norms appropriate to a particular situation.

A literature survey shows that interpersonal projecting clauses have been mainly approached syntactically and semantically. The syntactic approach concentrates on the relationship between the projecting clause and the projected one whereas the semantic approach on how the projection realizes the speaker's subjective modal assessment of a given proposition. However, no satisfying attempt has been made to offer a systematic investigation into the phenomenon vis-à-vis intersubjectivity. Considering the fact, the study identifies and classifies interpersonal projecting clauses based on observation of authentic data, and establishes a framework for analyzing interpersonal projecting clauses. It is proposed that the syntactic and semantic features specific to interpersonal projecting clauses justify their status as intersujectivity boosters. The study also suggests that the discursive behavior of interpersonal projecting clauses is constrained by generic identities of a given type of text.

Four categories of interpersonal projecting clauses are identified by the current study. The study identifies and categorizes interpersonal projecting clauses by examining the visibility of the interactant in the text and whether and how the interactant is construed by the Projector. To be specific, in *I*-type interpersonal projecting clauses, the Projector explicitly construes the interactant through *I/you*. In *we*-type interpersonal projecting clauses, the Projector is inclusive of the interactant through its realizing resources of *we/one/reader*. In the third type of interpersonal projecting clauses, namely, no-interactant interpersonal projecting clauses, no Projector appears in the projection construction. In the last type of interpersonal projecting clauses, namely, non-interactant interpersonal projecting clauses, the Projector construes a third party rather than the interactant.

The body of the book examines the lexicogrammatical realizations of each category of interpersonal projecting clauses with respect to the three metafunctions of language. The study also conducts a cross-genre investigation of interpersonal projecting clauses. By studying the discursive features of interpersonal projecting clauses in the genres of English linguistics book reviews and English linguistics journal editorials, the project argues that the discursive behavior of interpersonal projecting clauses is constrained by the generic identity and social and communicative functions of the particular genre. The study also explores how interpersonal projecting clauses function to boost intersubjectivity by specifying their functions of writer-reader aligning, position setting and interpersonal coherence, etc.

The main findings of the project include:

(i) The literature survey reveals that, although the phenomenon of IPC has been approached under various terms by different schools, there are four points worthy of particular notice. One is that IPC has not been considered from the perspective of projection until very recently. Another is that few studies have focused upon the intersubjectivity-boosting function typical of such devices. The third is that little attention is given to the discursive behavior of IPC with respect to particular genres, especially different genres within the same discipline. Fourth, ELBR has escaped deserved attention with respect to its close connection with IPC.

(ii) The study identifies four categories of IPC by examining whether and how the Projector in IPC construes the interactant. The primary concern for the classification is linked with the aim of the study, i. e., exploring IPC as an intersubjectivity booster. *I*-IPCs construe the writer as the interactant in the most explicit way. *We*-IPCs indicate the presence of either the writer or the reader or people in general, or any combination of them. No-interactant IPCs refer to constructions in which no Projector is present. Thus, no interactant is directly construed in this type of IPC. Thus, the visibility has to be inferred. Non-interactant IPCs do not display the presence of any interactant. Instead, they construe the presence of non-interactants. However, by genre-specific ways, this type of IPC suggests the presence of the interactant, the writer in particular, by infusing her voice into that of a third party. It is observed that the four types of IPC form a continuum in that the visibility of the interactant varies from the most obvious to the least observable.

(iii) The research observes that the discursive behavior of IPC is of close connection with specific genres. It is found that within the genre, the writer is expected to inform the reader of the content of the book under review while simultaneously evaluating it in an objective and convincing way. Thus, the close connection between IPC and the genre is found to be linked to the fact that the writer will resort frequently to IPC for interactant alignment and joint attention regulation, since in the genre the interpersonal stake is higher than that in others.

(iv) The study also notices that IPC resources vary to a great extent in terms of frequency, lexicogrammatical realizations with process types, tense and modalization, and the GSP elements in particular, and genre variation. It is also found that each type of IPC devices performs a multiple functions in terms of intersubjectivity enhancement.

(v) Across the genres of ELBR and ELJE, IPC resources are found to behave differently as well. Generally speaking, the differences attribute to different purposes the genres expected to fulfill. In ELBR, IPC is used primarily to enhance intersubjectivity at the moment when the writer predicts interpersonal conflicts. By contrast, in ELJE, IPC is employed mainly to invoke and sustain the reader's interest in the articles and hence to impress the reader in a favorable way for the ultimate purpose of promotion.

The significance of these observations can be elucidated in the subsequent dimensions.

(i) The current study provides a comprehensive and constructive survey of how IPC has been dealt with in traditional schools and other approaches and constructs a preliminary framework for the identification and classification of IPC resources in the language of English.

(ii) The study offers a detailed investigation into ELBR and examines the interconnection between IPC and the concept of genre. In addition, the analysis of IPC across the genres of ELBR and ELJE contributes to the study of genre from the intra-disciplinary perspective. Furthermore, the cross-genre analysis of IPC provides a feasible way to approach other linguistic phenomena.

(iii) Finally, the study exhibits how IPC behaves on the plane of discourse across different genres within the same discipline. The distribution and allocation of the lexicogrammatical realizations of IPC show how the strategy is employed in ELBR and ELJE to facilitate the writer's different social and communicative purposes. Thus, the study offers a complementary contribution to the current prevailing cross-disciplinary studies. Pedagogically speaking, the findings will shed light on EFL teaching and in particular teaching academic writing.

The study concludes that interpersonal projecting clauses are an effective investment of the language user for the purpose of intersubjectivity enhancement.

Key words: interpersonal projecting clauses; academic book reviews; intersubjectivity booster

List of Abbreviations

ABR	academic book review
CC	context of culture
CS	context of situation
DIST	distancing indirect speech or thought
ELBR	English linguistics book review
ELJE	English linguistics journal editorial
FG	Functional Grammar
FPG	Functional Procedural Grammar
GSP	Generic Structure Potential
IPC	interpersonal projecting clause
RAI	research article introduction
SFL	Systemic Functional Linguistics
SLDM	second-level discourse marker

Chapter 1

Introduction

The present study aims to achieve a multidimensional exploration of the interpersonal projecting[1] clause (henceforth abbreviated as IPC) from the vantage point of Systemic Functional Linguistics (henceforth abbreviated as SFL). The main concern will be both with the conceptual clarification and with the empirical investigation of IPC. Therefore, a corpus-assisted analysis will be conducted to scrutinize the distribution of various types of IPC and their lexicogrammatical realizations in English linguistics book reviews[2] (henceforth abbreviated as ELBR). The corpus research serves to test and testify the central hypothesis of the study, that is, IPC serves as an intersubjectivity-boosting resource employed by the speaker[3], with

---

[1] The definition and related terms will be introduced and discussed in Section 1.1 below.

[2] In order not to arouse ambiguous understanding, it is of necessity to state that English linguistics book reviews investigated by the current study are linguistics book reviews written in English.

[3] By "speaker" and "hearer", the present study means the interactants in the text. That is, the former refers to the speaker, the writer, the addresser, or any other utterer of any text, written or spoken. The receiver of the text is referred to as the hearer. As the current study focuses on written texts, "speaker", "writer" and "addresser" are used interchangeably and so do with "hearer", "reader" and "addressee".

which she invites the hearer to take a desired perspective specified by the projecting clause towards the information in the projected clause. This chapter consists of five sections dealing respectively with the background, the rationale, the objectives, data collection and methodology, and finally the organization of the book.

1.1 Background of the Study and Definition of IPC

This study takes IPC as its focus. However, it is of necessity that the concept of interpersonal projection be introduced first because it is the prerequisite to the understanding of IPC. Interpersonal projection as a fairly new term is proposed by Halliday & Matthiessen (2004: 626) when they argue that "there is [...] a fundamental relationship between modal assessment, including modality, and projection. To bring this out, we can interpret modal assessment as interpersonal projection". Seen in this way, interpersonal projection adds interpersonal meaning to the clause either by providing a second chance for the speaker to add her judgment or express assessment about the clause as a whole (Eggins, 2004: 160-61).

One striking feature of interpersonal projection is that the speaker's intrusion is always implicitly realized by modal adjuncts, i.e. clause constitutes such as *probably*, *usually*, *frankly*, and *unfortunately*. That is, the speaker does not "show up" in the clause. Therefore, the implicit realizations may be interpreted as the typical and unmarked realizations of interpersonal projection. However, human language has evolved to make it possible for the grammar to construe interpersonal projection by "co-opting ideational resources to do interpersonal services" (Halliday & Matthiessen, 2004: 626). That is, interpersonal projection can be "disguised" as ideational projection. The direct motivation is to make interpersonal projection explicit. For instance, in *Perhaps Mary knows*, the interpersonal assessment signal *perhaps* serves as the projection manifestation, assessing the possibility of the proposition *Mary knows*. This is the typical expression of interpersonal projection where the speaker does not show up. Instead, in *I think Mary knows*, there is the hypotactic projection① of

α②   *I think*
β   *Mary knows.*

Here the logico-semantic relationship of projection is employed to realize the interpersonal function of probability. The difference lies in the fact that in the ideational projection, the speaker is "visualized" through "I". In this way, the speaker directs the hearer to coordinate with her in a way specified by the projecting clause (in this case *I think*). The current study defines this type of interpersonal projection as IPC. In IPC, interpersonal projection is not manifested through interpersonal functions but through ideational projection.

Here three aspects need to be elaborated. First, modal assessment is an interpersonally cover term for mood and comment. The system of modal assessment is best illustrated in Figure 1.1. The project will return to the system several times in the subsequent chapters.

---

①   Hypotactic projection belongs to the domain of ideational projection which will be elaborated in Chapter 3.

②   In SFL, "α" and "β" are labels used to indicate the hypotactic relationship between clauses within a clause complex. The former designates the dominant clause while the latter the dependent clause.

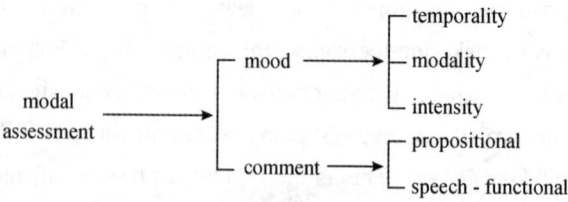

Figure 1.1 The System of Modal Assessment (after Halliday & Matthiessen, 2004: 126)

Modal assessment is interpersonal in function and therefore realized by an interpersonal adjunct (e.g. mood adjunct, comment adjunct) which is lexicogrammatically typically realized by an adverbial group or a prepositional phrase. For instance, in *Perhaps Mary knows*, *perhaps* is a mood adjunct, expressing probability; in *Frankly speaking, I can't stand Henry James*, *frankly speaking* is a comment adjunct, expressing the speaker's attitude.

Second, projection in SFL refers to the type of logico-semantic relationship in complementarity with expansion. That is, when describing the interdependency between connected clauses, the system of logico-semantics offers a choice between expansion and projection. In projection, one of the clauses comes to function not as a direct representation of (non-linguistic) experience but as a representation of a (linguistic) representation (Halliday & Matthiessen, 2004: 441). To put it in a simpler way, as Eggins (2004: 271) interprets, the projecting clause indicates that someone or something says something or thinks of something; any other clauses in the clause complex express what the person or thing says or thinks of (i.e. the projected clause), as in the subsequent example.

(1) *I think* Mary knows.

In Example (1), *I think* is the projecting clause whereas *Mary knows* is the projected clause, which is "filtered" through the projecting clause and therefore functions as an indirect representation — it is the "something" thought by "I". The dominant clause provides a specified manner with which the content of the dependent clause is to be entertained.

Hypotactic projection is always explicit while interpersonal projection is always implicit "unless it is made explicit" (Halliday & Matthiessen, 2004: 626). That is, logical projection clearly points out the source of the projection — the projector. Interpersonal projection, on the contrary, is realized by modal adjuncts, such as *perhaps*, which do not specify the Projector. However, out of certain communicative purposes, the speaker may intend to make the projection orientation explicit. In the context, the speaker turns to other manifesting devices such as hypotactic projection. In this way, IPC functions to construe the speaker's deliberate construction of dynamic intersubjective space between her and the hearer.

Third, IPC is explicit interpersonal projection. The fact that interpersonal projection is implicit unless it is made explicit indicates that implicitness is its default sense, hence the unmarked type. The pair "explicit" and "implicit" is directly related to ORIENTATION in SFL. The system of ORIENTATION is presented in Figure 1.2.

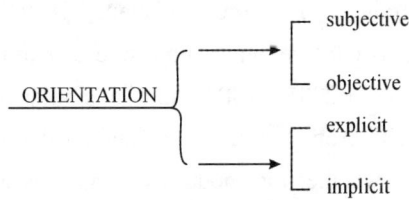

Figure 1.2　Types of Orientation (after Halliday & Matthiessen, 2004: 619)

As the figure shows, when ORIENTATION is concerned, there are the options of subjective explicit, subjective implicit, objective explicit, and objective implicit. Take modality for instance. Table 1.1 is an illustration of options in the system.

Table 1.1 Options in the System of ORIENTATION (after Thompson, 2004: 72, with a specification of IPC added)

		Modalization	Modulation
IPC	Explicit subjective	I'm sure we should sell this place.	I don't advise you to drink it.
	Implicit subjective	She might have written to me.	I mustn't go there any more.
	Implicit objective	We probably won't repay it.	A cathedral is supposed to be old.
IPC	Explicit objective	It's likely that they've heard by now.	It is essential that you leave.

In Thompson's (2004: 71) interpretation, explicitness and implicitness denote the extent to which the speaker openly accepts responsibility for the assessments being expressed, namely, implicit when the modality is expressed in the same clause as the main proposition (as *might* in *She might have written to me*); explicit when it is expressed in a separate clause (as *it's likely* in *It's likely that they've heard by now*). This separate clause is an IPC expression. Therefore, an IPC is either explicit subjective or explicit objective.

Martin & White (2005: 130) hold a similar view on how to distinguish "explicit" from "implicit" by stating that "explicit-implicit distinction turns on whether the modal assessment is given prominence through being encoded by means of a matrix clause (e.g. *I believe that*; *It's probable that*... = explicit) or whether it is but one element of the clause (e.g. *probably* in "He's *probably* lying" and *may* in "He *may* be lying" = implicit)".

The explicit nature of IPC is directly related to its intersubjectivity orientation. On the one hand, the two separated clauses construe two orders of representation: one projecting the other. That is, the projecting clause filters and frames the projected clause, being the dominant clause. The double-layered structure makes it possible to construe the reality in a two-order way. On the other hand, the speaker can directly instruct the hearer to entertain the proposition or proposal in the dependent clause by choosing between personal and depersonalized perspectives①.

Although IPC is a new term, its various realizations have been approached occasionally in the literature. Here are some IPC realizations.

(2) *I guess* he might be late.
(3) *It is likely* that he knows.
(4) *It is obvious* he is right.
(5) *We are convinced* that the girl is innocent.
(6) *It is important* for you to lock up.

Traditional grammar centers on the grammatical structure of these clause complexes②. Thus, there are the following familiar expressions of "complex sentence" to refer to these IPC realizations. Examples

---

① Instead of using "subjective" and "objective" to refer to the two types of explicitness, the study prefers "personal" and "depersonalized" since both "subjective" and "objective" are in essence intersubjective. From an intersubjective perspective, it is not appropriate to dichotomize the concept.

② In SFL, "clause" and "clause complex" are used instead of "sentence". A clause in meaning terms typically expresses a single proposition. Sentence is a unit in writing. Orthographically the sentence begins with a capital letter and is terminated by a full stop. In meaning terms, the typical role of the sentence is to express one or more ideas or propositions.

(2) and (5) are termed "complex sentences". Examples (3), (4) and (6) are instances of extraposition. The traditional analysis focuses on the syntactic features of these IPC expressions and assigns syntactic roles to the matrix clause and the subordinate clause.

In addition to the traditional descriptive approach, the phenomenon is studied as well by linguistics from functional descriptive perspectives. Hyland (2005a) includes some IPC expressions in his model of metadiscourse, assigning functions of hedging (*it is likely*), boosting (*it is obvious*), or self mention (*I*) to these expressions. Siepmann (2005) regards them as discourse markers and classifies them according to their syntactic features and functions in the discourse. Hunston & Francis (1999) describe their approach to these clause complexes as "corpus-driven", and abandon the formal analysis. To them, these are patterns in their own right, with certain meanings associated with them. In the studies of modality, Givón (1995) and Nuyts (2001) tend to consider these expressions as modality expressions and focus on the modal functions they perform. This approach is somewhat closer to the present understanding of IPC.

However, their orientation is from the subjective approach. That is, an IPC is considered either subjective or so-called objective in orientation. Little is considered from intersubjective perspectives. Little has been said from the perspective of discourse negotiation between the speaker and the hearer. Besides, these studies fail to provide a truly grammatical description and functional interpretation of IPC. The functional analysis, though contributing to the understanding of IPC, can neither escape being fragmental nor over generalize the phenomenon. Consequently, only some examples or patterns of high frequency were described and discussed. Being lexis study in nature, these studies fail to approach this kind of clause complexes in the following aspects.

First, these studies do not provide an SFL comprehensive description and interpretation.

Second, their focus is merely on lexical expressions. Therefore, there are only examples and illustrations. What is the working mechanism behind the phenomenon has not been touched.

Third, the phenomenon has not been approached from the intersubjective perspective. In essence, IPC is an intersubjectivity augmenting device.

Fourth, although some linguists, such as Siepmann (2005), have examined the phenomenon by considering its function in the discourse, few have attempted to explore IPC in genuinely discoursal environment, or to analyze IPC from the vantage point of interpersonal coherence.

Fifth, although some studies have shown their concern for similar phenomena related to genres, they fail to provide a general picture. Besides, to the knowledge of the current study, few have conducted thorough research in the genre of academic book reviews (henceforth abbreviated as ABR).

Sixth, although some empirical studies have been conducted, those solely on IPC are rare in the literature since they fail to give special focus on IPC. It follows that empirical research is of necessity.

On the whole, there has not been a general systemic functional grammatical category to cover all these expressions so that the inner connection can be shown. A survey of the literature shows that approaches to IPC are neither systematic nor exhaustive. IPC has not been given the importance it deserves. Although some empirical studies are conducted to observe the patterns in certain texts, they are generally in want of theoretical guidance. It is out of this consideration that the present research approaches IPC within the framework of SFL. Special attention is given to the working mechanism behind the phenomenon. That is, IPC is seen as an intersubjectivity enhancement strategy employed by the speaker. Also, IPC will be examined on the level of discourse so that its discursive features and functions will be brought out.

1.2 Rationale for the Study

In SFL, the semantic system comprises three metafunctions, namely ideational (construing human experience of the external and internal world), interpersonal (enacting social relationships among social actors), and textual (enabling the exchange of information to be a message). Taken together, the three metafunctions open up the path towards grammatically-based text analysis (Thompson, 2004: 10). Each metafunction is composed of its own system, i.e. the system of TRANSITIVITY of the ideational metafunction, the systems of MOOD and MODALITY of the interpersonal system, and the system of Theme-Rheme in the textual metafunction.

These systems do not move across metafunctions. However, some semantic motifs do manifest themselves either ideationally or interpersonally. Projection is one such motif. Ideationally, projection may be construed as an aspect of human experience. Thus, experientially, projection can be construed through mental processes, verbal processes, and relational processes, etc. Logically, it is not hard to see the hypotactic relationship between the projecting clause and the projected one. Interpersonally, as was discussed above, projection is enacted as an assessment of the projected clause.

The trans-metafunctional characteristics of projection makes it possible to combine different systems of different metafunctions to realize projection. In the case of IPC, the systems within ideational metafunction and those within interpersonal metafunction co-work to construe a special kind of projection. That is, the typical implicit interpersonal assessment is upranked to the level of clause instead of clause constituent. The result is that a separate clause serves to construe the interpersonal meaning. The "raising" of the syntactic status makes interpersonal assessment distinct. This separate clause, i. e. IPC, as Verhagen (2005) states, is the most straightforward expression for making perspective-taking explicit. It is time to draw a conclusion that the trans-metafunctional nature of projection partly attributes to the intersubjectivity orientation function of IPC.

The second attributing factor is grammatical metaphor. Matthiessen (1992: 56) treats grammatical metaphor as "second-order" use of grammatical resources. That is, one grammatical feature is used as a metaphor for another feature; and since some features are realized by structures, one grammatical structure comes to stand for another. In the case of IPC, for example, a mental, verbal or relational clause is used to represent the interpersonal adjunct whose typical representation is an element within a clause. Due to the working mechanism of grammatical metaphor, a clause replaces a clause element to construe the interpersonal assessment on a separate dimension. On this dimension, the grammar offers the speaker more potential choices than a clause constituent for her to manage her relationship with the hearer.

Halliday & Matthiessen (2004: 626) rightly suggest that it is the pressure to expand the meaning potential that in fact lies behind the development of metaphorical modes of meaning. In IPC, where a clause constituent is replaced by a clause, the metaphorical construction makes it possible to make the orientation explicit in IPC expressions such as *I guess* and *it is likely that*. Thus, grammatical metaphor construes a conspicuous layer in the syntactic structure of IPC to mark the speaker's stance towards the issue or claim. At such a clausal layer, the hearer is invited to adopt the perspective explicitly shown by the speaker.

Another ingredient that deserves full consideration is the prosodic structure of interpersonal meaning, which is strung throughout the clause as a continuous motif or coloring (Halliday, 1979/2002: 205). Prosody is a characteristic of spoken language, which is usually realized by tone, pitch and intonation. In written language, prosody can be realized by three structures (Martin & White, 2005: 19-24). One of them is "dominant prosody", which is shown in Figure 1.3.

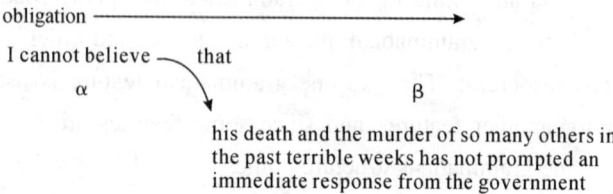

Figure 1.3　The Prosodic Domain in English (after Martin & White, 2005: 23)

The illustration shows that the structure of prosodic domination sets up the modality expressed by the IPC *I cannot believe* as the head clause on which the modalized proposition depends. This shows that the language semantic system has evolved to establish a particular type of prosodic structure to realize interpersonal modes. This includes the prosodic structure in which IPC manifests, i.e. prosodic domination. In this type of structure, IPC takes the leading position of the clause complex, which as the arrow indicates, interpersonally "tints" the following clause. In this way, IPC functions as a frame within which the projected dependent clause is expected to be interpreted.

Thus, it is reasonable to argue that the special structure of prosodic domination makes it possible for the manifestation of IPC. In the structure, IPC is given the leading position, with which the speaker may display her stance towards the proposition adjacent to the head clause. The construction as a whole allows the speaker to be involved and simultaneously to be informative, by redirecting the hearer to a new position which is more informative (cf. Verhagen, 2005: 8).

The discussion above aims to argue that IPC, realized by grammatical elements and syntactic constructions, has its well-founded functions on the dimension of intersubjective coordination. In this study, these general insights are incorporated into an examination of the academic English discourse. The study will focus mainly on the dominant discursive features of IPC while simultaneously examining the relationship between IPC and the generic organization of particular text types. The SFL theory-oriented approach will highlight the discoursal organization of the compared text types in connection to their most important IPC peculiarities. This will prove to be fairly promising from a pedagogical perspective.

The choice of ABR as a subject of investigation has been determined by the following considerations. To begin with, ABR is a widespread and important genre that plays a significant role in promoting new knowledge within scientific communities, both national and international. Second, despite its significance, ABR remains a "relatively neglected academic genre" (Tse & Hyland, 2006: 767). Finally and the most important, the genre of ABR involves much higher "interpersonal stakes" (Hyland, 2000: 41) than other academic genres, e. g. journal editorials. As Hyland (2000) observes, the context of interaction is an important element here as it plays a vital role in determining the accepted form and the pragmatic force of the evaluation employed. Book reviews are more interactively complex than journal editorials. While journal editorials mainly focus on informing the reader and promoting the articles under question, ABR is centrally evaluative. Although most academic genres are more or less evaluative, ABR is "most explicitly so" (Hyland, 2000). Therefore, interpersonal considerations are crucial in ABR.

It is under this consideration that the study proposes that ABR has a striking feature which points out the ways with which the writer and the reader are linked. As IPC is an interpersonal strategy serving intersubjectivity orientation, it is expected that IPC be prevalent in the genre. A lexicogrammatical analysis of IPC will bring out the distributions and hidden features of IPC in ABR. This, in turn, will contribute to people's understanding of IPC from the theoretical perspective. Although the current study takes ABR as the center, it is different from Hyland (2000), Tse & Hyland (2006), and Motta-Roth (1998) in that they focus on disciplinary variations and differences, while the current study exclusively concentrates on one discipline, i. e. English linguistics. It is hoped that the empirical research will facilitate a general comprehension of the discourse community within the discipline. Meanwhile, scrutinizing operations of the IPC system in ELBR will definitely shed light upon the understanding of IPC as an intersubjectivity boosting device.

1.3 Objectives of the Study

As was stated above, the aim of the present research is to explore and explain IPC as an intersubjectivity indicator within the framework of SFL. The study will be both qualitative and quantitative. From the qualitative angle, IPC will be scrutinized from semantic and functional aspects, with special consideration on its discursive manifestations. From the quantitative angle, IPC will be approached by examining the distribution feature of its lexicogrammatical realizations within the particular academic genre of ELBR. Thus, the research generally fits into the theory-application model. Centering on the main aim of the study, there are five objectives derived partly from a reflection on the literature review and partly developed from studying the current literature. They are summarized here in the form of a list and demonstrate the issues that this study attempts to address. They are meant to serve as guidance that structures the study of IPC.

- A. Review and comment on previous studies with reference to SFL framework;
- B. Present the SFL theoretical framework for the analysis of IPC;
- C. Explore and establish the relationship between the genre of ELBR and IPC;
- D. Describe IPC with regard to its metafunctional, discoursal and generic structural features within the theory of SFL, on the basis of information revealed by the corpus of ELBR; and
- E. Depict and explain the discursive behavior of various types of IPC identified across the genres of ELBR and English linguistics journal editorials (henceforth abbreviated as ELJE).

It is hoped that this detailed study of a specific text type can improve people's understanding both of IPC in the context of ABR, in particular, and of IPC in general.

1.4 Data and Methodology

As was mentioned above, the present study is both qualitatively and quantitatively oriented. As McEnery & Wilson (1997/2001) state, a stage of qualitative research is often a precursor for the quantitative analysis, since, before linguistic phenomena are classified and counted, the categories for classification must first be identified. These two form two different perspectives on corpus data. The qualitative analysis offers a rich and detailed perspective on the data while the main disadvantage of qualitative approaches is that their findings cannot be extended to wider populations with the same degree of certainty. That is, in the qualitative study, it is hard to decide whether the results are statistically significant or more likely to be due to chance.

On the other side of the coin, the quantitative analysis of a particular corpus does allow for its findings to be generalized to a larger population and, furthermore, it means that direct comparisons may be made between different corpora. Therefore, it enables one to discover which phenomena are likely to be genuine reflections of the behavior of a variety and which are merely chance occurrences. In a word, the qualitative analysis can provide greater richness and precision, whereas the quantitative analysis can provide statistically reliable and generalizable results.

On the basis of the considerations above, this research attempts a study combining qualitative and quantitative analyses of IPC. The project will analyze IPC variations in the academic genre of ELBR on the basis of reviews published in the international linguistics journals written in English. In addition, a corpus of linguistics journal editorials written in English has also been built for comparison and contrast within the same genre colony which "represents groupings of closely related genres serving broadly similar communicative purposes, but not necessarily all the communicative purposes in cases where they serve more than one"(Bhatia, 2003: 59).

Thus, the data consist of two corpora. The first is composed of 100 ELBR texts retrieved from 19 international linguistics journals published between the years of 2004 and 2008. This corpus is composed of 205,984 words in 6,437 dependent written units①. The second corpus consists of 100 ELJE texts taken from 13 international linguistics journals published between the years of 2004 and 2008. This corpus consists of totally 230,588 words in 6,782 dependent written units.

There are several considerations for choosing these journals. The first is their accessibility. The contents of these journals are available either online or in paper. The second is their reliability. These journals enjoy wide popularity and high academic reputation in the circle of linguistics. The third is that the publications and contributions to these journals stand for accepted academic English. It stands to reason that their English fits into the norm of English linguistics journals.

Machine-readable versions of the corpora are first made by scanning or format-changing the original materials. A number of stages are necessary to identify IPC expressions in the corpora. In the first stage, the corpora are examined by retrieving the clause complexes containing IPC signals of person (*I*, *my*, *me*, *we*, *our*, *us*, *one*, *the reader*, etc), and those of depersonalized (*it*) and other possible structures. In the following stage, Wordsmith is used to work out a list of IPC expressions according to their frequencies. In the third stage, the list is examined item by item using Koncordancer. This makes it possible to investigate these items in their extended context. Finally, the study concentrates on projecting clauses identified, trying, in particular, to identify their patterns of usage and distribution. Based on the statistic results, the intersubjectivity-orientating function of IPC will be examined.

---

① That is, "sentence" in the traditional sense.

1.5 Organization of the Book

This study falls into 7 chapters. The current chapter briefly introduces the skeleton of the whole project, i.e. background information, terminology consideration, rationale, objectives, material and methodology, and finally the structure of the book.

Chapter 2 "Literature review" conducts a survey of the literature with an aim to establish theoretical foundations for the subsequent study. This overview will serve as the background against which the present research can compare the patterns and distributions found in the ABR data.

Chapter 3 "Theoretical framework" unfolds with a framework with which IPC will be analyzed in this study. The chapter then focuses on SFL theories which are necessary for the analysis framework. To be specific, the theoretical considerations are of four aspects, namely, metafunctions and their co-opting, projection, genre, and intersubjectivity.

Chapter 4 "Genre of ELBR" attempts to explore the generic identities of ELBR. This chapter begins with a working definition of ABR, which is followed by the discussion of the goals and social importance of ABR. After this, it is illustrated that research conducted in this field focuses on various aspects of ABR as an academic genre. Then the generic structure is highlighted by critically reviewing other scholars' contributions, based on which the generic structure potential (henceforth abbreviated as GSP) of ELBR is proposed. It is also shown that intersubjectivity orientation is a striking feature of ELBR. A preliminary examination reveals that IPC has a fairly close connection with each of the GSP elements of ELBR. The chapter ends with a brief discussion of ELJE for the purpose of comparison.

Chapter 5 "*I*-IPCs and *we*-IPCs in ELBR" and Chapter 6 "No-interactant and non-interactant IPCs in ELBR" apply the framework put forward in Chapter 3 to the analysis of the data. The two chapters examine and explain lexicogrammatical realizations of IPC, together with their distributions within ELBR and their genre-specific features across ELBR and ELJE.

Chapters 5 and 6 constitute the main body of the study. Together, the two chapters offer a comprehensive but exclusive study on IPC from different perspectives.

Chapter 7 "Conclusion" ends the project with a summary of the main findings and significance of the study, acknowledging limitations and pointing out the necessity for further research on the complex but fascinating phenomenon of IPC.

Chapter 2

Literature Review

This chapter conducts a literature survey so as to depict a general picture of how IPC has been treated and interpreted in various schools.

The literature shows that traditional descriptive grammarians are concerned with the formal features of IPC. Turning to more recent trends, there emerge phraseological studies and corpus-driven register-oriented approaches. Cognitive linguists focus on the position and function of IPC whereas rhetorics and stylistics take IPC as a rhetorical strategy to construct points-of-view or to create text-worlds. In the view of pragmatic linguists, IPC is a hedging device. Structural-functionalists are interested in both the semantics and grammatical features of IPC. Finally, SFL scholars are found to either focus on syntactic constraints of IPC or to take IPC as grammatical metaphor. In addition, the literature shows that scholars approach ABR by either attending to resources of evaluation deployed or to its text structure.

The review aims to highlight the merits of the previous studies which shed light upon the current research while simultaneously bringing into vision the necessity of examining the discursive behavior of IPC in ELBR.

2.1 Traditional Descriptive Approaches

This section reviews traditional grammar represented by Jespersen (1933), Quirk et al. (1972), Quirk & Greenbaum (1973), and Quirk et al. (1985). The present study starts from Jespersen (1933), attempting to show how the phenomenon of IPC is hinted, though being neglected in traditional descriptive grammar, and what insightful ideas can be induced with regard to the present study.

2.1.1 Jespersen (1933)

Jespersen (1933) notices the syntactic relationship between IPC and its projected clause. However, his prime interest is in the latter. He (1933: 349-53) considers the projected clause as a grammatical "primary", that is, "a clause containing a statement which is not a sentence by itself, but is made part of a sentence, i.e., subject[①] or object either of a verb or of a preposition". Jespersen focuses on the "primary" clause, which carries the content of the clause complex, and its grammatical functions. Taking a traditional perspective, Jespersen considers only content meaning, or propositional meaning, while neglecting interpersonal meaning. Consequently, he tends to take the dependent clause, or the content clause in his term, as a constituent of the main clause, not treating the sentence as a combination of two clauses which are linked through logical relationships. Consider the following examples.

[①] In the section, "subject", "object", "extraposition" and other terms are used in the traditional sense. It is done so just for convenience of reviewing traditional approaches.

(7) *I believe that* he is dead.
(8) *It is to be regretted that* he should have come just now.

From his constituent perspective, in Example (7), the primary clause *he is dead* is a sentence constituent (i.e., the object of the verb *believe*). Similarly, in Example (8), *he should have come just now* is the subject of the entire sentence.

However, he does notice the functions of the conjunction *that* which introduces the content clause and thus links IPC to the ensuing clause. Jespersen (1933: 352) points out that *that* is often desirable, in some cases even necessary to "make the connection between the two ideas perfectly clear".

Jespersen (1933: 154) also stresses the function of the "preparatory *it*" as in the subsequent IPC examples.

(9) *It was splendid that* you could come today.
(10) *It seems to me that* he must be wrong.

According to Jespersen, this *it* in Examples (9) and (10) "represents a whole group of words which it would not be convenient to put in the place required by the ordinary rules of word order without causing ambiguity or obscurity". Therefore, the content clause comes afterwards in "extraposition"① as the subject, as is shown in the examples above.

2.1.2 Quirk *et al.* (1972; 1985) and Quirk & Greenbaum (1973)

Quirk *et al.* (1972; 1985) also take a syntactic approach to IPC.

---

① It is Jespersen who introduced extraposition for the placement of complement at the end of the sentence (Kiparsky & Kiparsky, 1971: 346).

Disjunct is the term which covers IPC. According to Quirk *et al.* (1985: 503), "disjuncts have a superior role as compared with the sentence elements". To be specific, disjuncts are syntactically more detached and in some respects "super-ordinate", in that they seem to have a scope that extends over the sentence as the grammatical functions of disjuncts in relation to the clause in which they operate. Consider the following example.

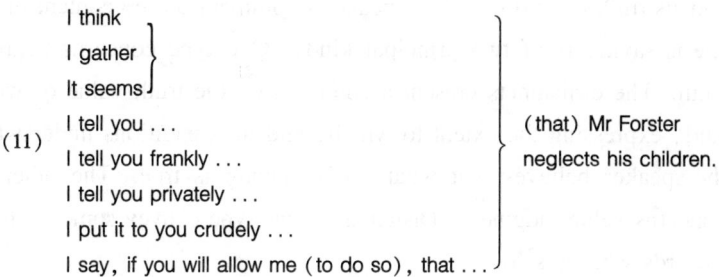

In Example (11), each of the italicized forms is regarded by Quirk *et al.* (1985) as an adverbial in a clause. Seen in this way, IPC expressions are taken as clause adverbials and have in some sense a super-ordinate role in relation to the sentences in which they function.

Quirk *et al.* (1985) classify disjuncts into two groups in accordance with their functions, as the following figure exhibits.

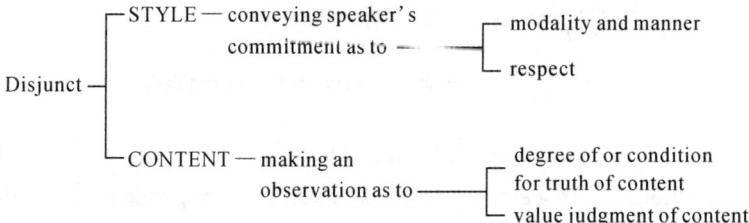

Figure 2.1 The Classification of Disjuncts (after Quirk et al., 1985: 614)

As Figure 2.1 indicates, disjuncts can be divided into two main classes: style disjuncts and content disjuncts. Style disjuncts convey the speaker's comment on the style and form of what she is saying, defining in some way under what conditions she is speaking as the "authority" for the utterance. Content disjuncts, also known as attitudinal disjuncts (Quirk *et al.*, 1972: 508; Quirk & Greenbaum, 1973: 242), make observations on the actual content of the utterance and its truth conditions. The speaker's comment on the content of what she is saying is of two principal kinds. One type concerns degree of truth. These disjuncts present a comment on the truth value of what is said, expressing the extent to which, and the conditions under which, the speaker believes that what she is saying is true. The other type concerns value judgment. Disjuncts of this type convey some evaluation towards what is said.

Quirk etal point out that adverbs as style disjuncts correspond to a clause with a verb of speaking, and that many adverbs as content disjuncts correspond to certain structures. Seen in this way, IPC constructions are simply clausal corresponding constructions of adverbial disjuncts. The difference merely lies in their structural representations. This is shown in the following expressions.

(12) $\begin{pmatrix} \text{Certainly} \\ \text{Clearly} \end{pmatrix}$ she consults her lawyer regularly.

(12a) = It is $\begin{pmatrix} \text{Certain} \\ \text{Clear} \end{pmatrix}$ that she consults her lawyer regularly.

As these examples indicate, Quirk *et al.* regard the IPC constructions *it is certain/clear* as clausal correspondences of the adverbial disjuncts *certainly/clear*. Quirk & Greenbaum (1973: 242-46) hold the same idea. They state that many of the adverb phrases are paraphrasable by constructions in which "the adjective base is subject complement, expressing an attribute of the subject" while the subject is the content of the original postposed.

Similarly, they argue that the same or similar notion can be expressed by a variety of clausal disjuncts. As the following examples indicate, they consider the IPC constructions *it is regrettable*, *I regret* and *one regrets* in the following constructions as almost the same in conveying meaning.

(13) *It is regrettable* that James refuses to speak.
(13a) = *I regret* that James refuses to speak.
(13b) = *One regrets* that James refuses to speak.

To Quirk *et al.*, therefore, IPCs are more or less equivalent to adverbial disjuncts. They take a transformation view over the complementing constructions. They also notice that disjuncts are syntactically more detached and "super-ordinate", having a scope that extends over the rest of the sentence. To them, *I regret* and *It is regrettable* are not by themselves complete clauses. Therefore, what follows should be analyzed as part of the same clause. This reveals that their study falls into the scope of traditional constituent approach.

2.2 Phraseological Approaches

Moving away from the traditional structural analysis, phraseological linguists take a straightforward pattern analysis. They go beyond intuition and attempt to discover phraseological units that occur in far greater numbers than previously thought. Sinclair (1991: 110), for instance, puts forward "the idiom principle", whereby "a language user has available to her a large number of semi-preconstructed phrases that constitute single choices, even though they might appear to be analyzable into segments". The phraseological approach argues that

> syntactic rules account for only a minimal part of the grammar of a language, and that the more important part is composed of the phraseological constraints upon individual lexical items. Thus, syntax is not a system independent of lexis: lexis and syntax must, ultimately, be described together. (Hunston & Francis, 1999: 13)

Considering the aim of the present study, it is of necessity to find out how phraseological researchers treat the patterns related with IPC. This section will mainly focus on Hunston & Francis (1999), Charles (2006a) and Siepmann (2005), while mentioning en route other contributions.

2.2.1 Hunston & Francis (1999) and Charles (2006a)

Hunston & Francis (1999) notice pattern behaviors of some IPC constructions. Pattern is defined as all the words and structures which are "regularly associated with the word and which contribute to its meaning". They set up three principles for pattern identification. A pattern can be identified if a combination of words occurs relatively frequently, if it is dependent on a particular word choice, and if there is a clear meaning associated with it.

Hunston & Francis (1999: 151-77) focus on the formal components of a pattern rather than on the structural interpretation. They find out that in IPC patterns with introductory *it*, there is always a finite or non-finite clause occurring at the end of the pattern, as shown in Examples (14) and (15) respectively.

(14) *It is obvious that* he is right.
(15) *It is difficult to* generalize.

According to them, IPC expressions such as *it is obvious* in

Example (14) and *it is difficult* in Example (15) have to be followed by a clause.

Different from the traditional descriptive way, Hunston & Francis (1999) argue that their authentic data observation indicates that Example (14) and Example (15) are patterns in their own right. Therefore, the clause complex should not be regarded as a version of something that "hardly ever occurs" (Hunston & Francis, 1999: 157). Thus, it is clear that they are against the traditional transformational approach to the interpretation of IPC.

Another point closely relating to IPC is that they regard the ensuing *that*-clause as in a sense the "main" clause of the sentence, with *I think* in Example (16) or *It is clear* in Example (17) as a contextualizing "preface" (Hunston & Francis, 1999: 156).

(16) *I think* he is right.
(17) *It is clear that* he is right.

In addition, they argue that it is "more useful" to adopt the straightforward pattern analysis approach than the traditional structural analysis of complementation constructions. This analysis, according to Hunston & Francis (1999), has the additional advantage of presenting language as a dynamic process. It presents the speaker moving, in a metaphorical way, from one clause (*I think* or *It is clear* in the examples above) into the next new clause (*he is right* in the examples above).

They also identify an IPC pattern "*it* followed by the verb *be* (or another link verb), followed by an adjective or adjective group, and a *that*-clause or infinitive clause" as an adjective pattern which involves evaluative adjectives (Hunston & Francis, 1999: 189). The meanings of these adjectives are all within evaluative scales such as good/bad, easy/difficult, probable/responsible, etc. According to Hunston & Francis (1999), the effect of using such patterns is so strong that the appearance of an adjective at this point is enough to identify it as evaluative. This is because

> we have a mental stereotype of this *it* pattern and we know the common currency of evaluation from which it deviates. The pattern is basically a chunk of meaning, involving the co-selection of items in a predictable way. [...] shows the productivity of such patterns: we always have recourse to the paradigms of the possible as an alternative to relying on the syntagms of the typical.
>
> [...] all word-classes can be identified in terms of their patterns — we know for example what an evaluative adjective is by looking at its immediate environment.
> (Hunston & Francis, 1999: 191)

As Francis (1993: 141) stresses, the chief orientation of the phraseological approach towards IPC constructions is that "these lexical patterns are closely connected with the communicative function of the structure", which is to present a situation in terms of how it is evaluated, putting the evaluation straight after the verb or the adjective. It is the way in which people typically evaluate situations. Therefore, using this particular structure (i.e. IPC) is "stereotyped". This viewpoint supports the statement that phraseology is crucial from a pedagogic perspective and that patterns are a valuable way of finding useful generalizations among a mass of information about individual lexical items.

It is worth mentioning that Charles (2006a) conducts a similar phraseological study of IPC from an interdisciplinary perspective. Following the work of Hunston & Francis (1999), Charles examines IPC expressions with *that*-clause complement and draws upon two corpora of theses written by native speakers of English in contrasting disciplines. She examines the verb patterns "V that" (e.g. *X argues that* ...) and "it be V-ed that" (e. g. *It has been reported that*...) and attempts to find out the most frequent phraseological patterns associated with them.

Charles identifies three clause types according to the grammatical subject of the IPC expression: a noun group with human reference; a noun group with non-human reference; and introductory *it* followed by passive voice. She suggests that such patterns are featured by an IPC with a *that*-complement to comment on the work of other researchers. Her research underlines the importance of phraseology in academic writing. Following Hunston & Francis (1999), Charles argues for the pedagogic significance of working with patterns. Furthermore, she elucidates that the IPC construction makes the pattern "well-suited to the positioning of self and others" (Charles, 2006a: 326).

Her analysis evidences that IPC patterns can open up space which allows for the writer to comment on the proposition in the complement clause, that the pattern can facilitate comments on individual researchers and studies, and that the present tense in the matrix clause conveys comments by the writer on the following content clause, and indicates the writer's stance towards the content clause.

To sum up, Charles's (2006a) highlights the fact that IPC allows the writer to attribute explicitly a stance to the content or the proposition and thus enables the writer to establish intersubjective space to convey her[①] modal orientation to the reader. Another noteworthy contribution made by Charles is that she rightly observes that investigation of the patterns is of particular value in the sense of "genre and/or disciplinary purposes" (Charles, 2006a: 329), since recurrent forms

---

① For the convenience of reference, the study uses "she" and "her" to refer to the writer and "he" and "his" the reader, if not specified.

of expressions are brought to the surface. Theses formulaic expressions display, in most cases, generic and disciplinary characteristics. Therefore, it is reasonable for her to argue that it is not sufficient to merely know the grammatically correct formulae. What is more vital is the understanding of what lies behind the sets of specific linguistic choices evident on the page. Charles furthers her discussion by suggesting examining the wider context of these patterns. It should be borne in mind that the different functions of the patterns under her discussion are very frequently related to their adjacent texts. This awareness of incorporating IPC into text hints at the necessity of considering IPC at the level of discourse.

2.2.2 Siepmann (2005)

Within the phraseological approach, Siepmann (2005) tackles the phenomenon of IPC by proposing "second-level discourse markers" (henceforth abbreviated as SLDM). SLDMs are "medium-frequency fixed expressions or collocations composed of two or more printed words acting as a single unit" (Siepmann, 2005: 52). In his interpretation, IPC constructions are SLDMs.

Siepmann (2005) establishes a framework of lexicogrammatical realizations of SLDMs in English (cf. Table 2.1), in which the category of "sentence fragments" concerns, to a certain degree, the concept of IPC. Sentence fragments, or "sentence builders" (i.e. items which provide a framework for the whole sentence) in Nattinger & DeCarrico's (1992: 39) interpretation, are sub-classified into four groups.

Table 2.1 Overview of Lexicogrammatical Realizations of SLDMs in English with a Specialization of Sentence Fragments (after Siepmann, 2005: 55-57)

Category	Example
A Set expressions...	...
B Sentence fragments	
1 anticipatory it + verb/adjective phrase (+ complement clause fragment)	
1.1 it + be + V – ed + that-clause	it will be seen that it is conceded that
1.2 it + V + complement + that-clause/to-inf	it seems arguable that it is my contention that it is easy to see how
1.3 it + V + (to/from n) that	it appears that it follows (from this) that it seems (to me) that
1.4 it + V + complement + – ing	it is worth noting that it is worthwhile looking at (also: to look at)
2 existential clause (+ complement clause fragment)	there is no denying the fact that there are good reasons for believing that
3 personal pronoun (I/we/one) + (auxiliary) verb phrase (+ complement clause fragment)	one must acknowledge that I must point out that we find out that
4 noun phrase + [+ (...)] + copular be + that-clause	a first point is that a further difficulty (for such an approach) is that my guess is that
5 – 15...	...
C Sentence-integrated markers...	...

As the table exhibits, for Category 1.1, the verb group often contains a modal auxiliary such as *will*, *must*, *can* or *could*. This fact is taken as an important factor in establishing idiomaticity in academic writing, and more specifically, in marking writer stance. For Categories 1.2 and 1.1, the relationship is seen by Siepmann as word formation rules, for instance, *it is arguable* ↔ *it can be argued*. A similar relationship is held between the impersonal *one* construction in Category 3 with Category 1.1: *one might say that* ↔ *it might be said that*. Categories 1.1 and 1.2 connect to Category 2 via intralingual class shifts: *it is increasingly recognized that* ↔ *there is increasing recognition that*. Category 4 comprises nominal constructions built around general abstract nouns and a copular verb. Given these lexico-syntactic criteria, Siepmann assigns various pragmatics functions to these "sentence fragments", such as emphasizers, e.g. *it must be noted that*, *it must be emphasized that*; informers, e.g. *it should be recognized that*, *a first point is that*; suggestors, e.g. *it is widely accepted that*; hypothesis and modal markers, e.g. *it is a fair guess that*, *I hypothesize that*; referrers and attributors, e.g. *it has been seen that*, *it has been proposed that*.

It is obvious that Siepmann (2005), Nattinger & DeCarrico (1992) notice and observe the syntactic and pragmatic behavior of some IPC constructions. They argue that an adequate use of these multi-word discourse markers is pivotal in making academic and other prose texts comprehensible and effective. Their phraseological-discourse-marking perspective highlights, to the last resort, the formulaic and discursive features of IPC.

2.3 Frequency-Driven Register-Oriented Approaches

This corpus-based approach is similar to the phraseological approach in that both agree that a comprehensive study of use cannot rely on intuition, or small samples. Instead, they require empirical analysis of large databases composed of authentic texts. Both approaches advocate that lexicography and grammar can be studied from a use perspective by applying corpus-based techniques. Represented by Biber et al. (1998) and Biber et al. (1999), however, this approach differentiates itself from the pattern grammar approach.

One striking difference lies in the fact that the frequency-driven approach strongly suggests that corpus-based analysis should be seen as a complementary approach to more traditional approaches, rather than the single correct approach (Biber et al., 1998: 9). Therefore, Biber et al. associate their frequency-driven investigation of syntactic constructions with register variation. Their corpus-based perspective explores how grammatical structures such as IPC can have strong association patterns with other grammatical structures, and how these patterns behave across registers.

2.3.1 Biber et al. (1998)

In Biber et al.'s (1998: 69-83) corpus-driven study of English grammar, the part most closely connecting to IPC is the pages that deal with the differing distributions of IPC-framed *that*-clauses and *to*-clauses vis-à-vis register variation. One reflection of this difference is their use in "extraposed"① versus "non-extraposed" constructions. Consider the following examples.

(18) *I think that* you might be wrong.
(19) *I want to* sleep here.
(20) *It's possible that* it'll happen again.
(21) *It's possible to* adjust the limit upwards.

According to Biber *et al.*, Examples (18) and (19) are non-extraposed whereas Examples (20) and (21) are extraposed. Seen from the perspective of IPC, Biber *et al.* actually distinguish two types of IPC, though their starting point is syntactic consideration.

Biber *et al.* focus on different frequencies of these two types of IPC in different text types, such as spoken texts, news texts, and academic prose. From the vantage point of the present study, according to Biber *et al.*'s data observation, IPC constructions like *it is possible to* in Example (21) have a very strong association with adjectival predicates in academic prose. These constructions are especially common with adjectives such as *possible*, *impossible*, *difficult*, and *hard*. They also find that IPC devices *I think* in Example (18) and *I want* in Example (19) are less favored in academic writing than those represented in Examples (20) and (21).

The frequency discrepancy, according to Biber *et al.*, helps explain the general preference for *to*-clauses over *that*-clauses in academic discourse. They suggest that these patterns fit well with the general pattern of academic discourse. Academic prose has a preference for static rather than dynamic packaging of information, which is

---

① Extraposed constructions here are defined as constructions which have a complement clause occurring after the verb phrase, with a dummy *it* as the subject of the clause.

reflected in more frequent nominalizations and noun-to-verb combinations. What is to be added, academic discourse has a preference for generalized states and processes, in contrast to the description of specific people performing actions in fiction and conversation. IPC constructions with adjectival predicates serve both of these functions. On the one hand, they present a proposition that cannot be attributed to any particular person; on the other hand, they frame the proposition in terms of static condition with an adjectival predicate such as *possible* or *difficult*, rather than in terms of a dynamic action or process such as *think* or *feel*. Thus, the typical grammatical associations of *to*-clauses fit well with the typical communicative priorities of academic prose, resulting in a greater reliance on *to*-clauses in that register.

As was illustrated above, Biber *et al.* (1998) examine the discursive behavior and register distributions of some realizations of IPC. They point out that the frequency differences across registers are due to the general preferences of the registers. Their frequency-driven investigations indirectly highlight, on the one hand, the register-bound features of IPC, and co-occurring grammatical associations of the lexicogrammatical realizations of IPC on the other hand.

2.3.2 Biber *et al.* (1999)

In Biber *et al.* (1999: 966-86), the phenomenon of IPC is more systematically analyzed in the part titled "the grammatical marking of stance". In this part, IPC is classified into "grammatical stance markers". Stance is necessary when "speakers and writers commonly express personal feelings, attitudes, value judgments, or assessments". Seen in this way, IPC is a grammatical device used to express a stance relative to another proposition. IPC can express speaker stance with respect to the proposition in the complement clause. Biber et al. (1999) approach IPC from its structure, meaning and register distribution.

From the structural perspective, Biber et al. distinguish three types of IPC, represented by the following instances.

(22) *I just hope that* I've plugged it in properly.
(23) *I'm very happy that* we're going to Sarah's.
(24) *It's amazing that* judges can get away with outrageous statements.

According to Biber et al., Examples (22), (23) and (24) are indicative of three types of IPC, controlled by a verb, an adjective, and extraposed structure respectively. Biber et al. observe that in such complement expressions, the stance marker occurs in the main clause, i.e. the IPC expression, whereas the propositional information is expressed by a complement clause. Whatever type, IPC as a grammatical stance expression sets a frame for understanding the proposition expressed in the complement clause. With such IPC, stance is separately expressed grammatically. Consequently, the grammatical structure overtly shows to the hearer that some stance is explicitly presented.

Biber et al. (1999) also notice that in most cases IPC precedes the structure expressing the informational proposition. This ordering, according to Biber et al., reflects the primary function of IPC as a frame for the interpretation of the propositional information. That is, the speaker first identifies her personal perspective, or attitude towards the proposition, thereby encouraging the hearer to process the following propositional information from the same perspective.

Semantically, Biber et al. group stance markers into three major semantic categories, namely, epistemic, attitudinal and style of speaking. Epistemic ones are used to present speaker comments on the status of information in the ensuing clause. Attitudinal ones report personal attitudes or feelings. Style of speaking stance presents speaker comments on the communication itself. Related with IPC, the three semantic types are illustrated by the following sentences respectively.

(25) Indeed *it seems that* girls very quickly replaced boys at the task.
(26) *I was curious to* see why it had happened.
(27) *I shall argue that* a state that accepts integrity as a political ideal has a better case for legitimacy than one that does not.

As is illustrated, the IPC in Example (25) indicates that the speaker chooses to avoid direct commitment. The IPC in Example (26) conveys the speaker's personal feelings to the ensuing proposition. The IPC in Example (27) marks the speaker's style of speaking, i.e. arguing.

In addition to the semantic criteria discussed above, Biber *et al.* also set up the parameter of "stance attribution" to distinguish stance markers. That is, stance markers differ in the extent to which they can be attributed to the speaker. Many are overtly attributed whereas others express stance without overtly identifying the speaker. Some stance markers are ambiguous as to whether they are reporting the stance of the speaker or of some third person. Thus, with regard to the source of attribution, Biber *et al.* classify stance markers into three categories, namely, explicit attribution, implicit attribution, and ambiguous attribution. Consider the following examples.

(28) *I am sure* this is completely untrue.
(29) *It is perhaps more likely that* they were associated with locomotion from the beginning.
(30) *It has been suggested that* at least five alleles are concerned.

In Example (28), the IPC *I am sure* overtly attributes the stance to the speaker. In cases such as Example (29), the attribution of stance is not overly but can be easily inferred as that of the speaker.

Example (30) is ambiguous as to whether the IPC marks the stance of the speaker or that of some third party.

Finally, Biber *et al.* compare IPC devices across spoken and written registers, inclusive of conversation, written texts, news, fiction and academic texts. The frequencies and features of IPC across registers (cf. Biber *et al.*, 1999: 984-86) are summarized in Table 2.2.

Table 2.2 Comparison of Frequencies of Stance Complement Constructions Across Genres (after Biber *et al.*, 1998: 984)

Stance Complement Constructions	Conversation	Academic Prose
Verb + complement clause	Extremely common	Rare
Extraposed complement clause	Rare	Common

As is shown in Table 2.2, the specific grammatical devices preferred in academic prose are nearly the opposite of those in conversation. As is demonstrated in Table 2.2, "verb + complement clause" is extremely common in conversation but relatively rare in academic prose. On the contrary, extraposed complement clauses show rather lower frequency in conversation while common in academic prose. It should be rementioned here that Biber *et al.* (1998) observe that extraposed *to*-clause is especially common in academic prose. In conversation, however, stance marking heavily relies on *that*-clause constructions, typically with the complementizer *that* omitted. These constructions are especially common when controlled by verbs *think*, *know*, and *suppose*.

To sum up, Biber *et al.* take IPC as a type of grammatical devices that assign emotional or attitudinal stance to a given proposition. They attempt to elucidate the phenomenon from the aspects of structure, semantics and register.

2.4 Cognitive Linguistic Approaches

The phenomenon of IPC is also noticed and discussed by scholars working in the field of cognitive linguistics. The literature shows that two trends deserve particular attention of the present investigation. One trend, represented by Langacker (1991/2004), takes a constitutional view and regards complement clause as one IPC clause participant. The other trend, represented by Verhagen (2005), Thompson (2002) and Diessel & Tomasello (2001), argues for the equal prominence of the complement clause. The assumption is that IPC and the complement clause simply function differently within the complementation construction.

This section will focus on these two cognitive approaches. It is hoped that some light be shed upon the understanding of IPC from a cognitive perspective. Meanwhile, the current study suggests that merits and limitations of the cognitive investigations can be both drawn upon, so as to enrich the SFL interpretation of IPC.

2.4.1 Langacker (1991/2004)

To Langacker (1991/2004: 436), IPC and its ensuing complement clause are different with respect to "profiling". That is, IPC as the main clause in a clause complex is the head of a particular level of organization, the clause that lends its profile to the composite structure of a multiclausal expression. The subordinate clause is one clause whose profile is overridden by that of the main clause. For instance, in

I know she left, the main clause *I know* is obviously the profile determinant. Therefore, the complement clause is not viewed as an independent object of thought (Langacker, 1991/2004: 440). Instead, it is viewed primarily as a main-clause participant.

In certain ways the relationship between an IPC and its complement clause is analogous to the one between the ground (the vantage point from which a linguistically coded scene is viewed) and the grounded structure. Grounding defines a kind of viewing frame that represents what is immediately accessible for focused observation. This frame of viewing attention constitutes the onstage region, or immediate scope of prediction, for the grounded structure. The analogy is strongest when the subject functions as the conceptualizer with respect to the contents of the subordinate clause, e. g. with verbs like *say*, *believe*, *imagine*, *see*, *want*, *enjoy*, and *realize*. Thus, the semantics of a complement construction may specify the subject's vantage on the subordinate structure.

Langacker's statements can be summarized into the following points. First, he considers the relationship between the clauses in complementation construction as one of conceptual dependence. Seen in this way, IPC and the projected clause hold a relationship of dependence and subordination. Second, Langacker prefers to see the role played by the complement clause as one main-clause participant. That is, he interprets the complementation construction from a top-down perspective, in which the complement clause is taken as subordinate to the main clause, i. e. IPC. This view is similar to the traditional interpretation discussed in Section 2.1 above. Third, Langacker proposes the concept of viewing frame to highlight the conceptually onstage status of the main clause in a complementation construction. This view, as will be seen from below, fully elaborated by Verhagen (2005), stresses the perspective-setting role of the main clause over the "subordinate clause". From the perspective of the present research, IPC devices play the role of perspective-setting over their dependent clauses.

2.4.2 Diessel & Tomasello (2001), Thompson (2002) and Verhagen (2005)

Diessel & Tomasello (2001), Thompson (2002), and Verhagen (2005) also engage themselves in the cognitive study of linguistic phenomena inclusive of IPC constructions. However, their viewpoint is different from Langacker's in that they do not regard the complement clause as subordinate to IPC. Instead, they argue that, based on evidence drawn on the process of language development and interaction in conversation and cross-linguistic corpus, IPC and the complement clause are equal in prominence. In this approach, IPC is covered under the terms "matrix clause", "main clause" or "complement-taking clause" within a complementation construction.

It seems to them that the main clause and the complement clause simply shoulder different functions. The former expresses certain perspectives or some epistemic/evidential/evaluative frames for the understanding of the latter which contains the single proposition of the whole structure. The matrix clause, in view of its separate status, are termed complement-taking clause or predicate.

Diessel & Tomasello (2001) observe that children's earliest complex expressions very often include finite complement clauses. In their use of the complementation construction, the main clause does not express a full proposition; rather it functions as an epistemic marker, attention getter, or marker of illocutionary force. The whole construction thus contains only a single proposition expressed by the apparent complement clause (Diessel & Tomasello, 2001: 97). They propose that these initial complex constructions are learned early, stored separately, and with specific properties of their own, and contain more abstract, rule-like schemas. They further propose that these constructions are concrete instances of the complementation construction capability of human beings.

Diessel & Tomasello's (2001) conclusion finds its echo in Thompson's (2002) studies of the role of complementation construction in conversation. Thompson uses interactional and grammatical evidence to argue against the traditional complement-as-subordination view. Instead, she shows that the complement clause is not in any insightful or useful sense subordinate to the matrix clause. Thus, in contrast to the view of many grammarians, including cognitivists, such as Langacker, Thompson holds the point that complement clauses in conversation function to profile the situation they denote with at least the same degree of prominence as their matrix clauses. Thompson argues that the matrix clause like *I guess* provides a certain type of perspective or stance toward the action, i. e. assessments, claims, counterclaims, and proposals, being done in the associated utterance. Consider the following example.

(31) (at a birthday party, after Kevin was discovered to have lettuce on his tooth, everyone has jokingly commented on it, and Kendra has asked for a toothpick)
WENDY: ... everybody's getting uh,
Tooth obsessed.
KEN: I guess we a = re. (Thompson, 2002: 132)

With this example, Thompson demonstrates that Ken aligns his agreement to Wendy's summary of the previous turns by the complement clause *we are*, and that it is not the IPC (here *I guess*) that constitutes the actual action of the turn.

Here is another example.

> (32) (talking about a photo collage on the wall)
> TERRY: I think it's cool.
> ABBIE: it i = s cool.
> MAUREEN: it i = s great. (Thompson, 2002: 132)

Thompson observes that the complement (here *it's cool*) provides an assessment of a common object of attention, or a proposition, while the IPC (here *I think*) provides a stance or perspective on that assessment. It should be noted that this view is also shared by Biber *et al.* (1999) (cf. Section 2.3.2). Thompson then argues that since exchanges are perfectly normal, there is no point in maintaining that a complement clause has lower prominence than the matrix clause, i. e. the IPC. Thompson therefore comes to the suggestion that what has been termed the main clause in much linguistic research simply serves as a stance frame for the clause with which it occurs. Such frames or fragments may be epistemic, evidential, and/or evaluative and provide a certain type of perspective or stance toward the actions, i. e. the assessment, claims, counterclaims, and proposals, being done in the associated utterance. Thompson proposes that this is typical for relations between complements and their matrix clauses.

Inspired by Diessel & Tomasello (2001) and Thompson (2002), and drawing on Langacker's viewing frame theory, comparing data from English and Dutch, Verhagen (2005: 78-155) aims to synthesize theories of cognition, syntax and discourse in interpreting finite complements. In contrast to most ideation-oriented cognitive studies, Verhagen takes communication as his focus of consideration, seeing human language as a system for mutual influencing rather than a system of information exchange (Verhagen, 2005: 7-8). From this starting point, he argues that the complementation construction as a whole allows the speaker to be relevant, and at the same time to be informative, by redirecting the hearer to a new position which is more informative. Thus, he assigns matrix and complement clauses to the intersubjective[①] and objective level respectively. To be specific, in his proposal, the matrix clause of a complementation sentence invites the hearer to identify with a particular perspective on an object of conceptualization that is itself represented by in the "embedded" clause (Verhagen, 2005: 79). This is shown in Figure 2.2.

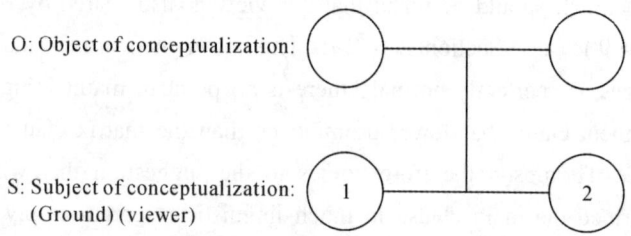

Figure 2.2　The Construal Configuration and Its Basic Elements (after Verhagen, 2005: 7)

As the figure displays, the matrix clause functions in the intersubjective dimension of the construal configuration. That is, it operates at level S rather than level O. The matrix clause, therefore, differs systematically from the complement in that it operates in the intersubjective dimension of the construal configuration. From this perspective, Verhagen argues that the primary function of matrix clauses in complementation constructions is located at level S. They

---

① Verhagen (2005: 1-27) defines intersubjectivity from a cognitive approach as "mutual management of mental state".

provide specifications of perspectives rather than descriptions of events or situations. Therefore, the grammatical functions of subject, object and predicate of a simplex clause can not be applied straightforward in these constructions. When IPC, or the complement-taking clause, is taken as a representation of a communicative event, it should be clear that it may just as well be taken as an instruction, from the speaker to the hearer, that the ensuing clause is to be conceptualized in a particular way.

This view holds, Verhagen argues, for complements traditionally considered as objects of their matrix clause, as well as for complements traditionally analyzed as subjects, as in *that ... is obvious/ unfortunate*, and *it is obvious/unfortunate that ...* In his framework, the complementation constructions have the primary function of instructing and directing the hearer to coordinate cognitively in a way specified by the matrix clause, with another subject of conceptualization (i.e. the conceptualizer) in construing the object of conceptualization, and not that of representing an object of conceptualization. Seen in this way, the prototypical function of IPC is to specify the manner in which the hearer is to coordinate cognitively with another subject of conceptualization, without this process of coordination being made into an object of conceptualization itself. It should be noted, however, the ultimate point concerns cognitive coordination between the receiver and the producer of the discourse, albeit more indirectly.

Within his framework, Verhagen distinguishes personal complementation constructions and impersonal ones. Since these two types are of particular relevance to the present research, some elaborations are of necessity here. Figure 2.3 displays the personal complementation construction.

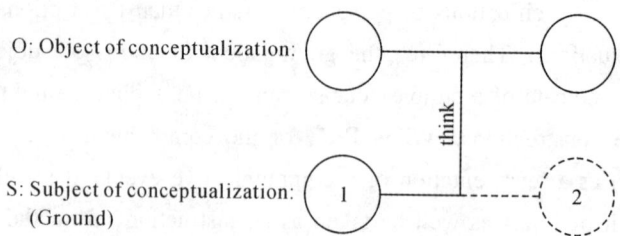

Figure 2.3   Construal Configuration for First-Person Perspective (after Verhagen, 2005: 106)

As Figure 2.3 demonstrates, in first-person complement constructions, the complement-taking clause does not operate at level O of the construal configuration, but at level S and its relation to O. The construction explicitly invites the hearer to entertain the object of conceptualization in the way the speaker does. The reason is that under the condition, the complement-taking clause has in one way or another marked the speaker's stance towards the issue or claim. In this construal configuration, the hearer and the speaker are engaged in cognitive coordination with respect to the same object of conceptualization. The object is a thought of Conceptualizer 1, that is, the speaker's own state of mind. In this way, the hearer is invited to adapt to the perspective of the onstage conceptualizer *I*. Verhagen (2005: 109) points out that the argumentative force of the first-person, present-tense utterance is maximal, compared to other personal complementation constructions as well as impersonal ones, as the cognitive coordination between the speaker and the hearer is explicit and direct.

Whereas personal complement-taking clauses explicitly invite the hearer to entertain the object of conceptualization in the way someone else does, impersonal ones invite the hearer to entertain it in a particular way. This is due to the fact that impersonal complement never attributes a thought directly to one of the conceptualizers in the ground, as there is no onstage conceptualizer, as is shown in Figure 2.4.

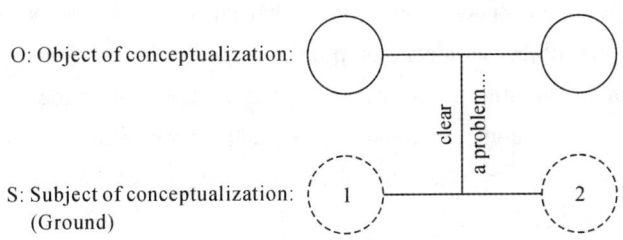

Figure 2.4 **Construal Configuration of Impersonal Complementation Constructions (after Verhagen, 2005: 134)**

Verhagen (2005: 132) considers impersonal expressions of IPC such as *it is only a hypothesis that...* and *it is clear that ...* as "extensions from the prototype". That is, in such constructions the subjectivity is not as immediately obvious as in the case of personal complements. However, he argues that it is undeniable that they evoke the idea of a conceptualizer. Only a subject of conceptualization can entertain something as clear, just as only a subject of conceptualization can consider something as a hypothesis. Being clear or hypothetical is never a property of an object, but always an aspect of the way it is being entertained. Consider the following example.

> (33) However, there is an urgent need for new models. *It is true* that the duo-relationship is an ideal for many homosexuals, but *It is clear* that this will be quite different from the traditional marriage. (Verhagen, 2005: 134)

In interpreting Example (33), the reader will normally attribute to the writer of the text, i.e. Conceptualizer 1, the responsibility for the claim that something is true or clear. Nonetheless, as is indicated in Figure 2.4, this is not an obligatory semantic feature of the construction, as the clause itself contains no reference to a participant who is the source of the judgment. Rather, it is a "default option" given the fact that Conceptualizers 1 and 2 are always available for use in interpretation. The assumption is that since this is the person who presents the object as clear, or problematic, to the receiver, she may be taken as holding those views in the absence of evidence to the contrary. If the context contains an explicit reference to another subject of conceptualization, then the attribution of responsibility for the claim is easily changed.

As was shown above, Verhagen examines IPC from the perspective of persuasion rather than information. Seen from this perspective, IPC functions differently from the complement clause in that IPC provides perspectives or "viewing frames" to the hearer to entertain the content of the complement clause. Both the personal and impersonal constructions of IPC function to invite the hearer to take the epistemic stance or attitude marked by the same clause.

2.5 Rhetoric and Stylistic Approaches

Both functional stylistics and cognitive stylistics have noticed the vital role played by grammatical structures in expressing modality, inclusive of IPC expressions. Although not specified or systematized, the phenomenon of IPC is constantly discussed and interpreted as a constituent of the modality network. Simpson (1993) proposes a modal grammar of point of view in narratives. His analysis highlights the functions and frequencies of various IPC patterns in different types of narratives. Werth (1999) and Gavins (2007), inspired by Simpson's modal grammar, postulate that in using modality, the speaker creates conceptually modal-worlds distant from their originating text-world, thus IPC expressions such as *I think* and *it is regretful* can be interpreted as an necessary part of the world-building elements of the modal-world.

2.5.1 Simpson (1993)

In Simpson's (1993) "modal grammar of point of view", IPC is considered as grammatical realizations of modality. From the stylistic perspective, IPC reveals genre-related differences in its frequency and distribution pattern relating to its shadings and lexicogrammatical realizations.

Modality is defined by Simpson as "attitudinal" features of language. Broadly speaking, modality refers to "a speaker's attitude towards, or opinion about, the truth of a proposition expressed by a sentence" (Simpson, 1993: 47). He identifies four modal systems of English, as exhibited in Figure 2.5.

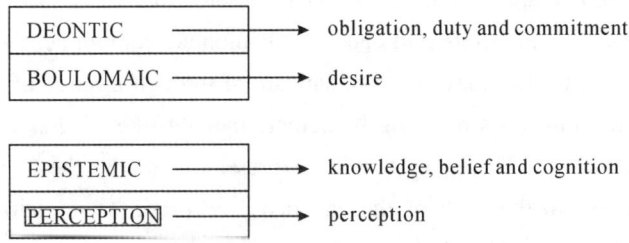

Figure 2.5 Functions and Interrelations of Modal Systems of English (after Simpson, 1993: 51)

As the figure indicates, there are the deontic system, along with the closely related boulomaic system, the epistemic system with its subsystem of perception system. Deontic modality is concerned with the speaker's attitude to the degree of obligation attaching to the performance of certain actions. The deontic system is of crucial relevance to the strategies of social interaction, especially to tactics of persuasion and politeness. Closely related to deontic modality is boulomaic modality, which indicates the wishes and desires of the speaker. The epistemic system is concerned with the speaker's confidence in the truth of a proposition expressed. Perception modality is regarded as a subcategory of epistemic modality. It is distinguished by the fact that the degree of commitment to the truth of a proposition is predicated on some reference to human perception, normally visual perception.

For each category of modality, Simpson discusses its favored IPC constructions, or grammaticalized expressions in his term. First, deontic expressions may combine IPCs such as *it is possible that* ... and *it is possible to*... to represent a comparable continuum of commitment from permission through obligation to requirement. In the boulomaic system, IPCs containing modal lexical verbs (e.g. *wish*, *hope*, *regret*) are central. Simpson also notes that IPCs such as *it is good/ hoped/ regrettable that* can carry boulomaic commitment as well. Epistemic modality may be grammaticalized through a range of devices similar to those ones realizing boulomaic modality (e.g. *I suppose*, *it is doubtful*). These epistemic expressions mark the speaker's commitment to the truth of the encoded proposition as modalized and qualified. As for the category of perception, Simpson stresses that IPCs represented by *it is clear/ obvious/ apparent that* constructions are especially important.

Based on this modal framework, Simpson categorizes and analyzes English fictions, as is shown in Figure 2.6.

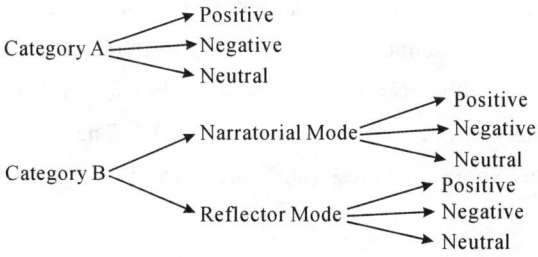

Figure 2.6 Modal of Point of View
(after Simpson, 1993: 56)

In this point-of-view network, Category A narratives are those which are narrated in the first person by a participating character within the story. These narratives can be divided further on the basis of three broad patterns of modality. These patterns are referred to as positive, negative and neutral. Category B narratives possess a third-person narrative framework and are subdivided into two modes, depending on whether events are related outside or inside the consciousness of a particular character or characters.

It is argued that the modal systems are distributed unevenly across the point of view categories and that certain modalities are specific to, or at least dominant in, particular categories. Seen in this way, IPCs specific to each type of modality are dominant in different categories of fictions. For instance, in A positive (A + ve), i. e. the first of the category A narratives, modality displayed is "positive shading". In general, the deontic and boulomaic systems are prominent, foregrounding a narrator's desires, duties, obligations and opinions vis-à-vis events and other characters. The epistemic and perception systems, by contrast, are suppressed. Thus, IPC constructions with modal lexical verbs and evaluative adjectives and adverbs are dominant. In the category of "A negative (A - ve)", epistemic and perception modalities are found which are absent form "A + ve". Therefore, IPCs conveying epistemic modal are much in evidence. This category is also featured with IPCs which have some basis in human perception (e. g. *it seems that...*, *it appears ...*). The reason is that, according to Simpson, these structures are intuitively negative in shading.

2.5.2 Werth (1999b) and Gavins (2007)

In cognitive stylistics, IPC is approached from the perspective of text-world theory, which was piloted by Werth and developed by Gavins. In the theory, IPC is also considered a modal device. However, different from Simpson (1993), the text world theory regards IPC as a device which facilitates to create text worlds. The underpinning concept is the notion of psychological remoteness and that of text-world accessibility. According to Werth and Gavins, human mind manipulates simultaneously hierarchical mental representations by creating and transcending ontological boundaries between discourse world and text worlds. In this way, IPC helps to establish modal worlds which define "degrees of certainty and reliability about knowledge and its sources".

Gavins (2007) distinguishes and discusses two types of IPC which create different text worlds for the reader with respect to remoteness and accessibility of these worlds. The first type is IPC appearing in first person, as in *I honestly believe that...* In such IPC cases, text-worlds are created by participants in the real discourse world (i.e. *I*) and the levels of accessibility to these text-worlds are the highest. Therefore, the hearer is constrained to take it as a truthful report by the speaker on what she believes. Nonetheless, by using impersonalized constructions

(e. g. *it becomes clear that*, *it appears that*), the speaker does not ascribe these mental perception processes to a specific senser. It remains therefore unclear whether the situation described becomes clear and appears to the speaker or to some other unnamed enactor. It is consequently impossible to assess whether the content of the epistemic modal-world is participant-accessible or enactor-accessible.

The text-world analysis of IPC type of modality can be shown in the interpretation of the following fragment of text.

> (34) *I think that* what's called resignation game is out of hand now. (Gavins, 2007: 112)

In Example (34), the epistemic nature of the IPC *I think* used to frame the statement positions the relational process contained within it at a conceptual distance from its originating text-world. Therefore, the comment is not a statement of opinion in the speaker's "here and now". Instead, it is a statement of opinion on that "here and now". As such, it produces a distinct text-world in which the proposition can be played out in the minds of the participants while remaining unrealized in their immediate spatial and temporal surroundings.

When *I think that...* is employed, the particular epistemic modal construction draws the reader's attention to the fact that this proposition is only a mental construction and that a different state of affairs may be actualized in the real world. If *I'm certain that* ... is used, the resulting text-world, although still modalized, is much closer to its originating discourse-world. This is because the modal item selected here does not act as a direct report of mental activity in the same way as *I think* does. It expresses a greater degree of speaker confidence in the truth of the proposition in the dependent clause and thus decreases the epistemic distance between the modal-world in which it resides and the discourse participants' "here and now".

To sum up, this section has introduced the stylistic investigations of grammatical modality, with the aim to highlight those constructions relating to IPC. It shall be borne in mind that both functional stylistics and cognitive stylistics treat modality as attitude-conveying devices that can be realized by grammatical structures. It seems that it is agreed that these grammaticalized modality expressions create a special layer of meaning, either in the sense of value indication (i. e. positive, negative, or neutral) or in creating a modal-world.

2.6 Pragmatic Approaches

This section will review studies from the approach of pragmatics relating to the present research of IPC. Three aspects are considered, namely, commitment modification, speech acts and metadiscourse. For the first category, Prince et al. (1982) consider IPC constructions as commitment modifiers. Holmes (1984) identifies boosting and attenuating as two external modifiers of illocutionary acts. Both can be realized by IPC. Myers's (1989) analysis of scientific texts for their positive politeness and negative politeness strategies also touches IPC. Finally, Skelton (1997) distinguishes Minor Truth Judgments from Major Truth Judgments, with the former realized by clause elements, and the latter by IPC.

In the second category, Stubbs (1986) recognizes and acknowledges that IPC can be used by the speaker to perform intended speech acts and to express her attitudes towards the proposition, ranging from full commitment to full detachment. Similarly, Meyers (1997) conducts a systematic investigation into the mechanisms and strategies of hedging speech acts realized by IPC. In a similar vein, Namsaraev (1997) works within the pragmatic/communicative sphere, focusing on the illocutionary force intensity of IPC expressions. Her study echoes, to a great extent, Givón's (1995) interpretation of IPC as communicative modality.

In the third category, Vande Kopple (1985), Crismore *et al.* (1993), and Hyland (2005a) attempt to construct metadiscourse networks in which some IPC realizations are discussed and assigned different socio-pragmatic functions, such as attitude markers, and boosters. That is, IPC is interpreted under the umbrella of "metalinguistic operators" (Schröder & Zimmer, 1997: 254).

2.6.1 Prince et al. (1982), Holmes (1984), Myers (1989) and Skelton (1997)

In this approach, IPC is taken as a type of hedging commitment modifier. Prince *et al.* (1982), inspired by Lakoff's definition of hedges as devices that make things fuzzy, classify hedges into two types of fuzziness. One is fuzziness inside the meaning of the proposition itself, the other exists between the speaker and the proposition, conveying the speaker's commitment to the content of the proposition. From this perspective, the second group of hedges are often realized by IPC expressions, being modifiers of the speaker's commitment to the truth-value of a whole proposition.

According to Prince *et al.*, the two categories of hedges are termed approximators and shields respectively. Consider the following examples.

(35) His feet were *sort of* blue.
(36) *I think* his feet were blue.

In Example (35), the approximator *sort of* affects the truth-value of the proposition whereas the IPC *I think* in Example (36) is a shield which indicates the degree of the speaker's commitment to the truth-condition of the whole proposition. Some scholars simply refer to "shields" as hedging (cf. Hübler, 1983; Markkanen & Schröder, 1997). This hedging is treated as the realization of interactional strategies employed by the speaker. To be specific, the function of the IPC is to modify the speaker's responsibility for the truth-value of the proposition, to modify the weight of the information given, or to express or hide the attitude of the speaker to the content of the proposition.

Similarly, IPC to Holmes (1984) is a modifying strategy for the speaker to express various degrees of illocutionary force. Holmes introduces the notion of "boosting" and "attenuating" to differentiate IPC resources. He stresses that boosting and attenuating are not components of the illocutionary force, but its external modifiers. Consider the following examples.

(37) *I'm not at all sure* Mary is coming.
(38) *It is definite that* Mary is coming.

As is shown in the examples above, the speaker may modify her commitment to the truth of a proposition by attenuating IPCs such as *I'm not at all sure* in Example (37) or boosting ones such as *It is definite* in Example (38).

In addition, Holmes distincts two types of commitment modifiers expressed by IPC, i.e. modal meaning modifiers and affective meaning modifiers. The former has to do with the speaker's attitude towards the proposition whereas the latter her attitude toward the hearer.

Myers's (1989) research also identifies and interprets some IPCs in terms of hedging modifiers. He conducts a written-discourse-oriented analysis of hedges on the theoretical basis of politeness (Brown & Levinson, 1987). Myers suggests that in scientific writing politeness is the motivating factor for hedging. His discourse analysis shows that in scientific writing, IPCs such as *we believe that...* and *it is unlikely that...* reflect the relation between the writer and the reader, rather than the degree of the probability of the statement. In Myers's (1989: 12) words, one purpose of such hedging modifiers is not to make knowledge claims uncertain, but rather to mark the claim as "unacknowledged by the discourse community". Therefore, Myers argues that the amount of hedging the writer employs depends on such factors as her position within the scientific community, and the potential readership. Myers also discusses the functions of these IPC constructions. He sees them as "introductory phrases" that inform the reader what weight the statement is to have. In academic writing, this kind of framing is used in particular to indicate to the reader the writer's commitment to or rejection of a statement.

In parallel to Myers's empirical exploration, Skelton's (1997) diachronic study also sheds light upon the understanding of IPC. He interprets IPC expressions as commitment-modifiers by using the concept of "comment". Comments are divided into judgments on the proposition they govern, on either its truth value or its emotional value, as is shown in the following instances.

(39) *I suspect the moon is made of green cheese.*
(40) *It is good to hear that the moon is made of green cheese.*

According to Skelton, the IPC *I suspect* in Example (39) is of the former type of comments, which comments on the ensuing proposition vis-à-vis its truth value. By contrast, the IPC *it is good* in Example (40) is grouped into the latter type which modifies the emotional value of the subsequent proposition. Skelton narrows the concept of hedging to cover only the former type, i. e. those comments which mitigate the speaker's responsibility and/or certainty to the truth value of a given proposition.

Also related with IPC is the notion "the domain of comments" proposed by Skelton (1997). That is, as items modulating the force of what follows, there is difference in the domains they govern. Consider the following examples.

(41) My car is *quite* big.
(42) *It is possible that* you are young.

According to Skelton, although both *quite* in Example (41) and *it is possible* in Example (42) are truth-judgments which govern propositions, a distinction exists between a judgment whose domain is less than a clause, i. e. *quite*, and one whose domain is a clause or more, i. e. *it is possible*. He therefore terms the former "Minor Truth Judgments", the latter "Major Truth Judgments", or simply "Truth Judgments". According to him, Minor Truth Judgments are not of great significance. He is interested in Major Truth Judgments. In IPC-governing structures such as Example (42), the IPC functions to modify the speaker's commitment to the proposition it governs. It acts to place the modifying marks (here *it is possible*) around the proposition.

From Prince *et al.* to Skelton, IPC is partly covered under the concept of commitment modification. This is in essence a functional approach to the interaction of syntactic forms and hedging. In addition, it is noteworthy some researchers have examined interaction with regard to specific text types, such as academic discourse. Their observation indicates that the behavior of IPC is sensitive to particular genres.

2. 6. 2 Stubbs (1986), Meyers (1997), Namsaraev (1997) and Givón (1995)

This group of scholars understand IPC from the vantage point of speaker commitment and detachment relating to the performance of speech acts. According to them, the ultimate sociopragmatic function of IPC expressions is to make statements more acceptable to the hearer and thus increasing their chances of ratification (Hübler, 1983).

Relating to IPC is Stubbs's (1986) discussion of indirect speech acts in scientific communication. With respect to vague and indirect language, Stubbs argues that there is a commitment continuum from complete commitment to complete detachment. The speaker chooses between the end points to shift her commitment to the illocutionary acts. Seen in this way, IPC is one such "hedging performative" the speaker employs to realize the commitment shifting.

Most closely related to the concept of IPC is his analysis of "explicit illocutionary prefaces", such as *I emphasize that* ... and *I would suggest that* ... Stubbs declares that the common surface form is "modal plus lexical illocutionary verb" (e. g. *I think* we should decline our offer, *I would advise you that* ...). According to his observation, these explicit performatives tend to appear in formal academic discourse and have the function of presenting personal beliefs and position adoption, or disassociating the speaker from points of view. Another important aspect of hedging performatives links with those "private verbs" (e. g. *believe*, *think*, *suspect*, and *expect*). Stubbs presents the psychological and modal interpretations of these verbs. From the perspective of IPC, constructions such as *I believe* and *one suspects* can be used to make statements about internal psychological state as well as to disassociate the speaker from total commitment to particular propositions.

Comparatively speaking, Meyers (1997) depicts a clearer picture of IPC through his categorization of hedging speech acts, basing his analysis on written academic discourse. From the perspective of IPC, Meyers's findings can be summarized into the following points. First, IPC expressions represented by *I would like to* are termed volitional hedges, indicating inclination or desire. Such IPCs are adopted when the speaker predicts that a speech act might be face-threatening to the reader. Second, IPCs such as *I suggest* and *it is hard to see* are often used to reduce or to avoid commitment to the proposition. Their employment is due to the inherently weak illocutionary force such IPCs convey. Third, IPCs with modal operators such as *can* and *may* and coming-to-know verbs (e.g. *be found, be identified*) may be used to weaken the illocutionary force of a claim.

Meyers suggests that the motivation behind these various hedging performatives realized by IPC has to do with the norm and convention of the genre of scientific writing. That is, the strength of the speech act reflects the certainty of knowledge. Therefore, it is only when research activities fail to provide a basis for unhedged statements that language comes in to compensate for the lack of certainty.

A similar interpretation of IPC is found in Namsaraev (1997), who discusses the illocutionary force intensity of hedging expressions. The particular consideration is given to indetermination, subjectivization and depersonalization. Her study indicates that the strength of a hedged speech act decreases when its protective function increases. Therefore, Namsaraev argues that these hedgings work to convey the speaker's communicative intentions and should be interpreted within the pragmatic and communicative sphere. Unfortunately, Namsaraev does not further on these "communicative modality" devices.

However, Givón's (1995) functional interpretations of modality provide a theoretical complement to Namsaraev's observations. IPC is found to be an important part in Givón's classification of modalities. He abandons the traditional truth-condition approach to modality and takes modality as communication-defined. He criticizes the logical tradition for its treatment of modality as a property of propositions detached from their natural communicative context. From a communicative pragmatic perspective, in terms of the epistemic states and communicative goals of the two participants in the communicative transaction — speaker and hearer, he categorizes modalities into presupposition, realis assertion, irrealis assertion and NEG-assertion.

Closely related with the concept of IPC is Givón's discussion of irrealis. He argues that irrealis functions in both cognitive and communicative aspects. Cognitively, irrealis orients towards subjective certainty rather than logical truth. Communicatively, irrealis concerns more with pragmatic and interactive meaning involving both speaker and hearer than speaker-oriented (semantic) meaning.

According to Givón, the hedged illocutionary force of irrealis can be typically realized by IPC constructions with perception/cognition/ utterance verbs or adjectives, such as *I believe*, *I prefer*, and *I am sure*. One striking common feature of these modalities is that they are non-factive and therefore do not presuppose the following complements. It can be concluded that Givón prefers irrealis to hedging in describing modified illocutionary forces which might be realized by IPC expressions. Nonetheless, his communication-oriented interpretation is in fairly close affinity with the ideas of the other scholars in this panel.

To conclude this part, as Flowerdew (1991) verifies, when a modified speech act is performed through IPC, the illocutionary act is heavily tinted by social negotiation and interpersonal orientation. The mechanism for achieving this is primarily the hedging device or "modality marker" (Kreutz, 1997: 225) realized by IPC which constitutes the linguistic form necessary to perform the act.

2.6.3 Vande Kopple (1985), Crismore *et al.* (1993) and Hyland (2005a)

In this socio-pragmatic approach, IPC is partly covered in the discussion of metadiscourse. Vande Kopple and others consider linguistic activities primarily as processes in which the interactants acknowledge, construct and negotiate social relations. The central concept for the study of discourse negotiation is metadiscourse. Metadiscourse is also termed metatext, or text about text (Vande Kopple, 1985; Moreno, 2003). Vande Kopple (1985: 83) defines metadiscourse as the linguistic material of texts that does not add propositional content but rather signals the presence of the author. In a similar vein, Hyland (2005a: 37) offers a more refined definition, namely, metadiscourse is the cover term for "the self-reflective expressions used to negotiate interactional meanings in a text, assisting the writer (or speaker) to express a viewpoint and engage with the reader as members of a particular community".

In essence, metadiscourse involves writer intervention into the discourse. Hyland & Tse (2004) postulate three key principles of metadiscourse. First, metadicourse is distinct from propositional aspects of discourse. Second, metadiscourse refers to aspects of the text that embody writer-reader interactions. Third, metadiscourse refers only to relations which are internal to the discourse. They distinguish interactive metadiscourse from interactional metadiscourse. Interactive metadiscourse functions to organize propositional information in such ways that the reader finds reasonable and convincing. In complementarity, interactional metadiscourse conveys to the reader the writer's perspective towards the proposition and the reader. According to Crismore (1989: 193), the mechanism of metadiscourse helps the writer affirm and/or assert control over the text and how it is to be read. From this perspective, metadiscourse attests to the writer's desire for control of the text and readership.

IPC constructions are regarded by Tse & Hyland (2006: 774) as metadiscourse which appears in clausal or sentence-level expressions. It is, in fact, not rare in the metadiscourse literature that realizations of IPC are discussed and interpreted (Hyland, 2000; Hewings & Hewings, 2002; Hyland & Tse, 2005). IPC is taken as a metadiscourse resource which has interactional features in particular and performs specific functions. In Hyland's model, IPC may serve functions such as commitment withholding (hedges), certainty emphasizing (booster), affective attitude expressing (attitude markers), explicit writer presence in the text (self mention), and/or explicit reader presence (engagement markers). In his interpersonal metadiscourse model, Vande Kopple (1985) assigns to IPC functions such as illocutionary markers, attitude markers and commentaries whereas Crismore *et al.* (1993) have functions of hedges, certainty markers, attributors, attitude markers and commentary for IPC constructions.

Vande Kopple *et al.*, therefore, see IPC as clausal metadiscourse which is indicative of the writer's response to the potential negatability of her own statement and an interpersonal professional intervention to engage the reader.

This section has conducted a review of studies in the field of pragmatics, in which IPC is seen as a communicative strategy adopted by the speaker to shift from complete commitment to complete detachment from the given proposition. To be specific, whether IPC is taken as a hedging device, an illocutionary force qualifier or metadiscourse, the analyses focus upon the effects of pragmatic factors on the grammar. That is, the degree of the speaker's confidence in truth of the proposition can interact with syntactic forms. Moreno (2003: 277) rightly points out that these modifying functions can not be detached from the formal status of IPC. The socio-pragmatic interpretation is in close relation to the grammatical structures where IPC devices occur.

2.7 Structural-Functional Linguistic Approaches

This section will offer a review on how IPC is coped with in the field of structural-functional linguistics. According to Butler (2003a; 2003b), there are mainly three branches of structural-functional linguistics, namely, Functional Grammar (FG) represented by Dik, Functional Procedural Grammar (FPG) represented by Nuyts, and SFL initiated by Halliday. This section will deal with Dik's research and Nuyts's study whereas the subsequent section focuses on SFL.

2.7.1 Dik (1997)

In FG, IPC is discussed in Dik's (1997) brief account of modality distinction. According to Dik, English modality can be distinguished at three levels. At the first level is inherent modality which is internal to the clause (e. g. *can, be willing to*). At Level 2 is objective modality. It can be further divided into epistemic objective modality and deontic modality. The former has its base on knowledge of possible situations in relation to reality or hypothesis whereas the latter on knowledge of possibility in relation to a system of moral, legal and social conventions. The speaker employs objective modality to indicate her evaluation of a given message. All objective modal elements can be realized by lexical devices or grammatical structures. At Level 3 is subjective modality with which the speaker can express her commitment to the truth of a given proposition.

Seen in Dik's perspective, IPC is a grammatical structure which realizes objective modality as in Example (43) or subjective modality as in Example (44).

(43) *It is possible that* he is right.
(44) *I think* he is right.
(45) *Possibly* he is right.

Dik's contribution to the exploration of IPC lies in two aspects. First, Dik discusses features of objective IPCs represented by *it is possible* in Example (43) with respect to interrogation, negation, and attribution, by comparing them with modal adverbs such as *possibly* in Example (45). Dik posits the view that objective IPCs can be questioned or hypothesized in a conditional sentence while modal adverbs cannot. For instance, the IPC *it is possible that* ... can be questioned as *is it possible that* ... ? or hypothesized as *if it is possible* ... However, *possibly* ... can not be questioned as ** possibly* ... ? or hypothesized as ** if possibly* ... ? In addition, objective IPCs can be formulated either positively or negatively whereas the modal adverb is constrained to positive terms. For instance, formulations such as *it is* *impossible that* ... are allowed whereas people do not use expressions like *∗ impossibly* ... Finally, objective IPCs and modal adverbs are different in terms of the attribution or the source of the information. For the former, the attribution can be questioned while it can not for the latter. For instance, in answer to a statement modified by *it is possible that*, *who says so* is perfectly acceptable. Nonetheless, in the case of *possibly*, it is inappropriate to ask *Who says so*? Instead, it is appropriate to ask *Do you think so*?

Second, Dik argues that subjective IPC is located outside the predication itself and that the source of the evaluation is the speaker herself. According to Dik, the *who says so/do you think so*? test confirms his argumentation. In addition, the subjective IPC is characterized by an element of modal performativity. That is, it creates a commitment of the speaker in relation to the propositional content of the utterance. Therefore, the subjective IPC belongs to the interpersonal organization of the clause.

2.7.2 Nuyts (2000)

Nuyts (2000) takes a function-to-form approach to IPC. According to his interpretation, IPC is included in the category of epistemic modality realized through modal adjectivals (e.g. *it is possible*) and mental state predicates (e.g. *I think*). He proposes several independent factors which contribute to the properties of IPC, as is exhibited in Table 2.3.

Table 2.3 Properties of Various Epistemic Modal Constructions①(after Butler, 2003: 476, which is based on Nuyts, 2001: 227)

Construction →Factor ↓	Adverbial	Adjectival	Mental state predicate	Modal auxiliary
Evidentiality: [inter]subjectivity②	−	+	+ +	(−)
Performativity: descriptive use	−	(+)	+	(−)
Information structure: focalized use	−	+ +	(+)	−
Discourse strategy: mitigation	−	+	+	−
Discourse strategy: argument management	+	−	−	+

According to Nuyts, as is indicated in Table 2.3, one of these factors is concerned with the type and quality of the evidence the speaker has for the epistemic judgment made. This evidence exists along a cline from purely subjective (available to the speaker) to highly intersubjective (widely known). As for modal adjectives,

---

① " + " means that the factor is frequently responsible for the selection of the relevant construction. " + + " marks the factor that may be considered most important for the expression adoption. "(+)" means that the factor can trigger the use of the construction. However, it is not a major factor. "(−)" means a slight tendency towards this feature. " − " means that the construction type is never triggered by the factor.

② Nuyts's concept of intersubjectivity is different from the one in the present study. To him, (inter)-subjectivity is an evidential category, referring to evidential markers that indicate the relevant evidence is to the speaker only to shared by a larger group. The former are subjective, including mental state predicates such as *think*; the latter are intersubjective, including epistemic adjectives such as *probable*.

Nuyts holds the opinion that it is the impersonal construction (e. g. *it is possible*) in which the modal adjective occurs that expresses an evidential meaning, but not the adjective itself. It is obvious that the speaker's choice of constructions with mental state predicates (e. g. *I think*) is of the most relevance to the factor of evidentiality.

A second factor is the distinction between performative and descriptive uses of modal qualifications. It depends on whether the speaker is reporting her own point of view, or describing/reporting someone else's. The degree of performativity has its obvious effect on the speaker's use of *I think* type constructions.

The third factor is the information structuring of the linguistic expressions in which the modal qualifications occur. Nuyts suggests that the adjective is normally used when the modal qualification is salient in the discourse. Consequently, the *it is probable that* ... type of constructions is employed for the purpose of focus indexing. According to Nuyts, constructions of the *it is probable that* ... type acts as something rather like a cleft version of *probably* ... since one major function of cleft constructions is focalizing. In contrast, the adverbial construction tends to occur where something other than the modality is salient in the discourse.

Nuyts's final factor in the differentiation of the various formal realizations of epistemic modality is the discourse strategy used by the speaker. This factor primarily operates at the speaker's interpersonal relationship with the hearer. Table 2.3 shows that IPC devices with modal adjectives and mental state predicates are in complementarity with adverbs and auxiliaries when the discourse strategy is at work. In the case of argument managing, both types of IPC constructions are far less prominent whereas hedging, face-saving and other politeness concerns are involved. Consequently, the speaker will turn to constructions containing adjective or mental state predicates. Generally speaking, it appears that adjective and predicate constructions are of closer connection with the four factors taken as a whole.

It is seen that both Dik and Nuyts have noticed the IPC type of modality in English. Dik approaches modality from subjective-objective considerations. In his investigation, the parameters of questioning, polarity, and information source are proposed to distinguish subjective modality from objective modality. Nuyts suggests that external factors such as evidentiality, performativity, focalization and communicative strategy affect the speaker's choice of modal constructions realized by IPC.

2.8 SFL Studies

This section focuses on studies in the field of SFL, which contributes to the interpretation of IPC. The relevant works are mainly of two types. One type is on the syntactic features of IPC whereas the other on the semantics of IPC. Therefore, the present study observes, on the one hand, Hudson's (1972) syntactic analysis of IPC. On the other hand, Halliday and Matthiessen (Halliday, 1994; Halliday & Matthiessen, 2004) interpret IPC as interpersonal grammatical metaphor. To Halliday and Matthiessen, the working mechanism of IPC is in essence interpersonal meaning expressed by the variation of clausal constructions.

2.8.1 Hudson (1972)

Hudson (1972) identifies and distinguishes IPC of reaction types and of cognition types, and within the latter factive types and modal types. His focus is on the lexicogrammatical realization possibility differences between the pairs.

First, Hudson shows his interest in distinguishing two types of IPC, i.e. those specify the modality of the "noun clause"[①] and those specify the subjective reaction to the fact stated in the noun clause. He terms the former cognition type and the latter reaction type, represented by Examples (46) and (47) respectively.

(46) *It seems that* no-one had locked the door.
(47) *Everyone regrets that* she pushed him.

The IPC *it seems* in Example (46) is of cognition type and *everyone regrets* in Example (47) is of reaction type. According to Hudson (1972), the two types of IPC are different in the following six aspects in terms of their grammatical constraints.

The first is related to finiteness of the noun clause. For both types, the noun clause can be finite. The second is related to the presence of Subject. If the noun clause is infinitival, the presence of Subject is optional in reaction type constructions while obligatory in the cognition type. The third is related to fronting of Subject. If the noun clause is infinitival, and contains Subject, this must be fronted in cognition type IPC, but must not be fronted in a reaction type. The fourth is related to question fronting. In an IPC where the noun clause is semantically factive, question fronting is often not possible. The fifth is related to negative-raising. In cognition type IPC, the negative marker of the noun clause can be transferred to the IPC. However, this

---

[①] Hudson's (1972) noun clause can be regarded as equivalent to the dependent clause.

is not allowed in reaction types. The final one is related to infinite noun clauses. Reaction type IPC allows infinite noun clauses which can contain *should* or *ever*, which are not allowed in cognition type IPC.

Hudson (1972) then divides the cognition type constructions into factive and modal constructions, represented respectively by Examples (48) and (49).

(48) *I realize that* he has left.
(49) *I think that* he has left.

The difference between the factive type of IPC represented by *I realize* in Example (48) and the modal type of IPC represented by *I think* in Example (49) lies in, according to Hudson, the speaker's commitment to the proposition defined by the noun clause. That is, in the former case, the noun clause is taken as a fact, while in the latter it defines a thesis whose reliability is defined by the IPC.

Hudson identifies the formal differences between factive and modal types of IPC. The first is related to the possibility of the fact. If the noun clause is finite, it can be put in apposition to the fact if the construction is factive, but not if it is modal. The second is related to the use of *so* in place of the noun clause. The modal constructions allow the clause substitute *so* which is not allowed in factive constructions. The third is related to extraposition. This is optional in factive constructions while obligatory in modal constructions if the noun clause is Subject in a clause which contains no complement.

2. 8. 2 Halliday & Matthiessen (2004)

Focusing on the semantic level, Halliday & Matthiessen (2004) regard IPC as a metaphorical expression of interpersonal meaning vis-à-vis the speaker's subjective assessment (Halliday & Matthiessen, 2004: 626-35). The most equivalent term for IPC is "modal clause" (Thompson, 2004: 70). Seen from the perspective of interpersonal grammatical metaphor, IPC is a non-congruent, clausal type of variation that expresses a given interpersonal meaning.

Halliday (1994) recognizes grammatical metaphor as variation in the expression of a given meaning, rather than variation in the meaning of a given expression. That is, of the same meaning, various lexicogrammatical configurations are compared as alternative realizations. Some of the realizations are considered congruent, while some others are transferred, or incongruent. The notion of congruency is characterized in terms of markedness. That is, congruent expressions are the unmarked, typical realizations of the given meaning. What is congruent conforms to the typical ways of saying things, as Halliday states:

> in all the instances that we are treating as grammatical metaphor, some aspect of the structural configuration of the clause, whether in its ideational or in its interpersonal function or both, is in some way different from that which would be arrived at by the shortest route—it is not, or was not originally, the most straightforward coding of the meanings selected. (Halliday, 1994: 366)

Thus, incongruent expressions are taken as grammatical metaphorical realizations. Lexicogrammatically, if the interpersonal meaning is expressed outside the clause[1], according to Halliday

---

[1] Bloor & Bloor (2004) seem to hold a different view in stating that interpersonal grammatical metaphor is involved in the alternation between the use of a modal verb, and modal adverb, adjective, and nouns. For instance, they consider *there may be three major indicators of generic integrity* as a more congruent version of the grammatically metaphorical *possibly there are three...* and *three possible major indicators of ...*

(1994), interpersonal metaphor is involved. Consider the following examples.

(50) It is *probably* going to rain.
(51) *I think* it's going to rain.

In Example (50), *probably* is used to express the interpersonal meaning of modality. It is an internal element of the clause. It is the congruent way of expressing the modal meaning. In Example (51), the modality is realized by an additional clause, i. e. the IPC *I think*. In this way, the modal meaning is explicitly realized.

In fact, the speaker can express her opinions in separate clauses in various ways. Halliday & Matthiessen (2004) point out that for one congruent expression, there might be a variety of incongruent alternatives. For instance, for *probably* in Example (50), there are multiple IPC possibilities. The subsequent expressions given by Halliday & Matthiessen (2004) include: *it stands to reason that... nobody tries to deny that... it is particularly difficult to avoid that... there can be no doubt that... the impartial spectator will surely agree that ... any teacher will agree that... most people would agree that... and everyone knows that ... no sane person would pretend that... not... commonsense determines that... all authorities on the subject are agreed that... you can't seriously doubt that...*

In SFL, two categories of IPC are identified (cf. Halliday, 1994; Halliday & Matthiessen, 2004; Thompson, 2004), namely, explicit subjective modality and explicit objective modality as the following examples indicate respectively.

(52) *I expect* that he is ill.
(53) *It is quite possible* that he is ill.

The IPCs *I expect* in Example (52) and *it is quite possible* in

Example (53) are metaphorical expressions of the congruent form *probably*. The difference lies in that the former is subjective and the latter objective. According to Halliday *et al.*, however, both types of IPC function in essence to express the speaker's subjective judgments and/or attitudes vis-à-vis given propositions.

It is widely accepted in SFL that there are two features which suggest that these modal meanings expressed in separate clauses (i. e. IPC expressions such as *I expect*, and *it is quite possible*) are metaphorical. The first is tag adding, as in (52a) and (53a).

(52a) *I expect* he is ill, isn't he?
(53a) *It is quite possible that* he is ill, isn't he?

The tag adding test shows that *he is ill* is the main proposition. That is, the tag invites the hearer to agree with the basic proposition *he is ill*. The difference between the two metaphorical versions lies in that the subjective one highlights the speaker's personal assessment of probability whereas the objective one treats the main proposition as a definable chunk of meaning that can have qualities attributed to it (in this case the quality of being possible).

The second is negation transferring. These modal clauses do not really express the main proposition for it is these modal clauses that do the job of Finite by establishing polarity. Consider Examples (52b) and (53b).

(52b) *I don't expect* he is ill.
(53b) *It isn't possible that* he is ill.

It is obvious that in the examples above, IPC expresses the negation of the main proposition. As Thompson (2004: 71) states, in speech, it is more commonly the modal clause that is negated. In such cases, IPC is characterized with transferred polarity instead of negation expressed in the proposition itself.

To sum up, in the field of SFL, Hudson notices IPC of reaction and cognition types. His interest lies in the lexicogrammatical possibilities of IPC. Halliday and Matthiessen, however, tend to interpret IPC from grammatical metaphorical perspectives. IPC is taken as a clausal realization of the interpersonal meaning.

2.9 Approaches to ABR

ABR, or published peer reviews (Hyland, 2000: 41), or scholarly book reviews, are defined by Osburn (1989: 729, cited in Nicolaisen, 2006) as "the process whereby authorities in a given field determine the validity and assess the relative significance of a particular contribution of a scholar or scientist within that field". Lindholm-Romantschuk (1998: 40) concurs with Osburn in stating that peer reviews are book reviews "published in a disciplinary journal or a general academic journal, written by a member of the academic profession". Seen in this way, peer reviewing essentially involves evaluation of the scholar's production by expert judges who are professional peers. In the academia, the system of peer reviewing is regarded as the most prevalent form of evaluation of scholarly work (Lindholm-Romantschuk, 1998: 17; Motta-Roth, 1998).

Despite its vital role in the academic community, the genre of ABR has not received deserved research attention until very recently. A survey of the literature shows that there are primarily two trends with respect to ABR studies. One is led by Hyland (2000) and Tse & Hyland (2006), who are interested in bringing out the evaluation resources employed in the genre. The other is represented by Belcher

(1995) and Motta-Roth (1998), who strive to formularize text structures of ABR.

2.9.1 Hyland (2000) and Tse & Hyland (2006)

This group of scholars aim to find out how ABR texts deploy lexicogrammatical resources for the purpose of evaluation. Wilss (1997) displays the linguistic devices deployed in German ABR texts which function to "hedge" criticism. Philip (2004) makes a notable endeavor to bring into academic vision the implicit or covert evaluation in ABR. Hyland (2000), Low (2005), and Groom (2005) find their common interest in comparing and contrasting the resources for realizing positive and negative comments across disciplines and/or academic subgenres (e. g. ABR and research articles) whereas Tejerina (2005) and Römer (2005) work on evaluative resources within a single discipline. In addition, the cross-cultural and cross-linguistic vantage point attracts Moreno & Suárez (2008) whose studies shed light upon the cultural influence (in their case English versus Spanish) on the reviewer's employment of critical strategies.

Similarly, Tse & Hyland (2006) apply the model of metadiscourse (Hyland, 2005a) to a sample of ABR texts. Table 2.4 exhibits the resources Tse & Hyland (2006) analyze in their sample.

Table 2.4 Interpersonal Model of Metadiscourse (after Hyland, 2005a: 49)

Category	Function	Examples
Interactive	Help to guide the reader through the text	Resources
Transitions	express relations between main clauses	in addition; but; thus; and
Frame markers	refer to discourse acts, sequences or stages	finally; to conclude; my purpose is
Endophoric markers	refer to information in other parts of the text	noted above; see Fig; in section 2
Evidentials	refer to information from other texts	according to X; Z states
Code glosses	elaborate propositional meanings	namely; e.g.; such as; in other words
Interactional	Involve the reader in the text	Resources
Hedges	withhold commitment and open dialogue	might; perhaps; possible; about
Boosters	emphasize certainty or close dialogue	in fact; definitely; it is clear that
Attitude markers	express writer's attitude to proposition	unfortunately; I agree; surprisingly
Self mentions	explicit reference to author(s)	I; we; my; me; our
Engagement markers	explicitly build relationship with reader	consider; note; you can see that

However, it is Hyland (2000) who classes most of the mentioned aspects of evaluation in ABR texts into six categories. Table 2.5 summarizes these aspects.

Table 2.5 Categories of Evaluation in ABR (after Hyland, 2000: 47)

Focus	Description
Content	
(i) General	Overall discussion: e.g. coverage, approach, interest, currency, quality
(ii) Specific	Argument: e.g. insight, coherence, explanatory or descriptive value
Style	Exposition: clarity, organization, conciseness, difficulty, readability and editorial judgments
Readership	Value or relevance for a particular readership, purpose or discipline
Text	Extent, relevance and currency of references, the number, usefulness and quality of diagrams, index items, tasks and exercises
Author	Writer's experience, reputation, qualifications or previous publications
Publishing	Price, quality and production standards of the book

Tse & Hyland (2006) and Hyland (2000)'s studies of metadiscourse in ABR texts show that metadiscourse is discipline-sensitive. Across soft disciplines (e.g. Politics, Philosophy) and hard ones (e.g. Physics, Chemistry), disciplinary conventions play a determinant role in the allocation and distribution of these resources in ABR.

2.9.2 Belcher (1995) and Motta-Roth (1998)

From the perspective of text structure, Belcher (1995) describes three types of structures found in her sample of ABR. In another vein, working in the move-analytic tradition represented by Swales (1990) and Bhatia (1993), Motta-Roth (1998) and Nicolaisen (2006) strive to generalize an applicable rhetorical move structure of ABR.

Approaching text structures from a rhetorical strategic perspective, Belcher (1995: 140) examines ABR texts and article reviews from 14 different fields and subfields identifies and identifies three types of "text structure", in terms of the arrangements of summary and critique, the necessary structural elements serve the vital informative and evaluative roles played by reviews. Belcher (1995) recognizes two types of critical review text structure, namely, the discrete summary/critique review and the cycling summary/critique review. The discrete type of review is usually composed of introduction, summary, and critique. According to Belcher's data, the discrete review may consist primarily of summary and conclude with a final evaluative overview which states the reviewer's position.

Cycling reviews are structured as introduction, summary, critique, summary, critique, summary, critique, and so on. The cycling review is fraught with clear, reader-friendly summative evaluations. However, sporadic commentary on specific sections of the book under review precedes the final evaluation.

In the third type of review, the introductory component is extensively developed vis-à-vis background information. As Belcher observes, this type of review may, in fact, devote a third to a half of the entire review to "scene setting" before launching into the review. Her samples show that their seemingly excessive and indirect introductions preface either extremely negative or extremely positive critiques.

Motta-Roth (1998) provides a genre analytical study of ABR from the fields of Chemistry, Economics and Linguistics. Following Swales (1991) and Bhatia's (1993; 2002) move analysis methodology, she formulates a schematic description of the invariable structural organizations of ABR texts, as is shown in Table 2.6.

Table 2.6 Rhetorical Moves in ABR (after Motta-Roth, 1998, modified by Nicolaisen, 2006, who adds Subfunctions 12 and 13)

Move 1.	Introducing the book
Sub-function 1.	Defining the general topic of the book
Sub-function 2.	Informing about potential readership
Sub-function 3.	Informing about the author
Sub-function 4.	Making topic generalizations
Sub-function 5.	Inserting the book in the field
Move 2.	Outlining the book
Sub-function 6.	Providing general view of the organization of the book
Sub-function 7.	Stating the topic of each chapter
Sub-function 8.	Citing extra-text material
Move 3.	Highlighting parts of the book
Sub-function 9.	Providing specific evaluation
Move 4.	Providing evaluation of the book
Sub-function 10.	Definitely recommending the book
Sub-function 11.	Recommending the book despite indicated shortcomings
Sub-function 12.	Neither recommending nor disqualifying the book
Sub-function 13.	Disqualifying the book despite indicated positive aspects
Sub-function 14.	Definitely disqualifying the book

According to Motta-Roth (1998) and Nicolaisen (2006), the four-move rhetorical pattern of English ABR reads in this way. The initial section of most ABR texts encompasses 1/the first move, which may provide five pieces of information about the book under review: central topic and format, readership, author, topic generalizations, and locating the book in the broader field of study to which it relates. The 2/second move is usually the longest one. It typically includes a detailed description of how the book is organized, which topics are treated in each chapter, with what approach, and what kind of additional information is included in the book (graphs, pictures, tables, etc.). During the 3/third move the reviewer concentrates on specific aspects of the book, giving a positive or negative comment from very mild criticism to praise. Move 4/four rounds up the text, breaking up with the detailed perspective adopted in move 3. It provides a final evaluation of the whole book and additionally serves the purpose of closing the review text.

The description, in the same vein with many others (Swales, 1990; Flowerdew & Dudley-Evans, 2002), follows Swales's pioneering move-analytic model. It is no doubt that Motta-Roth (1998) offers a valuable attempt in bringing into vision the structure of ABR. However, as was limited by the methodology per se, the formula is far from being exhaustive in describing possible generic structures of the given genre.

2.10 Comments on Previous Studies

This chapter has conducted a literature review of how IPC is dealt with in different linguistics approaches, ranging from traditional ones to recent developments. The major branches under review include traditional grammar, phraseological approaches, frequency-driven register-oriented perspectives, cognitive linguistics, rhetoric and stylistic studies, pragmatic investigations, structural-functional approaches, and finally

SFL. It should be borne in mind that each of the approaches, despite its limitations in either theoretical or practical consideration, has its peculiar contribution to the present study of IPC. Therefore, it is of vital significance to sum up the contributions and limitations of the previous studies so that light will be thrown upon the current investigation.

First, like other traditional grammarians, Jespersen considers only content meaning, or propositional meaning while neglecting interpersonal meaning. In addition, he tends to take the dependent clause as a constituent of the main clause, not treating the sentence as a combination of two clauses. However, his contribution lies in the fact that he notices the importance of the conjunction *that* and the introductory *it*. This hints at the fact that Jespersen notices the link between IPC and its ensuing clause in the complex. Therefore, it is fair to say that Jespersen makes his contribution to the study of IPC, though indirectly and unconsciously.

Quirk *et al.* interpret IPC expressions and adverbials as equal in conveying the writer's comments or observations of the subordinate clause. This indicates that they have noticed that clauses can be employed to express the writer's modal assessment of the dependent clause. Unfortunately, they do not point out the difference between the two versions (i. e. clausal expressions and adverbials). Quirk *et al.* also rightly notice that IPC disjuncts are syntactically more detached and "super-ordinate", having a scope that extends over the rest of the sentence. However, they do not show much interest in this aspect. Consequently they do not put at the centre the reader-orientating functions of IPC.

Another demerit lies in the fact that Quirk *et al.* do not distinguish between what is possible and what is typical. Their paraphrasing interpretation of adverbial disjuncts and clausal disjuncts blurs the distinctions between them. One of the distinctions is that, as Halliday & Matthiessen (2004) indicate, the adverbial is typical in expressing modal assessment, and the clausal construction is the marked since additional considerations are always involved, such as the need to expand meaning, to enhance negotiation between the writer and the reader.

Second, phraseologists' pattern analysis greatly improves the accuracy of IPC which are more established or formulaic linguistic resources. They contribute to the study of IPC by revealing systemic patterns at a "greater degree of delicacy than had been recognized hitherto" (Halliday, 2008: 71). The patterns are anchored at an intermediate point between the most generalized systemic options at the grammatical end of the lexicogrammatical continuum and the collocational regularities that are associated with the lexis. However, it should be pointed out that patterns, such as realizations of IPC, do not exist in isolation as constructions independent of grammar. As Halliday (2008: 72) points out, to understand how these patterns work, we need a general pattern of the grammar.

Third, Biber *et al.* regard IPC as a grammatical stance marker. They touch on the syntactic and semantic features of IPC. More important, Biber *et al.* introduce the concept of register into the interpretation of IPC. They notice that the linearity of IPC and the ensuing clause makes it possible for the speaker to first foreground her intended perspective, and then to identify the propositional information which is, due to the linear order of the clauses, supposed to be interpreted with respect to the given perspective. It should be stressed, as later-on chapters will show as well, the paradigmatic feature is a necessary ingredient of IPC. Variations concerning frequency and distribution are compared across registers. The different grammatical realizations of IPC are therefore explained with relevance to the controlling parameter of register. This sheds much light on the present study, in particular, on the relationship between BLBR and IPC.

Fourth, cognitivists develop the concept of "viewing frame" to highlight the conceptually onstage status of IPC. Verhagen *et al.* are right in noticing that IPC sets up a frame or perspective for the understanding of the following propositional clause. From an SFL perspective, this suggests that Verhagen *et al.* stress the interpersonal negotiation function enacted through IPC. However, semantic and discursive features of IPC deserve much more in-depth investigations, as will be shown in the coming chapters.

Verhagen's work is of particular significance in that it attempts to generalize the pragmatic functions of IPC by turning to the construction of intersubjectivity. However, his interpretation seems overgeneralizing. Therefore, for the investigation into projection constructions, it is far from being sufficient or convincing to ascribe everything to intersubjectivity. In addition, seen from above, the clause complex of projection is the grammatical realization of the semantic level of language. Thus, it is of necessity to turn to the three metafunctions of language (namely, ideational, interpersonal and textual) for more satisfying answers in the case of IPC, since it is grammatically realized by complement constructions.

Fifth, both functional stylistics and cognitive stylistics treat IPC as a grammatical realization of attitude-conveying modality. It seems that it is agreed that these grammaticalized modal expressions create a special layer of meaning, either in the sense of value indication or in creating a modal-world. However, scholars in this field limit their studies to the analysis of fictions. Their conclusions need be tested in actual discourse, with contextual elements taken into consideration. Another demerit lies in the fact that the stylists fail to provide a systematic framework for the analysis of such modal structures. It appears that they are picked up at random. All in all, their claims are in want of real-and-large corpus support.

Sixth, in the field of pragmatic use of language, IPC is seen as a communicative strategy adopted by the speaker to shoulder commitment or to avoid commitment. This language-user-oriented, functional approach on the one hand highlights the interaction between grammatical structures and the speaker's communicative intentions, and backstages systematic interpretation of the lexicogrammatical realizations of these communication-serving grammatical structures, on the other hand. Meanwhile, it seems the convention in the field that much theoretical research is based on introspection. That is, the pragmatic literature on IPC does little with regard to the discursive behavior of IPC and the co-occurrence of IPC with other linguistic devices. Consequently, no general picture of the discoursal patterns of IPC is afforded, despite the fact that some scholars (cf. Section 2.6) do mention that specific text types should be considered in investigating the phenomenon.

Seventh, the structural-functional approach gives an account of the semantics of IPC types of complex constructions. However, as Butler (2003b) observes, much of the study is more oriented to the effects on formal realization than to the contribution made on the discourse. The priority of the researches conducted by Dik, Nuyts and others is given to the characteristics of IPC which are independent of concrete contexts, ignoring what the speaker is doing in the discourse. It is perhaps beyond their interest and consideration. If the investigation priority were given to the intersubjective aspect of IPC in certain types of texts, their theories would have been much enriched.

Eighth, in SFL, IPC is coped with in more in-depth investigation. The grammatical metaphorical perspective foregrounds the nature of IPC and the tentative categorization of IPC is more convincing and practical than the other approaches. Meanwhile, as Halliday's grammar is always oriented towards what the speaker is doing in the discourse, the analysis of IPC is directed by what and how the speaker contributes to the ongoing discourse. Seen in this way, whether explicit subjective or explicit objective, IPC is conveying the extent to which the speaker openly accepts responsibility for the subjective assessment being expressed.

However, it is not always easy or convincing to pin down every realization of IPC to grammatical metaphor. Halliday (1994: 365) recognizes that in many cases "it is by no means easy to decide which are metaphorical and what are congruent forms". Therefore, the concept of IPC deserves much deeper and multi-perspective exploration and interpretation. For one thing, the current study proposes that it will be light-shedding if IPC is approached from the concept of projection. In addition, one important function of IPC that has been overlooked is its intersubjectivity-boosting function. It will, therefore, be revealing if the discursive behavior of IPC is examined, with special consideration given to the parameter of genre.

Finally, with respect to ABR, there emerge studies concerning evaluative devices used in the genre, and studies of the text structure of the type of text. Nonetheless, Hyland et al.'s studies overlook the role of grammatical constructions such as IPC in conveying evaluation in a give genre. Belcher's classification of text structures of ABR texts is out of mere observation and intuition. It does not provide convincing theoretical support. Meanwhile, the move-analytic approach fails to capture the dynamic nature of the genre. That is, in reviewing, more variations concerning the moves are notified. That is why Motta-Roth's (1998) formula encounters constant elaborations (Nicolaisen, 2006). Besides, little attention has been given to ELBR, a particular type of ABR. The correlation between IPC and the genre is rarely touched, as the literature survey has shown.

Overall, the previous studies provide extensive overviews of IPC types of grammatical constructions in general and, consequently, only touch upon either individual expressions to mark the speaker's individual, subjective opinions or attitudes, or theoretical considerations detached from authentic texts. The current study builds on this foundation to bring in the intersubjective aspects of IPC in actual, naturally-occurring discourse.

2.11 Summary

This chapter has primarily reviewed previous studies on IPC. In the traditional grammatical school, IPC is taken as the clausal disjunct. It is approached from a transformational, constitutional perspective. The clause complex composed of IPC and the "content clause" is analyzed as a single sentence. Phraseologists totally abandon the traditional way, and take IPC as a functional lexical pattern instead. They start by identifying grammatical patterns and their functions in authentic data to establish categories of IPC. The frequency-driven register-based approach prefers terming IPC as a "stance marker". In this field, researchers try to reach a compromise between traditional grammar and corpus linguistics. Being traditional, the constituent perspective is kept. Being corpus-assisted and register-specific, their study highlights the affinity between the frequency of IPC use and register variation. In cognitive linguistics, the study of IPC sees a transition from Langacker's subjectivity orientation to Verhagen *et al.*'s intersubjectivity concern. Scholars in the field of stylistics and rhetoric see IPC devices as grammaticalized expressions employed by the writer to reveal to the reader fiction characters' attitudes or to create text worlds. From the perspective of pragmatics, IPC is interpreted as a politeness strategy both for the speaker and the hearer. Structural-functional schools interpret IPC as a modal expression. SFL scholars understand IPC as interpersonal grammatical metaphor, which is an incongruent variation of expression of a given meaning.

These previous investigations, taken together, are handicapped in the following ways. First, there has not been a systematic categorization of IPC. Second, the intersubjectivity boosting function of IPC has been overlooked[①]. Third, theoretical exploration is necessary when IPC is considered from the SFL concept of projection. That is, IPC is far from being theoretically interpreted. Finally, the observation and understanding of IPC in the discourse of ELBR has received insufficient attention. To date, to the knowledge of the present study, not full-length monographs or books are devoted to the discursive behavior and pattern distribution of IPC with respect to genre consideration.

The next chapter will establish a framework to analyze IPC, which is followed by a description of SFL theories which are necessary for the analysis of IPC.

---

① It should be mentioned that Verhagen (2005) does highlight the intersubjectivity aspect of complement-taking constructions. However, his interpretation focuses on intersubjectivity indexing instead of boosting. Meanwhile, his approach is different from the present study in that his is cognition-based.

Chapter 3

Theoretical Framework

Previous studies on IPC, as were reviewed in Chapter 2, have not systematically approached IPC by examining its discursive behavior within a given genre. Meanwhile, the genre of ELBR has not received deserved attention, in particular, its relationship with the distribution and allocation of IPC strategies. Taking these into consideration, the current investigation takes the argument one step further by examining the discursive behavior of IPC from the perspective of SFL, within the particular genre of ELBR. This chapter unfolds with the framework the present project establishes for the purpose of IPC exploration. The current study identifies four types of IPC. This chapter further outlines SFL theories which are related with the categorization and interpretation of IPC. In particular, the chapter focuses on the three metafunctions, the system of projection, the notions of genre and intersubjectivity.

3.1 The Framework for IPC Analysis

Based on the previous studies, this research argues for the intersubjectivity boosting function of IPC. This function is rooted in the features of IPC, both structural and functional. That is, the lexicogrammatical characteristics of IPC make it possible and feasible for IPC to boost intersubjectivity. Looking at the other side of the coin, it should be admitted that there are more than one linguistic realization of IPC to intensify intersubjectivity. As Halliday (1994: 355) states, the speaker has at her disposal indefinitely many linguistic options to express her attitudes and opinions. The motivations behind the speaker's choosing particular types of IPC to enhance intersubjectivity instead of other lexicogrammatical forms demand that the explanations be sought outside language, in the social and cultural context (Eggins, 2004: 204). Within such a perspective, this section attempts to establish a framework with which the current study is going to conduct an analysis of IPC.

3.1.1 IPC as an Intersubjectivity Booster①

From a sociocultural and sociocognitive perspective, intersubjectivity concerns with the relation between one interactant's subjectivity and another's (cf. Du Bois, 2007). Intersubjectivity is thus recognized as fundamental sociocognitive relations that organize language use. That is, making sense of intersubjectivity in interaction depends on a dialogic understanding of language use. It is essential to see linguistic activity as shaped by the complex interplay of collaborative acts by co-participants involved. Therefore, IPC expressions like *I'm glad* or *I know* can not be a simple matter of subjectivity in isolation, whether

---

① Booster in the present study simply carries the connotation of "enhancement" or "intensification". It is slightly different from the interpretation offered by Hyland & Tse (2006: 772) as "the metadiscourse expressions which express certainty and emphasize the force of propositions".

epistemic or affective. It is evident that linguistic act is at the same time a social act (cf. Halliday, 1978; 1994). In the discourse of communication, one speaker's subjectivity actively reacts to another's subjectivity (Du Bois, 2007). This dialogic relation sometimes is implicitly indexed and sometimes explicitly foregrounded or boosted. With foregrounding, an interactionally salient dialogic resonance is achieved between the participants.

Pragmatically and grammatically, the speaker is expected to actively engage herself in the alignment process with the listener, when they converge or diverge to varying degrees. In this light, IPC should be seen as an explicit part of an activity of alignment that calibrates and enhances the intersubjective relationship between the engaged co-participants. In Du Bois's (2007: 170) words, in such cases, IPC expressions like *I think* can be said to function as "intersubjective alignment markers". Besides inviting and involving the co-participant in stancetaking in the same way as has been shown, these "markers" gain added levels of significance through their juxtaposition with other intersubjectivity indexing devices.

Much has been done in revealing structural features of IPC (cf. Thompson, 2002; Quirk *et al.*, 1985). The previous studies rightly point put that IPC is often structurally super-ordinate and logically hypotactic, in relation to the clause containing the proposition or proposal. In this way, IPC forms a frame or a scope for the interpretation of the following information clause. The structural feature facilitates the speaker to signal and display her intended communication orientation to the hearer in advance.

In this way, IPC structurally "organizes" the modal assessment activity of the interactants. Frame containing, IPC provides the speaker the powerful linguistic device to invite the hearer to take into account the stance already explicit in discourse. At such points in interaction, IPC gains importance to such an extent that it impinges on the sequential organization of discourse. The speaker thus achieves establishing and increasing social solidarity between the interactants involved. It is therefore safe to conclude that the frame formed by an IPC is an essential part of the intended activity by the speaker in the ongoing discourse. An activity, such as an assessment or a claim, can be well accomplished without IPC, but it would constitute an essentially different type of assessment or claim. Thus, it is reasonable to argue that IPC signals, displays, and makes more explicit the kind of modal assessment action that is being done by the speaker.

Besides the framing feature, the functional properties of IPC make it possible for IPC to serve as the intersubjectivity booster. IPC has all the properties and functions of a clause, which indicates that IPC can be seen as a proposition or a proposal by itself. It therefore has its independent interpersonal systems of tense, aspect, person, modality, etc. Consequently, the proposition in an IPC can be further negotiated in a number of ways (cf. Hudson, 1972) and allows for a further interplay between the speech role and the wording choices. Consider the following examples.

(54) *I was just wondering* what time dinner was. [demand for information, with declarative annotating clause]

(55) *Tell me* what you saw. [demand for information, with imperative annotating clause]

(56) *I wouldn't advise* you to get too excited. [demand for goods-and-services, with declarative annotating clause] (Thompson, 2004: 235)

By choosing IPC to realize modal assessment, the speaker also has at her disposal a number of choices concerning processes with participants and optional circumstances. The following IPC realizations offer clear examples.

(57) *I think that* ... [mental process]
(58) *It is essential that* ... [attributive process]
(59) *There is a definite danger that*... [existential process]

These IPC choices as Examples (57), (58) and (59) represent offer the speaker more options to express herself best with respect to the interaction with the hearer.

In SFL, language is understood as a resource for making meaning by choices out of the meaning potential. This is clearly stated by Halliday:

> A system network is a theory of language as choice. It represents a language, or any part of a language, as a resource for making meaning by choosing. Each choice point in the network specifies:
>
> 1) an environment or context: an entry condition or the choices already made
>
> 2) a set of possibilities of which one is (to be) chosen
>
> The output of networks are structures. A structure is the realization of the set (s) of features chosen in passing through the network. (Halliday, 1985: xxvii)

Holding "choice is meaning", systemicists give theoretical priorities to paradigmatic relations. That is, in understanding how language makes meanings, the notion of choice, or oppositions is of fundamental importance (cf. Eggins, 2004). As the instances above show, the consequence or output of the choices (here IPC) are structures, captured through lexicogrammatical realizations. It has to be borne in mind, therefore, that systems of language are set up when there is structural difference. However, it is better to see that the structures develop along a cline from being similar in structure to a more delicate structural difference. The concept of system is fairly important because it captures what choices the speaker could make. As the examples above demonstrate, the speaker can choose among multiple options to realize IPC. There is always discrepancy between the speaker's linguistic potential and the choice she actually makes on a particular occasion.

It is the linguist's interest to find out why the speaker makes one choice rather than another. However, it is not sufficient to seek for the explanation only within the linguistic system. Otherwise the research will "go round in circles" (Eggins, 2004: 204). As language is a social semiotic (Halliday, 1978), it is necessary to explore dimensions of the context of situation where the speaker-hearer interaction occurs. SFL has, in fact, indicated the intimate interdependency of the social and the semiotic. Therefore, it is significant to explain the meaning choice by considering the relationship between the social role the speaker is playing and the discursive role she has access to.

To make it clearer, people with different social positioning tend to have significantly different patterns of linguistic interaction. These patterns are recognizable as genres which are defined by Martin (1985: 248) as "how things get done, when language is used to accomplish them". To understand how and why the speaker makes a choice out of her meaning potential, the genre she is involved in has to be under examination. In the present case, it is assumed that IPC choices by the speaker are determined by the genre under question and that the discursive behavior of IPC is expected to vary across different genres.

However, there is little substantial evidence for genre variation with respect to IPC use. Only a few studies have attempted to map the use of IPC across genres (cf. Biber et al., 1998; Herriman, 2000; Yang, 2006). However, their contributions concern only some type (s) of IPC. It follows that their investigations can not represent the overall discursive features of IPC. Meanwhile, to date, most studies that involve comparison and contrast across texts are cross-disciplinary.

Hyland (2004a) explores research articles in eight different disciplines whereas Charles (2006a) focuses on two contrasting disciplines. Therefore, more research is needed to map the genre variation of IPC vis-à-vis its lexicogrammatical realizations.

The present study assumes that the frequencies and patterns of IPC vary across genres. In some genres it is conventional for the writer or the reader to be visible. Such genres will witness a relatively high frequency of IPC in "explicit subjective" ways (e. g. *I suppose*, and *you are supposed to*). In other genres, however, it is not appropriate for the writer to be explicitly mentioned at all. It is therefore reasonable to assume that in genres such as legal documents, explicit subjective IPC expressions such as *I think* are not preferred. In addition to genre, discipline has been shown to play an important part in textual variation. With respect to linguistic signals to indicate intersubjective interaction, the speaker may choose to establish an involved or remote stance, or to adopt a convivial or indifferent interpersonal tenor. All these are at least partly influenced by the dominant ideologies of the discipline, which are conventionalized through the patterns of the genre the community members are participating in.

3.1.2 Categories of IPC and the Analysis Framework

It is argued that ABR is a genre where intersubjectivity has to be specifically considered and managed. It is also argued that IPC serves as a best linguistic strategy, both structural and functional, to facilitate and foreground the writer's special endeavor to create a "communicative space" (Thompson, 2001) or "interpersonal space" (Matthiessen, 2004) where intersubjectivity is managed and tailored with greater delicacy vis-à-vis lexicogrammatical manifestations of IPC.

Participant oriented, this study classifies IPC tactics in terms of the presence/absence of the interactant in the projecting clause. The present data reveal the following types of IPC:

Type 1: The Projector is the interactant;
Type 2: The Projector includes the interactant;
Type 3: No interactant appears in the IPC;
Type 4: The Projector is a third-person instead of the interactant.

In IPC of Type 1, the interactant (i.e. *I*, or *you*) participates directly in the process of projection. According to Halliday & Matthiessen (2004), this type is the typical interpersonal projection in the language of English. The following examples represent this type of IPC.

(60) *I think* the ambitions of the near future should be more modest. [R72]

(61) *I was surprised that* this book starts by posing the question why so many Germans could be persuaded to back the Nazis. [R11]

In IPC of Type 2, the interactant does not participate directly in the projection. Instead, the Projector is a general term whose reference range may cover the interacant. The subsequent sentences demonstrate this type of IPC.

(62) But then *one could also argue that* the already bulky size of the volume might militate against the inclusion of more material. [R61]

(63) Real semantics is understood to consist of something conceptual referring to something distinct, an object in the world, *we might say*. [R77]

In IPC of Type 3, there appears no Projector involved in the process of projection. Examples (64), (65) and (66) represent this type of IPC.

(64) *It seems that* the idea of objectivity is owed to this direct or integrated conceptual relation in the causal situation sustained by our stereotyped background knowledge. [R12]

(65) ...And although "semiotics" to some humanities scholars may have the ring of yesteryear's scholarly fashion, *there is no doubt that* semioticians

have always shown a theoretical interest in multimodal texts... [R72]
(66) *The problem is that* only the main text is indexed, while the extensive and informative end-of-chapter notes are not. [R78]

IPC of Type 4 is typically characterized by a projecting process in which the Projector is construed by a third-party rather than the participants in the interaction, as illustrated by the following examples.

(67) *As the author notes in the first chapter*, this is similar to Pomerantz's (1978) work on how people respond to compliments in American English. [R78]

(68) There is much to discuss, and more to criticize, and, *as Popper has taught us*, criticism is the crucible of intellectual progress. [R71]

The four types of IPC and their subtypes will be discussed in Chapters 5 and 6, with specific consideration given to metafunctional features, genre-specific characteristics and intersubjectivity-augmenting functions of each type. Figure 3.1 represents the framework with which these types of IPC are going to be analyzed in the subsequent chapters.

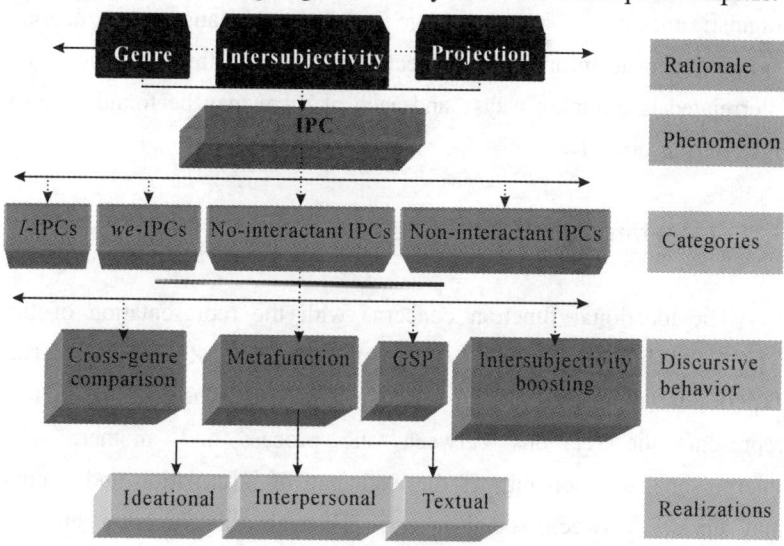

Figure 3.1 The Framework for IPC Analysis

As Figure 3.1 shows, IPC will be approached from the dimensions of genre, intersubjectivity and projection. For each category of IPC, its discursive behavior will be examined from four perspectives, namely, metafunctional features, cross-genre comparisons, distribution vis-a-vis GSP elements, and its intersubjectivity-boosting functions.

The following sections will introduce SFL notions necessary for the detailed analysis of IPC in the subsequent chapters.

3.2 Metafunctions and Metafunctional Complementarity

In SFL, language is viewed as a social activity which takes place in a situational context and fulfills different functions. It is well-accepted that language fulfills three metafunctions, namely ideational, interpersonal and textual. These reflect the different aspects of linguistic meanings (i.e. language as reflection, language as action, and language as information respectively). These three functions are interrelated in complex ways, and each of them may be found to shed light on the other two.

3.2.1 Metafunctions of Language

The ideational function concerns with the representation of the world and has two modes, the experiential and the logical. The experiential represents the processes themselves whereas the logical represents the relations between one process and another. The interpersonal function mirrors the exchange of information and goods-and-services between social actors. Through this function humans construct their social relationships with the various others. Textual metafunction concerns with the creation and organization of information within clauses, and through this, with the organization of the larger text. The three functions reflect respectively three parameters of register, or contextual variables, namely, field, tenor and mode.

3. 2. 1. 1 Experiential Metafunction

The experiential function is the one whereby the speaker expresses the propositional content of her statement, i. e. to refer to the entities in the world, both external and internal. These entities and their interrelations are construed in the grammar as figures, mainly through the system of TRANSITIVITY. In the system, experience is construed in terms of configurations of a process, participants involved, and circumstances. In English, six different types of processes are distinguished, as Table 3. 1 illustrates.

Table 3. 1 Process Types and Nuclear Participants

Process type and subtypes	Nuclear participants	Examples
material	Actor, Goal	I found the book
Mental: perception cognition affection desideration	Senser, Phenomenon	I saw the car I forget his name She liked his music I prefer the blue one
relational: attributive	Carrier, Attribute	The book is interesting
identifying	Token, Value	She is the leader
verbal	Sayer	He answered
behavioral	Behaver	They laughed
existential	Existent	There exist some objections

As the table shows, material processes construe doings and

happenings in the material world as well as change in abstract phenomena. The Actor in a material process is the one conducting the doing while the Goal is the participant impacted by the doing. Mental clauses construe a person involved in conscious processing, including processes of perception, cognition, affection, and desideration. The inherent participant, i. e. the Senser, is endowed with consciousness and involved in conscious processing. One important characteristic of mental clauses is that they can project. This will be discussed in Section 3. 3 below. The Phenomenon is being sensed. It can be any kind of entity entertained or created by consciousness.

Relational clauses construe being and do this in two different modes, i. e. attribution and identification. The essential difference between attributive and identifying is the difference between class membership and symbolization (Martin et al., 1997: 106). That is, Carrier and Attribute are of the same order of abstraction, but differ in generality as member to class. Token and Value are of different orders of abstraction; they are in symbolic relations. Verbal processes construe different modes of saying. The process can also project by representing the content of saying as a separate clause quoting or reporting what was said (cf. Section 3. 3 below). Behavioral clauses represent human behavior, including mental and verbal behavior, relating to human physiological processes. Existential processes express the existence of an entity. They are normally recognized because the Subject is "there". The Existent is the only one participant in such clauses.

The system of TRANSITIVITY makes it possible to explore transitivity structures of clauses in a given text. Therefore, the system is helpful and necessary to bring out different processes which construe IPC. To be specific, as Martin et al. (1997: 115-16) rightly point out, there are mainly three general considerations. The first is about the possible alternative verbs other than the particular one used in the given clause. This facilitates to find out verbs that can be used in more than one process. In addition, the same experience may be represented by more than one process. The second is about the obligatoriness of the participants. That is, to know whether two structures are related to each other, it is useful to see whether there are variations with the number of participants. The third is about alternative realizations of participants. Processes may be constrained in this aspect in terms of consciousness. These considerations on the one hand reveal the differences between processes, and on the other hand, provide the language user parameters for choosing types of processes to construe her intended meaning. Different processes chosen by the interactant to realize IPC in particular communicative contexts should be considered as dependent on a variety of factors, such as communicative purposes, metafunctional coordination, and the element the language user intends to give saliency.

3. 2. 1. 2 Logical Metafunction

The logical function construes relationships between the propositional ideas on an equal or subordinate basis. This function enables the speaker to produce complex configurations by combining two or more grammatical units (e. g. word, group, phrase, clause) into a larger whole, which is the complex (e. g. clause complex). In relation to the present study, the focus will be primarily on clause complexing. In SFL, two logico-semantic systems, those of DEPENDENCY and SEMANTIC RELATION, are used to describe possible relations between clauses within a clause complex. This is shown in Figure 3. 2.

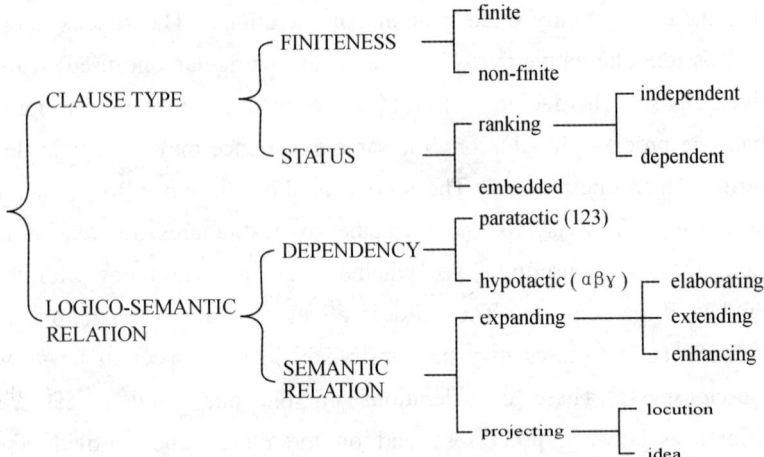

**Figure 3.2 Basic Systems for Clause Complexing
(after Thompson, 1996/2004: 214)**

In the figure, the systems of FINITENESS and STATUS are related to single clauses. That is, they describe whether an individual clause is finite or non-finite, and ranking or embedded. It seems that they were not appropriate here. The reason that they are included is that they clarify the structural forms that realize the components which enter into the logico-semantic relations of DEPENDENCY and SEMANTIC RELATION, as will be shown in Section 3.3 below. Therefore, in analyzing complexes, it is necessary to consider these aspects.

In terms of the two ways in which two clauses may be combined into a complex, each can be furthered in delicacy. The two options within the system of DEPENDENCY① are parataxis and hypotaxis ones which relate to notions of coordination and subordination in traditional grammar. When two clauses within a complex are in parataxis relation,

---

① For the terminological preference, TAXIS is chosen instead by Halliday (1994), Halliday & Matthiessen (2004), and Martin *et al.* (1997).

each stands as an independent functioning role. This relation is signaled by the Arabic numeral system of 123, as in Example (69).

(69) He replied quickly, ‖ "I can't complain."
         1   2

By contrast, if two clauses are in hypotactic relation, one clause is a principal or dominant clause and the other is dependent on it. The relation is signaled by the Greek alphabet system, as is shown in Example (70).

(70) α I think [dominant]
     β that is quite possible [dependent]

In addition to the system of DEPENDENCY, clauses within a clause complex can be linked in terms of two types of semantic relationship between them: expansion and projection. Within the relationship by which one clause expands the other, three semantic subgroups are identified: elaboration, extension and enhancement. An elaborating clause does not add any essentially new element to the dominant clause, relating to apposition or non-defining relative clause in traditional grammar. If one clause extends the other, it adds to it by addition through *and* or by replacement through *or*. Enhancing clauses are traditionally called adverbial clauses. They specify aspects of the dominant clause such as time, condition, etc. Projection, the other type of semantic relation between the clauses within a clause complex, typically concerns the relation between a mental or verbal clause and the content it quotes (i. e. locution) or reports (i. e. idea).

Of the various logico-semantic relations between the clauses within a clause complex, two points deserve elaboration.

First, the options of the systems may combine to result in more complex relations. The co-ordination of "projection" with the two options within the system of DEPENDENCY produces the semantic relations of paratactic projection and hypotactic projection.

Second, the options in the system of SEMANTIC RELATION may operate with options within the system of clause types. For instance, "projection" and "embedded" co-work to produce the semantic category of embedded projection. These will be fully elaborated in Section 3.3 below.

3.2.1.3 Interpersonal Metafunction

As was seen, the ideational metafunction construes human experience of the world through its two modes of experiential and logical functions. The ideational metafunction enables the speaker to realize IPC with a variety of processes and to construe the relationship between an IPC and its projected clause.

In addition to the ideational metafunction, there is the interpersonal metafunction, which enacts the speaker to participate in the speech situation via exchanging either goods-and-services (proposal) or information (proposition). The interpersonal component of the semantic system of language is also concerned with the social, expressive and conative functions of language. That is, language expresses the speaker's "angle", such as her attitudes and judgments, her encoding of the role relationships in the situation, and her motive in saying anything at all.

The grammar of interpersonal meaning is described by the systems of MOOD and MODALITY. As is demonstrated in Table 3.2, the system of MOOD is realized by the grammatical structure of Mood + Residue (+ Moodtag). Within the system, the Mood element makes the clause negotiable and consists of Finite, Subject and sometimes modal Adjunct. The Finite makes a clause negotiable by coding it as positive or negative and by grounding it in terms of time or modality. The Subject is the element in terms of which the clause can be negotiated. Modal Adjuncts add meanings related to the polarity of the Finite (Mood Adjunct) or to speaker judgment and attitude.

Table 3.2　The System of MOOD Realized on the Clause Structure

Perhaps	Luke	could	have	a walnut bun	couldn't	he?
Adjunct: modal	Subject	Finite	Predicator	Complement	Finite: neg	Subject
Mood			Residue		Moodtag	

From the perspective of IPC, the system of MOOD offers the possibility to increase delicacy and subtlety in expressing intended meaning. That is, in deploying IPC constructions, the speaker may resort to the system of MOOD to further modify the MOOD part of an IPC so as to achieve the best communicative effect. Consider the following examples.

(71) ... *there is no doubt that* semioticians have always shown a theoretical interest in multimodal texts... [R72]

(72) *There can be no doubt whatsoever* that a landmark publication such as this will be an asset to any library, pubic or private. [R61]

The IPC expressions in Examples (71) and (72) are different in the selection of the MOOD realizations, the Finite in particular, i.e. *is* in Example (71) and *can* in Example (72). The delicacy in MOOD selection makes it possible for the speaker to choose an appropriate resource along the polarity cline. The choices may be determined by the particular communicative purpose, or the relationship between the speaker and the hearer. Consequently, the writer in Example (71) chooses to claim the ensuing clause as a fact by employing the Finite *is*, whereas the writer in Example (72) chooses to make her claim less fact-like through *can*.

Through modality, the speaker presents her judgments, opinions, and explores the validity of what is being said. Figure 3.3 illustrates the system of MODALITY.

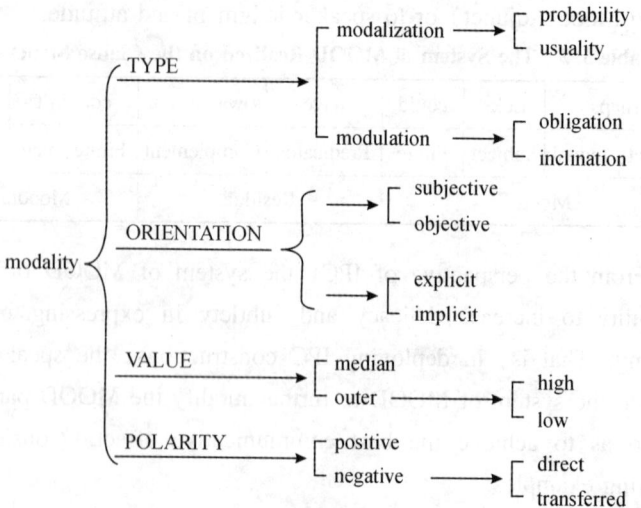

Figure 3.3 The Modality System in English (after Halliday, 1994: 360)

As the figure above shows, the system of MODALITY has two modes: modalization and modulation. Modalization is used to argue about the probability or frequency of propositions whereas modulation is used to argue about the obligation or inclination of proposals. Besides the categorization on the basis of proposition and proposal, modality can be approached in more delicacy in terms of orientation, value, and polarity, as Figure 3.3 illustrates.

As Halliday & Matthiessen (1999: 526-27) argue, modality is a rich resource for the speaker to intrude her own views into the discourse, e.g. her assessments of what is likely or typical, her judgments of the rights and wrongs of the situation and of where other people stand in this regard. Unlike ideational meanings, which tend to be located at definable locations in the grammatical structure, interpersonal meanings tend to be strung throughout the discourse.

There may be regular lexicogrammatical variants used to maintain different alignments of speaker and hearer. Such forms may be located at one point in each grammatical structure or dispersed prosodically throughout the wording of the clause. In fact, as Eggins (2004) notes, modal meanings can be expressed through modal operators (e. g. *might*, and *can*), Mood Adjuncts (e. g. *possibly*, and *usually*), or both. However, a third type of realization is done through IPC or "clause-like Adjuncts" (Eggins, 2004: 175) such as *I reckon*, *I'm sure*, and *it is possible*, as is shown by the following instances.

(73) *I reckon* Henry James wrote 'The Bostonians'.
(74) *I'm sure* Henry James wrote 'The Bostonians'.
(75) *It is possible that* Henry James wrote 'The Bostonians'.

As these illustrations suggest, these IPC strategies enable the speaker to express her judgment of certainty and usuality with great subtlety and delicacy. It should be noted, however, no matter how strong the use of modality, it makes a given proposition more tentative than it would be without any modality. As in Halliday's (1994: 362-63) own words, "[...] we only say we are certain when we are not".

So far it can be concluded that modalization is a way for the speaker to convey her judgments or attitudes about statements whereas modulation is there for the speaker to express her judgments or attitudes about actions or events. Under the label of modality, both represent complementary resources for the speaker to achieve the exchange of information or goods and services.

The present study has presented how the interpersonal meaning works through the systems of MOOD and MODALITY. These components of the interpersonal grammar enable the speaker to express her assessment of probabilities and attitude, to interact with others through language, and to negotiate with the counter-interactant. From the specific perspective of IPC, the systems provide rich meaning potential and lexicogrammatical resources to the language user for the purpose of delicacy and subtlety in particular communicative events.

3.2.1.4 Textual Metafunction

Through the textual function the speaker is firstly able to give a thematic structure to the elements of the clause content, thereby highlighting one or other element in first position and giving it thematic prominence. Second, the speaker organizes the clause content in terms of information units. Textually, language enables the flow of information as meaningful message. Here the systems of THEME and INFORMATION are central in the language of English. The former system gives the clause the thematic structure (Theme + Rheme) while the latter the informational structure (Given + New).

The two systems demonstrate the thematicity within a clause and newsworthiness within an information unit. The informational structure indicates the focal point of a given information unit. That is, it shows the "new" information the speaker expects the hearer to attend to. The new information usually comes at the ending position of the clause. In contrast, generally Theme is grammatically realized by the initial elements of the clause. This is best illustrated in Figure 3.4.

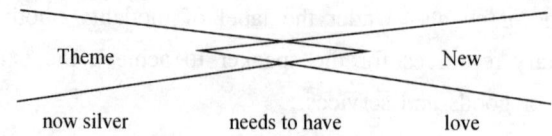

Figure 3.4 Textual Waves of Prominence and Non-prominence in the Clause (after Matthiessen, 1992: 42)

Almost all languages have a system of THEME and employ certain strategies to mark the Theme as prominent. In English, this is realized through sequence, as Figure 3.4 shows. From the speaker's point of view, a piece of information has a specific point of departure, this is Theme. In English, the Theme always includes one element that has an experiential function, typically a participant in the process. It may include other elements as well, such as an interpersonal expression of modality if the speaker is thematizing her own point of view.

The complexity of the Thematic systems in English is shown in Figure 3.5.

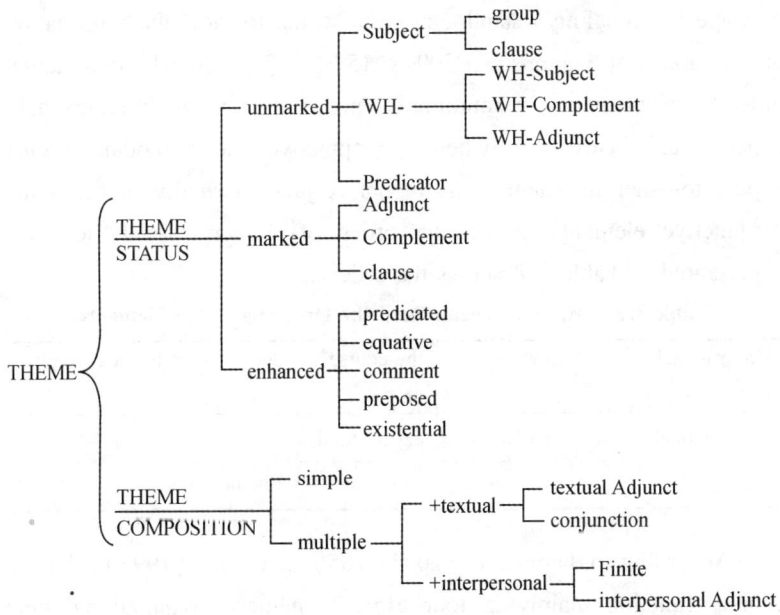

Figure 3.5 Thematic Systems in English (after Thompson, 2004: 164)

As Figure 3.5 displays, one way of signaling what is thematic is by putting it first in the clause, where everything up to and including the first experiential element constitutes the speaker's chosen point of departure. Thus, if anything precedes the experiential element in

Theme, i. e. textual or interpersonal elements, it is also part of the Theme. Theme of this type is termed in SFL a multiple Theme. The textual element is often realized by conjunctions, which signal that the following clause from part of a larger structural unit (i. e. a clause complex), and how the clause is related to the other clauses in the complex. The interpersonal element may be realized by the modal Adjunct. As was discussed in Section 3. 2. 1. 3, these modal Adjuncts may be interpreted as comments on the content of the message, rather than a part of the content. Therefore, they orient the hearer to the message by signaling s standpoint from which to view the information in the clause (Thompson, 2004: 157). The typical combination ordering of elements in multiple Themes " is textual ^ interpersonal ^ experiential". However, when a conjunctive and a modal Adjunct appear together in Theme, the modal Adjunct normally precedes the conjunctive element, hence the order of "interpersonal ^ textual ^ experiential". Table 3. 3 shows the ordering.

Table 3. 3 Multiple Themes and the Ordering of the Elements

Unfortunately, Not surprisingly,	however, then,	the course he	doesn't start till next week. was right.
interpersonal	textual	experiential	
Theme			Rheme

According to Thompson (2004: 165) and Fries (1995), Theme choices function mainly in four aspects, namely, maintaining topic progression through the choice of Subject; setting and changing the framework for the understanding of the following clause through the choices of marked Theme or multiple Theme; signaling boundaries of parts within a given text through changing Theme types; and finally, specifying what the speaker considers is a significant starting point through repetition, i. e. one element is chosen to appear in the Theme to highlight the speaker's focus at the point.

To sum up, the Theme functions to construct the framework of the text, or to establish the angle from which the content should be understood. The Rheme, on the contrary, functions to provide the content or the main information.

From the consideration of IPC, the textual metafunction is significant in the subsequent aspects. First, it makes it possible for the speaker to assign the Thematic position to IPC as in the following clause complex.

(76) *It is undeniable that* representatives of both genders can and do use both styles naturally... [R69]

In the example above, through the system of Theme-Rheme, the IPC *it is undeniable* is assigned the Thematic status. In this way, the speaker establishes her desired angle for the reader's interpretation of the ensuing clause in the Rheme.

Second, the system facilitates the speaker to arrange multiple Thematic patterns inclusive of IPC, in order to achieve her intended purposes in a particular communicative event. Consider the subsequent instances.

(77) However, *it is hoped that* research in this field will draw more attention.
(78) *It is hoped*, however, that research in this field will draw more attention.

The difference between Examples (77) and (78) lies in the linear arrangement of the textual Theme (i. e. *however*) and the interpersonal Theme (i. e. the IPC construction of *it is hoped*). This variety of multiple Theme arrangement has a dual function. On the one hand, it enables the speaker to initiate the clause complex by a textual Theme out of the consideration of textual conjunction. On the other hand, she may choose to begin the complex with an IPC in order to set up a frame for the understanding of the ensuing part of the complex, or to foreground the IPC for other reasons.

This section has discussed the three metafunctions of language and the major systems of each. In terms of the ideational metafunction, clauses are representations of meaning, construed mainly through the system of TRANSITIVITY. The system of logico-semantics accounts for the interrelationship between clauses when they combine to form complexes. In terms of interpersonal metafunction, clauses are exchanges between co-participants in social interaction. The social negotiation is enacted through the systems of MOOD, MODALITY and modal assessment. Finally, the textual metafunction enables the ideational and interpersonal meanings to be organized within a text, hence the clause as message.

It should be noted that the three distinct kinds of meaning are embedded in the structure of a clause. Figure 3.6 demonstrates how the three metafunctions operate on the clause.

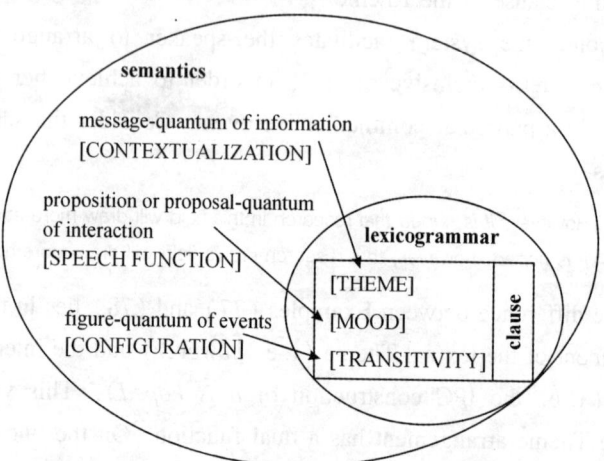

Figure 3.6　Clause as a Tri-functional Construct
(after Halliday & Matthiessen, 2004: 589)

As is shown in Figure 3.6, each of these three strands of meaning is construed by configurations of certain functions. Usually, as Matthiessen (2004) observes, the systems of each metafunction work within the respective metafunction, and do not cross metafunctions. According to Halliday (1994) and Halliday & Matthiesen (2004), within the clause in English, experiential selections are realized by constituency configurations of a process, participants and circumstances, textual selections are realized by sequential prominence, and interpersonal selections by prosodies of modality, phonology and so on.

3.2.2 Metafunctional Complementarity

The above section has shown how the three functions of language work in conveying different aspects of meaning. However, the significance of each function relies in its relationship to other functions. As Matthiessen (1992) argues, there is good reason for assuming that metafunctions map onto each other for realization out of various motivations. In fact, the grammar of English has evolved to allow for the co-opting of the metafunctions.

Matthiessen (1992) observes how the metafunction of textuality is mapping onto that of ideation. That is, textual meaning often turns to the systems in ideational function for meaning carrying. Consider the following examples.

(79) I saw the whole thing. [congruent, material process: event]

(80) This is what I saw. [incongruent, relational process: identification]

It is argued that the alternative configuration in Example (80) constitutes a textual alternative way of distributing information in the clause. By putting *this*, instead of *I*, at the initial position of the clause, the speaker may be considering topic progressing, highlighting the identifier, etc. In this case, the grammar turns back on itself to reconstrue itself for textual reasons. Thus, experiential grammatical metaphor is a strategy for creating a carrier of textual meaning.

In a similar vein, interpersonal meaning may be mapped on to ideational meaning at all points from the most micro to the most macro: from modality and speech function in the clause to settings affecting the whole of a particular register. Butler's (1985: 176) interpretation of the interpersonal system of MODALITY illustrates the interrelation between the grammar of ideation and that of social interaction. Of the two modes—modalization and modulation, modality is approached from the ideational function, but modulation arises from the interpersonal function. Modalizations are interpersonal because they represent the participation of the speaker in the speech event and that, not being subject to polarity and tense distinctions, they do not form part of the ideational content of the clause. However, modalities, though interpersonal, are oriented towards the ideational in that they express an opinion on the content of what is said. In contrast with modalizations, modulations show polarity and tense distinctions. Though ideational, modulations are oriented to the interpersonal in that passive modulations are concerned with the imposition of constrains on the Subject of the clause.

Therefore, there is good reason to argue that the interpersonal metafunction motivates ideational decisions. Ideational resources are often borrowed to construe interpersonal meanings. Transitivity selections may be made in such a way as to achieve an appropriate interpersonal meaning of a clause. For instance, instead of saying *Probably he is right*, the speaker may choose the mental process of *I think* to construe the interpersonal meaning of modality that is expressed by *probably*.

The motivations behind may be that through the mental process, the speaker is able to express her explicit subjective orientation. In this way, the speaker overtly conveys her active alignment with the reader. The following figure displays how the transitivity choices in the grammar of ideational construal come to stand for interpersonal enactment.

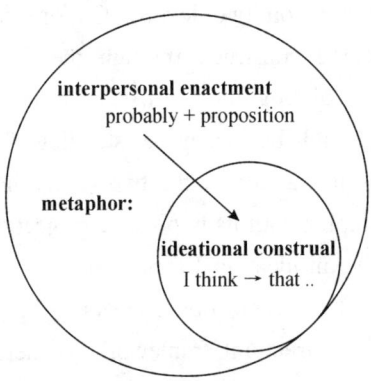

**Figure 3.7　Ideational Construal Standing for Interpersonal Enactment
(after Halliday & Matthiessen, 1999: 584)**

Figure 3.7 shows how ideational metafunction comes to construe interpersonal meaning. In Martin *et al.* 's (1997: 28) words, this way of metafunctional complementarity, among other things, opens up opportunities for verbal play. It is worth mentioning that elements of ideational systems are often found to co-opt to construct interpersonal meaning together with textual considerations. For instance, instead of saying *probably*, the speaker may choose *I therefore think*, *but I think*, or *then I think* to achieve both interpersonal meaning and textual conjunction. In addition, the speaker may arrive at greater delicacy of expression if she wishes through delicacy of transitivity choices in terms of tense and polarity, for instance, she may employ *I thought*, *I would think*, or *I don't think* to achieve accuracy of expression and appropriateness of interaction.

As with modality, speech functions are often observed to appear in transitivity disguises. Instead of the direct imperative utterance "Give!", the speaker may have her good reasons to say "I ask that you give". Such expressions, due to the interpersonal and ideational co-opting, must be read on two levels. On one level, there is the literal declarative mood construed through the first person, present tense mental process of cognition *I ask*. On the other level, this declarative mood should be taken as standing for the underlying command *Give*. The interaction of the two levels makes the meaning. Thus, the clause complex with its hypotactic projection deconstructs the meaning of imperative in ideational forms.

Similarly, thematic organization appears to be often exploited by the speaker to provide structural framework for her discourse, which relates back to her main intention and provides a perspective on what follows. Because textual metafunction employs a wave-like mode of expression, with peaks of prominence at the beginning and typically, the end of the clause, the speaker may put whatever elements she regards the most important in the initial position or the very ending position of the thematic structure.

Brown & Yule (1983: 133) use "thematization" to stress that what the speaker puts first will influence the interpretation of everything that follows. Thematization is regarded by them as a discoursal rather than simply a sentential process. Through the process, the speaker presents her statement from a particular perspective. Since the thematic peak is realized by sequential prominence, i.e. early position of a clause, the linear organization can be manipulated to bring some items and events into greater prominence than others. Therefore, it is reasonable to argue that the thematic arrangement of a piece of discourse must have a significant effect on the process of interpretation and on the process of subsequent recall. In this way, textual metafunction serves a potential carrier of interpersonal meaning. This is best illustrated by Thompson (2004) in his interpretation of thematized comment, as Table 3.4 demonstrates.

Table 3.4 Thematized Comment (after Thompson, 2004: 67)

It is true	that it took five years to do so.
It may be	that the news reporters are manipulating the truth for reasons of strikingness.
It's interesting	that you should say that.
It is difficult	to know exactly how to characterize what we have just noticed.
It is regretted	that the University is unable to provide continuous nursing or domestic care.
Theme	**Rheme**

Thompson (2004) shows in Table 3.4 how the interpersonal meaning expressed through IPC is mapped onto textual prominence. Through metafunctional complementarities, the speaker chooses from her linguistic meaning potential the device best serving her communicative purposes. In the present case, the speaker aims to explicitly express the special effort she is making (i.e. by upranking an interpersonal element within a transitivity process into a separate clause) to achieve intersubjective alignment.

As Matthiessen (1992: 57) suggests, textual metafunction co-opts with interpersonal and ideational metafunctions by turning the latter two into the meaning carriers of textual meaning. In the present study, it is argued that interpersonal meaning is carried by ideational meaning and textual meaning. Ideationally, the interpersonal metafunction may be carried by constituency, mapped on to sequence created by the overall linear sequence of the elements of the clause; textually, interpersonal meaning may be given prominence when carried by wave, mapped onto the initial position and often the end position (i. e. thematically prominent to information-new prominent). One main motivation behind all these metafunctional complementarities is closely related with what the speaker chooses to make prominent to the reader. It is of no doubt that in the case of IPC, the prominence is assigned to the interpersonal aspect. That is, the speaker invites the reader to pay special attention to what is done by the speaker to achieve co-participant interaction and negotiation.

3.3 Projection Manifestation Across Metafunctions

The previous section introduces the three metafunctions of language and the main systems of each. As was mentioned in Section 3.2.1.2, there are two modes of logico-semantic relationships between the clauses within a clause complex. One is expansion and the other is projection. In expansion, one meaning is expanded through another whereas one meaning is projected through another in projection. In relevance to the present study, this section aims to further the discussion on projection by defining the concept and categorizing what it covers. The particular focus is on the interrelationship between ideational projection and interpersonal projection.

3.3.1 Ideational Projection

This subsection serves two functions from the perspective of IPC.

First, the concept of projection will be introduced and elaborated. The primary concern is its ideational manifestation. Second, projection will be categorized and each category will receive a detailed discussion.

3.3.1.1 Definition of Projection

Projection, according to Halliday & Matthiessen (2004), is the logico-semantic relationship whereby a clause acts as the representation of something linguistic, rather than as a direct representation of some non-linguistic aspect of the world. Matthiessen (1995: 130) characterizes projection as "developing a clause complex by projecting one clause onto a plane of existence higher than the other clause, as the symbolic content of that clause". In projection, one of the clauses in the relationship represents experience not directly but instead designates linguistically processed phenomena. Therefore, projections are metaphenomena[①], they are representations of a (linguistic) representation. They represent phenomena already encoded in language which then participate in other linguistic structures.

Projection typically involves two clauses: the projected clause and the projecting clause. The projected clause represents the wording or meaning of the speaker represented in the projecting clause, not the speaker of the clause complex. It is thus a meta-representation, or a metaphenomenon. The metaphenomenon projected by a verbal clause is a locution, or mental clause as an idea (cf. Section 3.3.1.2). To make it clearer, the projected clause stands for a wording. That is, the

---

[①] Metaphenomenon is glossed by Halliday (1994: 115) as "something that is constructed as a participant by projection—that is, indirect or reported discourse".

phenomenon it represents is a lexicogrammatical one. Take for example "*I'm not sure*", *replied the Fat Controller*. While the projecting clause (here *replied the Fat Controller*) represents an ordinary phenomenon of experience, the projected clause (here *I'm not sure*) represents a second-order phenomenon of experience, something that is itself a representation, or a metaphenomenon. Thus, projections represent phenomena already encoded in language, which then participate in other linguistic structures.

Projection as metaphenomenon can be better interpreted in the following ways. In interaction, if the hearer intends to argue, the issue is not the content in the projected clause; it is the projecting clause. Therefore, for "*I'm not sure*", *replied the Fat Controller*, the possible questions could only be *did he?* or *did he not, say these words?* If the interactant aims to argue the content of the projected clause, he has to turn it into a first-order phenomenon.

In addition to the hierarchy of representation set by projection, projection involves human consciousness since only humans can project into second-order reality. That is, the content of the projected clause is either brought into existence in the course of the mental or verbal process of the speaker or impinges on the projector's consciousness. Consider the following examples.

(81) *It strikes me that* there's no-one here.
(82) *It worries me that* there's no-one here.

Of the two projections, the projected clause in Example (81) is brought into existence by the thinking of the speaker *I*. That is, it is a metaphenomenon which is projected by the consciousness of the projecting agent *I*. In Example (82), it is different. Here the content of the projected clause pre-exists before the conscious activity of the speaker. That is, the projected clause represents a fact which is not influenced by the interactant. Instead, the projected clause has an effect on the speaker (here *it worries the speaker*) as an external impact.

To sum up, projection involves either the projecting clause bringing the projected information into existence or the projector being under impact brought by the projected clause, which exists prior to the occurrence of the projector's verbal or mental processes.

3.3.1.2 Categorization of Projection

In SFL, projection may be classified into different categories according to different criteria. Halliday & Matthiessen (2004) group projection into paratactic projection, hypotactic projection and embedded projection in accordance with the relationship between the projecting clause and the projected clause (cf. Section 3.2.1.2 for the logico-semantic relations within clause complexes). If the two clauses are of equal status, it is said that the paratactic relationship is held. If the two clauses are of unequal status, they are either connected through the hypotactic relation or embedding with one clause downranked to act as one element within the other clause. In the cases of paratactic and hypotactic projections, the projection exists within the clause nexus whereas in the case of embedded projection, the projection involves only one single clause, since the projected clause participates in the projecting clause, performing a clausal element.

Closely related to the understanding of IPC is hypotactic projection and embedded projection. A hypotactic relation holds when one clause reports another, i.e. indirect quote or thought. As has been mentioned above, the status of the two clauses is unequal, i.e. the projected figure is dependent on the projecting one. It follows that the projected figure is construed as belonging to a second-order plane of reality. The projecting clause is construed as belonging to a higher status than the projected. There are three consequences of this.

First, in reporting, the projected clause has lost its first-order semantic features. Instead, the report is more fully incorporated into the projector's own message. This means the selection of mood, tense, reference, etc has to be dependent on the respective selections in the projecting clause.

Second, in a hypotactic relation, as one clause modifies the other, only one clause is dominant. That is, if two clauses are linked through hypotactic projection, the projecting clause is semantically the main proposition of the clause complex. This also holds with regard to the syntactic representation. The projecting clause is structurally the main clause as well.

This leads to the third, the sequential order of the two clauses within a hypotactic nexus is typically fixed, with the projecting clause governs the projected one. That is, the projected clause is projected through the projecting one, as is illustrated in Example (83).

(83) *I anticipate that* the lecture will be well understood.

As is shown in Example (83), the relationship that holds between the two clauses in a hypotactic projection is a hypotactically unequal status. It should also be rementioned that the hypotactic type of projection involves clause complexes or nexuses.

There is, however, a third type of projection, i. e. embedded projection, which involves the single clause. According to Halliday (1994: 264), embedded clauses are not projected by the process of the clause in which they function, but come as they were already packaged in projected form. That explains why embedded projection is also termed pre-projection (Halliday & Matthiessen, 2004: 608). To be specific, this type of projection is a semantic abstraction which is not created in anybody's consciousness, nor is it emitted by any signal source. It is simply there to function as a participant in some other processes. Embedded clauses are clauses that have been rankshifted in that they are made to function at a rank lower than that of the clause. Therefore, embedded projection differentiates itself from other types of projection in that only embedded or rankshifted clauses can function as constituents within another clause and serve a function in it. Thus, in embedded projection, one clause is embedded (as in Example (84) below) or structurally integrated as a constituent in another clause (as in Example (85) below).

(84) It's odd [that he didn't say anything about this one].
(85) They were aware of the possibility [that the whole project might collapse].

In SFL, embedded projections are interpreted as facts. As the examples above show, facts as projections which are not tactically related to the clause with which they are used, but are embedded in it as a constituent. In Example (84), the embedded clause serves as the Subject of the clause whereas in Example (85) the clause *that the whole project might collapse* is embedded to act as postmodifier to the head noun *the possibility*. As has been seen, all the embedded projections involve a projecting clause or a projecting noun.

A clause with embedded projection in it thus represents some form of interaction with a prepackaged proposition. That is, a fact may be an entity to be interacted with, or to be mentally manipulated, or the source of a specific affect. In a word, in the factive construction, the projected element is responded to or interacted with by the Subject of the clause.

To sum up, in SFL, from the vantage point of logico-semantic relation, three types of projection are recognized, i. e. paratactic projection, hypotactic projection and embedded projection. The first two involve the clause nexus whereas the latter concerns the single clause. The differences between embedded projection and that of taxis are illustrated in Table 3.5.

Table 3.5　Contrast Between Ranking and Downranked Clauses in Projection (after Martin et al., 1997: 181)

Ranking [hypotactic]	Embedded (downranked, exemplified by nominal groups)
idea: typically projected by processes of cognition [proposition] and affection: desideration [proposal]	fact (Phenomenon): typically configured with processes of affection: emotion
agnate with paratactic projection, i. e. can be quoted (although unlikely)	not agnate with paratactic projection
cannot be the Subject (since it is not a participant)	can be the Subject in agnate passive variant of the clause (since it is a participant)
cannot be the focus of Theme predication (since it is not a participant)	can be the focus of Theme predication (since it is a participant)
can be presumed by substitute so/not	cannot be presumed by substitute so/not, only by reference item such as *that*, *it*
cannot follow explicit fact noun as Head/Thing in nominal group	can follow explicit fact noun as Head/Thing in nominal group
She thought that she had painted the house: she thought " I painted the house": she thought so	she regretted (the fact) [[that she had painted the house]]: it was (the fact) [[that she had painted the house]] that she regretted: she regretted it

So far the manifestations of projection through the logical metafunction have been discussed. Paratactic/hypotactic/embedded projections are compared and distinguished. However, projection can be approached from the perspective of experiential metafunction as well. As Table 3.5 shows, projection has a close connection with various types of processes. Quotes typically contain a verbal process whereas hypotactic projection is typically projected through mental processes, as well as verbal processes. Facts, however, typically combine with clauses that contain mental and relational processes, and, less frequently, verbal processes. The projecting clause in different types of projection thus may be represented through various processes. Consider the following examples.

(86) *He said*, "I could fix that hot-water heater." [paratactic projection: verbal]
(87) *I think that* the State Government isn't necessary. [hypotactic projection: mental]
(88) *He said that* he adopted the name simply because it occurred to him at the moment. [hypotactic projection: verbal]
(89) *It seems that* the possible worlds are more precarious to deal with than previously assumed. [embedded projection: mental]
(90) *It is said that* he has already left. [embedded projection: verbal]
(91) *It is clear that* questions about data are more important than is sometimes assumed. [embedded projection: relational]

As Examples (86), (87) and (88) show, the processes of saying and sensing are characterized by their special power of setting up other figures as second-order semiotic reality through the creation of projecting sequences (Halliday & Matthiessen, 1999: 128-49). Examples (89) and (90) illustrate that these two processes (i.e. saying and sensing) convey the interactant's reaction towards the pre-projected fact. It must be noted that the relational process exemplified in Example (91) serves a similar function. The observation of the above examples therefore demands a scrutiny of the three processes vis-à-vis idea/fact projections. It is worth re-mentioning that with idea projection, the projector's thinking or saying brings the idea into existence whereas with pre-projection of facts, the interactant reacts towards the already existing facts.

Table 3.6 summarizes the distribution of the three processes and their subtypes in realizing ideas and facts as projections.

Table 3.6 Projection of Ideas vs. Pre-projection of Facts Across Process Types

process		idea	fact
mental	perceptive	–	✓
	cognitive	✓	✓
	desiderative	✓	–
	emotive	–	✓
verbal	indicating: declarative	✓	✓
	indicating: interrogative	✓	–
	imperating	✓	–
relational	intensive and attributive	–	✓
	intensive and identifying	–	✓

As is displayed in Table 3.6, within the overall category of mental processes, the classification given distinguishes those of perception (using the five senses), cognition (thinking, knowing, and understanding), affection (liking, hating, and fearing) and desiderativeness (wanting, wishing, and hoping) (cf. Halliday & Matthiessen, 2004; Halliday & Matthiessen, 1999: 137-44).

Cognitive and desiderative figures are distinguished from emotive and perceptive ones in that projection by the former involves bringing into existence of an idea: thinking creates the idea which is thought; wanting a situation brings it into hypothetical existence. Emotive and perceptive figures, on the other hand, are activated by pre-existing facts.

Verbal processes are typical in construing saying as the production of wording in the form of paratactic direct speech. In addition, the verbal process is also favored by idea projections. All of the three subtypes of verbal processes, i. e. declaration (saying, telling, explaining), interrogation (asking, enquiring) and imperating (commanding, ordering), are characterized by hypotactic idea projections. Verbal processes can also be followed by a fact. This is realized by the declarative type as in the processes of admitting, acknowledging, etc. Relational processes, as Table 3.6 displays, are characterized by pre-projections. The typical environment for a fact is a relational process clause of intensive type, either attributive as in Example (91) or identifying in Example (92) below.

(92) *The problem is that* he has already left.

A fourth type of process which construes pre-projections is the existential process. The process is not shown in Table 3.6, since it typically characterizes nominalization, as Example (93) illustrates.

(93) *There is evidence that* the water is severely polluted.

The current study has discussed the classification of projection from logical perspective and the types of processes favored by different categories of projection. The discussion attempts to describe the phenomenon of projection within the scope of information conveying, or the ideational function of language. Based on the discussion, in the following part, projection will be examined from the interpersonal point of view.

3.3.2 Interpersonal Projection

It has been justified that it is plausible for the three metafunctions of language to complement each other by mapping onto each other to construe human experience. The principle of complementarity also operates in the manifestations of projection. That is, although projection is primarily a system vis-à-vis ideational metafunctions of language, it does operate in the realm of the interpersonal metafunction through ideational projection. This part will focus on how ideational projection comes to stand for interpersonal projection.

3.3.2.1 From Ideational Projection to Interpersonal Projection

According to Halliday & Matthiessen (2004) and Thompson (2005), projection can be seen from two different ends. The view from the ideational end highlights the fact that a second-order linguistic phenomenon (i.e. the report of what was said or thought) is being projected through a first-order representation of a speech or thought event (i.e. the projecting clause). From this perspective, the projecting clause is both structurally the main clause and semantically the main proposition.

However, if viewed from the interpersonal end, the projecting clause serves as a "tag" attached to the main proposition in the projected clause. That is, the projecting clause loses its experiential function and gains its interpersonal function. IPC thus functions as a lexicogrammatical realization vis-à-vis the grammar of interaction with respect to validation, negotiation, attitude and attribution. In Thompson's (2005) words, as the tag to the projected clause, IPC frames the experiential proposition in interpersonal terms of how far the speaker is committed to it (i.e. modality), the speaker's comments on or attitudes towards the content in the projected clause, and/or the function of the expression, and/or the evidence for the main clause.

As Halliday & Matthiessen (2004) rightly point out, interpersonal projection is implicit unless made explicit through the co-opting of metafunctions of representation and interaction. That is, typically interpersonal projection is realized in lexicogrammar as interpersonal Adjuncts by adverbial phrases. Through mapping onto the ideational projection, where one process is projected through another process, the interpersonal projection gains a status of being clausal. Typically, meaning is projected by sensing and wording by saying. Thus, ideational projection construes human experience in figures of sensing and saying, projected by the Senser and the Sayer respectively. When this mode of construing moves from the ideational base into the interpersonal base, projection turns to be a mode of enactment, through which interactants enact propositions and proposals. That is, interpersonally, the potential of projection provides "interpersonal space" (Matthiessen, 2004) which is featured by resources for assessing the information being exchanged or for calibrating the relationship between the speaker and the hearer. Figure 3.8 illustrates how ideational projection comes to stand for interpersonal projection.

As Figure 3.8 shows, through the processes of saying and sensing which characterize ideational projection, projection manifests across metafunctions (i.e. meaning as construing and meaning as enacting) by bringing together the ideational and interpersonal aspects of human consciousness.

IPC thus brings into clear vision the interweaving relationship between the two modes of meaning construing, as in the case of interpersonal grammatical metaphor of modality. Through projection, the interactant simultaneously both enacts propositions and proposals interpersonally and construes this enacting in such a way that the

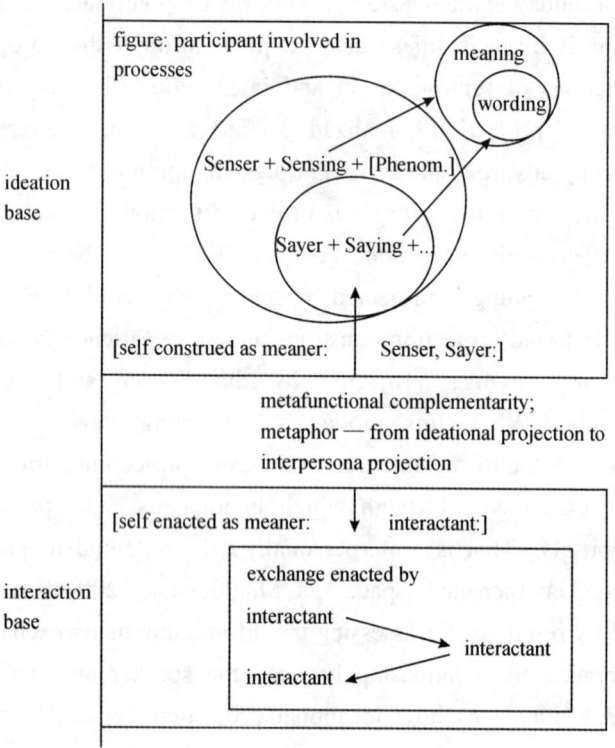

Figure 3.8   From Ideational Projection to Interpersonal Projection (after Halliday & Matthiessen, 1999: 601)

ideational construal comes to stand as a metaphor for the modal assessment aspect of the interpersonal enactment. Consider the following example.

(94) *I think* it's ready now.

In Example (94), the projecting clause *I think* ideationally construes the internal experience of the speaker through the mental process of cognition. Logico-semantically, the projecting clause and the projected one form a nexus through which the proposition *it's ready now* is represented as being a remove from reality rather than a direct representation. Semantically, the projecting clause *I think* connotes meaning roughly equivalent to *I suppose* or *I believe*. Interpersonally, however, the projecting clause functions to modalize the modal value of the projected clause, rendering the entire expression more tentative and as such perhaps more reasonable or palatable to the co-participant in the interaction.

Another implication of Figure 3.8 is that, instead of being clear-cut, projection allows for intermediate cases. The underlying principle is that all projection nexuses can be viewed from either the ideational or interpersonal perspective but that, if the experiential reading is more dominant, the interpersonal reading is correspondingly weaker, and vice versa (Thompson, 2005: 782). This means that there are numerous intermediate cases, and it can be difficult to decide which reading is stronger in particular instances. In fact, the more experientially tinted the interpersonal projecting clause becomes, the less clear the borderline between the two. Thompson (2007: 675) exemplifies this with clause complexes (95) and (96).

(95) It is certainly not too much to say that....
(96) It is a constant source of worry to me that....

However, as Thompson (2004) argues, such ambiguities are to be expected, because the process of ideational projection standing for interpersonal function involves a re-setting of the relationship between form and meaning. In the same vein, Halliday & Matthiessen (2004: 548-49) regard this kind of intermediacy as multifunctionality, which is inherent in the language of English. It follows that the intermediate cases do not undermine the basic validity of the categorization of projection.

It should be pointed out that the choice of seeing projection as ideational or interpersonal reflects whether the speaker stresses social exchange, or experience representation. That is, the interpretation of the projection depends on the interactant's primary concern at the moment of the communicative event. At any moment, the speaker may be more concerned to foreground real-world configurations, or to enact her awareness of, or explicitly guide, the hearer's reaction to what is under communication. As Thompson (2004: 79-80) rightly points out, not only that the grammar of any particular clause will be at least partly determined by its intended role assigned by the speaker in the interaction, but that the meaning of the clause can only be understood by comparing its grammar to this intended role.

3.3.3.2 Metafunctional Features of Typical Interpersonal Projection

It has been observed that from the vantage point of interpersonal function, IPC relies on the ideational projection to clausalize interpersonal modal assessment, which is typically realized by adverbial groups. Therefore, it is reasonable to predict that IPC is characterized by its peculiar features vis-à-vis the fundamental functions of language.

By mapping onto the ideational projection, IPC is featured by its explicit orientation of the assessment, either subjective or objective (Halliday & Matthiessen, 2004; Thompson, 2004). To be specific, a hypotactic projection is always subjective. The speaker is represented explicitly as the Senser or Sayer. A pre-projected fact in a mental clause resembles hypotactic projection in representing the assessment as subjective—the speaker is explicitly represented as the Senser. In contrast, a pre-projected fact in a relational clause represents the assessment as objective. The difference between subjective and objective orientation in the ideational manifestation lies in the fact that a projecting mental or verbal clause has a Senser or a Sayer whereas a relational clause does not have such a projector. This is best shown in the following instances.

(97) *I think* that he has already left. [IPC, hypotactic projection, explicitly subjective]

(98) *I regret* that he has already left. [IPC, embedded projection, explicitly subjective]

(99) *It is regrettable* that he has already left. [IPC, embedded projection, explicitly objective]

(100) *Regrettably*, he has already left. [non-IPC, non-projection, implicit in orientation]

Interpersonally, IPC is featured by choices of Subject, Mood and tagging. When the assessment is explicitly subjective, the Senser or Sayer has to be the speaker *I* or the hearer *you* (Halliday & Matthiessen, 2004: 629), e.g. *I think*, *I say*, *do you think*, and *do you say*. According to this basic principle, if it is a person other than the speaker, the clause will still be a projecting one. However, it will not characterize an interpersonal assessment. Consider the following example.

(101) *Manning regrets that* he has already left.

In this embedded projection, Manning's regret is construed as part of the experiential representation of a figure of sensing, i. e. emotive reaction. Nevertheless, the ideational projecting clause does not enact the speaker's regret. Therefore, it is not an instance of IPC.

IPC is also interpersonally constrained with respect to the nature of the Mood element of Finite, whose delicacy is either "temporal: simple present or modal: modulation (e. g. *can*, *may*, and *could*)"

(Halliday & Matthiessen, 2004: 629).

A third interpersonal parameter is the adding of a tag question to the given projection. Halliday (1994: 354) suggests that in a construction involving explicit interpersonal projection, a tag question picks up the projected proposition rather than the IPC expression. For instance, in the case of *I'm sure this is a muscle tear*, the most likely tag is *isn't it* rather than *aren't I*. The tagging shows that the proposition is with the projected clause while IPC frames the proposition in terms of interpersonal considerations of epistemic commitment. Therefore, the tag is regarded as a label which distinguishes an IPC from an ideational projecting clause[①].

Textually, it is typically not the IPC construction but the projected clause that enters directly into conjunctive relations (Thompson, 2005). Thompson (2005) is echoed by Verhagen (2005) who suggests that natural language use is characterized by its structural duality, i.e. the objective dimension (language as knowledge) and the intersubjective dimension (language as interaction), as is shown in Table 3.7.

---

① However, it should be mentioned that this test only works, as Thompson (2005: 789) states, when the subject is *I*. When the subject is *you* or inclusive *we*, the tag typically picks up the IPC: *you wouldn't think it was so painful, would you?*

Table 3.7 Textual Distribution of IPCs and the Projected Clauses in a Text (after Verhagen, 2005: 150, with slight changes and modifications)

IPC (language as interaction)	The Projected Clauses (language as knowledge)
I have reported before that	there has already been success in breeding clones of mammalian embryos
From the above it may be now be concluded that it will become impossible in the near future	to make new embryos with the DNA of full-grown animals as well
Some even expect that	this will happen as soon as next year
Others believe that	it may take somewhat longer
but nobody doubts that	the cloning of a full-grown sheep or horse will be a reality within ten years
The question is whether or whether	society is mentally and morally ready for this we will once again be hopelessly overtaken by the technical developments

As is shown in Table 3.7, IPC is invisible to the formation of patterns of Thematic cohesion. This contrasts with experiential projection, where the relations involve the projecting clause, or more precisely, the complex of "projecting + projected" clause, but with the projecting clause as the dominant element. Consequently, IPC is treated differently (cf. Thompson, 2007). Thompson (2004: 173) regards IPC as "contextual frame" or "orienting Theme". In this way, IPC is separated from the unmarked experiential Theme that contributes to thematic continuing. Thompson (2007) argues that as the contextual frame, IPC typically has the function of changing the textual framework in some way whereas the experiential Theme typically maintains the topic of the text. In many cases, it is the Subject of the projected clause that serves the primary continuative function.

As was discussed above, projection can be interpreted from both ideational and interpersonal perspectives. Ideationally, projection projects a metafunction through a representation of speech, thought or fact. Interpersonally, projection frames a proposition in terms of modal assessment. Interpersonal projection is made explicit by co-opting ideational projection to perform interpersonal services. Therefore, IPC is featured by the combination of ideational projection and interpersonal projection. It follows that IPC has its own metafunctional characteristics. However, it should be noted that these features only characterize typical IPCs. In particular situations of communication, marked or peripheral realizations may emerge. In a plain word, when a projection construction is employed to express interpersonal meaning, IPC is involved.

3.3.3.3 Split Projection

Along the continuum of ideational-interpersonal projection, extremely close to the end of interpersonal projection, there emerges a particular type of projection, namely, split projection (Harnett, 1995), as is shown by the subsequent instances.

(102) A Mac Plus — *I am certain* — is what he wrote the entire book with. (Mcgregor, 1997: 250)

(103) This advice, *we thought*, has been ignored by linguists.

The italicized expressions in both examples are obviously not ideational projections which require the projecting clause to be in structurally dominant position. Thus, their being subordinate in syntagmatic relations (Palmer, 2001: 109) deprives them of the experiential projection status. However, that does not mean that they are not realizations of IPC. The present study interprets them as departures from typical IPCs. Their being "interpersonal" can be accounted for by the fact that they can be fronted to the initial position and that they function as personal asides or digressions (Hyland, 2004). The position of split projection is related with local cohesion, end weight, highlighting and backgrounding of thematic structure (Hartnett, 1995: 200).

Obviously such "split projection"① is much closer to the interpersonal extreme rather than the ideational one along the continuum of projection manifestation. One striking feature of split projection is that the ideational meaning becomes vague or bleached while the interpersonal meaning highlighted. A second feature is that, as the examples above show, split projection operates at both local and global levels of the discourse (cf. Kärkkäinen, 2007). That is, it can indicate an inserted digression not only one sentence long, but also a sequence of several. A third feature of split projection is that it primarily frames and projects an upcoming viewpoint expressing action and simultaneously the onset of an interactive digression. A fourth feature is that split projection is syntactically detached from the rest of

---

① The literature sees a number of terms assigned to this phenomenon, primarily in the study of conversational discourse. The most frequent term is "discourse markers" (Schiffrin, 1987) and "parentheticals" (Chambon & Simeoli, 1998; Fetzer, 2008). Quirk et al. (1985) use "finite clause stance adverbials", "comment clauses", "inserts", and "discourse markers" interchangeably. To Thompson & Mulac (1991), they are "epistemic parentheticals". To Vandelanotte (2004), they are better to be seen as "distancing clauses" or "scopal distancing indirect speech or thought (henceforth abbreviated as DIST)". Whatever term, the prime consideration is that they are not integrated into the clause structures. It should be noted that most studies overlook their function in building up intersubjectivity (Kärkkäinen, 2007).

the sentence. One indicator of the syntactic detachment is the loss of the binder *that*. Thus, it has some discourse and sentence mobility.

To sum up this section, the nature of interpersonal projection is to upgrade the interpersonal meaning from group rank or preposition rank to the rank of clause. That is, the interpersonal meaning which is implicit in default within a simple clause is uplifted through projection to a separate clause. This mechanism enables the expansion of meaning potential. To be specific, given the status of a separate clause, the interpersonal meaning can be furthered in delicacy, and can be negotiated or negated. In this way, it opens up new domains of meaning.

3.4 Genre

Halliday (1979) argues that language is best regarded as a form of activity. Specifically, it is a form of activity of human beings in societies; and it has the property of being patterned. Thus, SFL adopts a social-semiotic view of language and is particularly suitable for investigating a text by relating it to its context in the discourse, and also to the general background of the text: who it is written for, what is its angle on the subject matter and so on (Halliday, 1990: 34). This text-analytic perspective concerns the social and cultural background wherein the language is set as well.

Under the same umbrella is found the participants' understanding of the predominant social meanings and cultural values (Morley, 2000). In SFL, all these are covered under "genre", which is a "staged, goal-oriented social process" (Martin & Rose, 2003: 7-8). That is, people participate in social interactions wherein they use genres to get things done in a few obligatory and/or optional steps. In a similar vein, Ventola (1987) defines genre as the plane, which is identified by the linguistic system, which organizes the ways social encounters unfold as generic structures. Within SFL, theorizing genre involves at least two considerations, i. e. its position within the whole system, and the GSP (cf. Hasan, 1984; Halliday & Hasan, 1985) of the genre. In addition to these two points, the genre of academic discourse to which ELBR belongs will be elaborated in the current study.

3. 4. 1 Genre, Register, and Metafunctions

As far as genre is concerned, most SFL scholars (Martin, 1992; Ventola, 1987; Eggins, 2004; Thompson, 2004) see it as the level above the plane of register①. SFL recognizes three planes of the linguistic system, i. e. genre, register and metafunctions (cf. Ventola, 1987). The plane of genre handles systems of social behavior. It is the plane whose expression form is register. Therefore, it controls the choices in register (Morley, 2000: 10). The components of register, i. e. field, tenor and mode, are then realized by the plane of language through the three metafunction systems. The relationship between genre, register and the three metafunctions of language is illustrated in Figure 3. 9 below.

---

① However, as Melrose (2003: 418) observes, Halliday (1978) sees genre as an aspect of mode. Therefore, often a question arises as to whether the concept of register and that of genre are distinct.

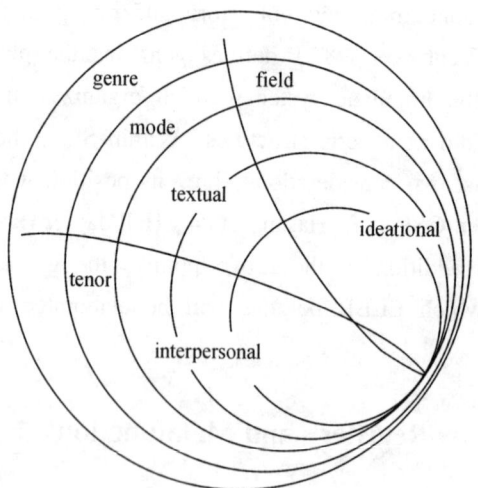

**Figure 3.9　Register Recontextualized by Genre
(after Martin & White, 2005: 32)**

Figure 3.9 demonstrates the relationship between genre, register and metafunctions. The relationship in essence reflects the interrelation between language and the social structure. Language is controlled by the social structure and the social structure is in turn maintained and transmitted through language. In this way, the concept of genre is similar to that of register in that both explain variation in texts by reference to variation in contexts. That is, explicit links are often made between features of the discourse and variables of the social and cultural context in which the discourse is enacted.

However, genre is different from register in the following aspects. To begin with, register describes the impact of dimensions of the immediate Context of Situation (henceforth abbreviated as CS) of a language event on the way language is used (Eggins, 2004: 9). Therefore, register is a CS index and accounts for use variation with respect to a specific CS. SFL identifies three key dimensions of the situation as having significant and predictable impacts on language use, namely, the register variables of mode (i. e. role of language), tenor (i. e. role relations of power and solidarity), and field (i. e. topic or focus of the activity).

By contrast, the concept of genre is concerned with the classification of types of social behavior within a given Context of Culture (henceforth abbreviated as CC) and with the impact of the context of culture on language. As Eggins (2004) illustrates, genre is characterized by the staged, step-by-step structure which is institutionalized as ways of achieving culturally established tasks and goals in social interaction. In addition, different from the traditional understanding, the concept of genre in SFL covers everyday genres, literary genres as well as academic genres like research articles and ABR. It follows that texts of different genres are texts deployed to achieve different purposes in a given culture. From this vantage point, a text's genre is identified by the sequence of functionally distinct stages or steps through which it unfolds.

Therefore, it is reasonable to come to the conclusion that two texts may be from the same genre, but show variation in register (Ansary & Babaii, 2005). Thompson (2004: 42-43) declares his support of the view in saying that "a genre deploys the resources of a register, or more than one register, in particular patterns to achieve certain communicative goals". Seen in this way, genre is simply "register plus purpose" (Thompson, 2004: 43). From this perspective, genre includes the more general idea of what the interactants are doing through language, and how they organize the language event, typically in recognizable stages, in order to achieve that purpose. To sum up, genre is made of appropriate type of register, cut and shaped in conventional ways to suit particular purposes of the interactants.

3.4.2 The GSP of a Genre

Genre theories, as Hyland (2005: 86-87) argues, locate the relationship of participants at the center of language use and assume that every successful text will display the writer's awareness of its context and the reader who forms part of the context. Text is a fundamental concept in SFL theory, which is defined as "an interactive event, a social exchange of meanings" (Halliday & Hasan, 1985: 11).

The generic identity of a text, i.e. the way in which it is similar to other texts of its genre, according to Eggins (2004: 56), lies in three dimensions: the co-occurrence of a particular contextual cluster, or its register configuration; the text's staged or schematic structure; and the realizational patterns in the text. The three variables of CS interpret the social context of a text, in which meaning is exchanged. The three metafunctions of languages realize the meaning under exchange and thus allows us to analyze the lexicogrammatical features in a text with respect to what the writer intends to do and mean.

A genre can also be defined, in SFL theories, in terms of the notion of GSP[①](Halliday & Hasan, 1985: 63-65) or "its obligatory elements of schematic structure" (Eggins, 2004: 65). The GSP is in essence the abstract representation of a genre, which includes paradigmatic options as well as syntagmatic orderings. It is featured by

---

① It is observed that there is some co-patterning between the GSP and Ventola's (1987) flowchart vis-à-vis genre analysis. However, the latter will not be covered since it falls out of the purposes of the present study.

the following points.

First, the GSP states the potential structure of every text appropriate to a particular context. Thus, it is a condensed formula representing the conditions under which a text will be seen as one that is appropriate to a specific context configuration (Ansary & Babaii, 2005: 276).

Second, the GSP exhausts all the possible actual textual structures of a given social activity. That is, individual texts may have different actual structures, but each realizes a possibility which is built into its GSP.

Third, the GSP is composed of a set of macro-elements. This derives from the fact that any given social activity in a given culture consists of a series of elements. A genre element is always specific to some particular activity structure. The GSP theory identifies three types of genre elements, i. e. obligatory elements, optional elements, and iterative elements. Obligatory elements define the genre, without which the text can not be interpreted as one instance of the genre to which the text belongs. By contrast, an optional element may or may not occur in actual texts. Its presence or absence does not affect the genre identity of the text. In Hasan's (1984/1996) interpretation, optional elements are "elaborative" in nature, that is, they contribute to the development of a more elaborated text, but are not essential to the creation of text identity. An iterative or recurring element is one that may occur more than once within the structure.

Fourth, the elements occur in specific sequential orders. This syntagmatic ordering is analogous to the sequence of steps of the particular communicative event. Hence the GSP of a specific social activity is characterized by predictable orders of the generic elements. They are predictable because the rules of a genre are in close affinity to social norms of interactions at a range of levels, from general to local, and the interplay between different levels (Thompson, 2005: 311).

Fifth, each component of the GSP, normally containing at least one proposition, can vary in size (Ansary & Babaii, 2005: 277).

Finally, the GSP is always definable with greater or lesser delicacy. The delicacy depends on a variety of parameters, inclusive of the degree of niceties the participants use language to orient to and interpret communicative situation, the interactant's singling out of certain stages for specific purposes, such as to explicitly invite the reader to give attention more than necessary, and/or to cater to the expectation of the discourse community.

To summarize, the GSP offers an exhaustive expression of possible text structures appropriate to the genre they are supposed to belong to.

To better describe the GSP of a genre, SFL scholars have developed some coding systems. The systems consist of symbols indicating generic stages and their sequential relations, as is shown in Table 3.8.

Table 3.8 Symbols Used to Describe Generic Structure
(cf. Eggins, 2004: 64; Halliday & Hasan, 1985)

SYMBOLS	MEANING
X^Y	stage X precedes stage Y (fixed order)
* Y	stage Y is an unordered stage
(X)	stage X is an optional stage
\<X\>	stage X is an recursive stage
\<{X^Y}\>	stage X and Y are both recursive in the fixed order X then Y
X · Y	more than one option in sequence (XY or YX)
[XY]	X and Y are of equal status in terms of a given feature

Given the systems, the GSP of a particular genre can be identified and described. One of the earliest GSP analyses is Halliday & Hasan's (1985) examination of a set of spoken texts within the specific contextual configuration of Service Encounter: Shop Transaction. They identify and establish the GSP of the genre as:

[(G) · (SI)^][<(SE ·) > <{SR^SC^} >^S^] P^PC(^F)①.

According to the GSP, any shop transaction in the culture of English is composed of the following generic elements: Greeting (G), Sale Initiation (SI), Sale Enquiry (SE), Sale Request (SR), Sale Compliance (SC), Sale (S), Purchase (P), Purchase Closure (PC), and Finis (F). Since the round brackets indicate optionality of enclosed elements, G, SI, SE, and F are optional and SR, SC, S, P, and PC are obligatory. If SR occurs twice, then SC must also occur twice.

The implications of the GSP is that it brings into vision the organized structure of the conventionalized, staged text types, which are driven by the common goals and purposes of a type of cultural events. In this way, the GSP can help to show different purposes of the writer, different assumptions she makes about her audience, and different kinds of interactions she creates with the reader. Meanwhile, it should be noted that the GSP theory is not only applicable to spoken discourse as Halliday & Hasan's (1985) analysis indicates.

The literature to date (cf. Section 4.2.2 below) has shown that the GSP is workable across a variety of text types inclusive of academic discourse, entertainment discourse, etc and the subgenres of each.

---

① There is a slight difference vis-à-vis the symbolic representation of recurring stages. In the original, ⌐is used instead of < >.

From the social constructive perspective, when the writer selects a genre, she also constructs the social occurrence of the genre, and the socially shared knowledge around it. This shared knowledge of the situation operates within the human activities of the community situation and the relationship which comes to be stabilized through genre. It is noteworthy that the GSP analysis is not simply concerned with describing text similarities, but with exploring the constraints which different contexts exercise on language patterns.

3.4.3 Genre of Academic Discourse

Academic discourse is defined as a discourse variety used in the construction and transfer of knowledge within and among scholarly communities engaged in tertiary education and advanced research (Giannoni, 2002: 27). It seems that the definition immediately tags the academic discourse as predominantly propositional, faceless and impersonal. However, as has been argued recently by Hyland (2000; 2005), Ädel (2006), Biber (1988), Fortanet (1998), Klinger & Müller (2005), Hunston & Thompson (2000), and other scholars, academic discourse has come to be seen as a persuasive endeavor as well as a rhetorical endeavor, involving interaction between the writer and the reader.

These researches verify and highlight the interpersonal dimension of academic writing. In fact, Hyland (2000: 12) even states that "in academic genres, a writer's principal purpose will be persuasive, [...] [for instance,] convincing peers to accept evaluation in a review". From this interactional perspective, academic discourse is a genre in which an orientation to the reader is crucial. One indication of this is that academic writing is primarily an act of inviting, aligning, and convincing an academic audience with respect to the reliability and acceptability of the writer's argument. Consequently, the writer is supposed to follow the GSP of the given academic genre and to make language choices which the audience will conventionally recognize as professional as well as persuasive.

Academic discourse is characterized by the features that describe genre as a general concept. Much related to the current study, the following aspects of the academic genre are worth foregrounding (cf. Paltridge, 2004: 86-87; Hyland, 2005).

To begin with, academic genres are of dual functions. On the one hand, they are informative. Thus, genres both stabilize experience and give it coherence and meaning. On the other hand, academic genres are dynamic rhetorical forms which have developed as a response to recurring communicative situations. Genre should be modified according to particular circumstances and the particular social setting of the text. The writer is supposed to consider the ways things are done in the situation in which she is writing, and orient her text to account for these expectations.

Second, genre knowledge is acquired through participation in the communicative activities of professional life. Thus, the writer is supposed to have learned what is needed for the successful performance of the genre before she contributes to the discourse community.

Third, genre knowledge includes both form and content. This includes a sense of appropriate content for a particular purpose. Also included are the ways chosen by the writer to best orient to and interpret routine communicative situations.

Fourth, as the writer uses genre and engages in communicative activities, she both constitutes and reproduces particular social structures, disciplinary communities and social relations.

Fifth, conventions of a genre reveal much about the norms and ideologies and beliefs of a discourse community. Transmitted through the repetition of writing activities, these community-specific ideologies serve at least two purposes: to regulate social interaction, and to simplify the communicative event by setting up expectations of how the event will proceed, and by providing ready-made forms.

These lead to the final feature of academic genres, that is, they are persuasive (Hyland, 2000; Bhatia, 2004). Texts produced under the name of academic genre are usually the result of a process of persuasion. The writer deploys certain choices from her language meaning potential in order to create a convincing reader-environment. As Hyland (2005a: 65-67) states, academic discourse is often perceived as a form of argument. Therefore, academic texts are not simply produced to represent the reality, but to use language to acknowledge alternative views, and to persuade the reader of the claims that are made. Hence academic discourse must be regarded as the use of appropriate devices to enhance persuasiveness for the purpose of social relation construction and negotiation.

Therefore, it is reasonable to state that the construction of academic discourse is primarily a purposeful social activity. According to Vergaro (2004: 182), "purposeful" means that, as in any kind of communication, academic discourse manifests a goal or an intent which, however ritual it may be, expresses a given community's way of making things happen through language.

This goal-oriented nature of academic communication determines the text patterning, or "pragmatic disposition" in Vergaro's (2004) term, at the macro-textual level and the linguistic choices at the micro level. From the writer's perspective, this connotes the assignment of different pragmatic functions to stretches of language and the construction of the schematic structure through which the writer expresses her social and communicative purposes.

To sum up, academic discourse characterizes its contributing writers in terms of at least two major parameters. First, the writer needs to consider general discourse community expectations and conventions, as well as particular expectations, conventions and requirements of the particular communicative setting. Second, the writer is supposed to consider the targeted audience. This includes how the audience will react to the text, and the criteria they will use to evaluate and respond to the text.

3.5 Intersubjectivity

As Du Bios (2007) states, the concept of intersubjectivity, in its broadest sense, deals with the relation between the subjectivities of the interactants engaged in a communicative event. In relevance to the present study, the concept is narrowed down to the ways in which the interactants "indirectly regulate participation and joint attention, and social norms for what can be seen as appropriate displays of emotion within a situated encounter" (Aarsand & Aronsson, 2008). The statement finds its echoes in Halliday's (1978) interpretation of an individual as a "social man", who uses language to establish and maintain his social relations. This section will focus on the academic interest orientation, turning from subjectivity to intersubjectivity in this sense. In addition, the genre of ABR will be considered with respect to intersubjectivity. It is verified that ABR is characterized by IPC, one most powerful intersubjectivity boosting device.

3.5.1 From Subjectivity to Intersubjectivity

The academic world has been witnessing the trend, advocated by both social philosophers (e.g. Bakhtin, 1986) and sociologists (e.g. Du Bios, 2007; Goffman, 1981), which argues for the intersubjective aspect of language use. In a similar vein, the tradition of SFL sees language as a form of interaction, which is learnt in interaction, and the existence of language is seen to imply the existence of "social man" (Halliday, 1978). The intersubjective meaning of language is explored by Thompson (2001; 2003), Martin & White (2005), Thibault (2004), Hunston & Thompson (2000), and Hyland (2005). Generally speaking, these studies attempt to reveal the intersubjective aspect of language use and discuss various ways natural language offers, in their structure and their normal manner of operation, to the writer to express her "awareness of the reader's attitudes and beliefs" (Traugott, 2010).

As was argued in the previous section, language is the ability to mean in the situation types, or social contexts, that are generated by culture (Halliday, 1970: 325). To study language is therefore to study "language-in-use, in a context of situation, and all of it relates to the situation" (Halliday, 1970: 324). Hence it is in the interorganism, sociological and functional perspective that SFL approaches and interprets language. This social approach regards the individual as an integral whole and looks at the individual from the outside. This functional and sociological rather than structural and psychological account means that learn to speak is interpreted as the individual's mastery of behavior potential. In this sense, language is a form of interaction, and it is learnt through interaction. In Hyland's (2005b:

175) words, meanings are ultimately produced in the interaction between the writer and the reader in specific social circumstances.

According to Morley (2000), the interpersonal function can be considered mainly in two ways, i. e. subjectively, personal mediation and modulation of the main idea/content, and intersubjectively, verbal interaction and exchange with others. There are three types of interaction: social interaction, instrumental interaction and informational interaction. In terms of social interaction, language serves to establish and maintain social relations, as is found in greetings and various form of phatic communion. The exchange of propositions is often featured by formulaic patterns which can be anticipated, and the language used merely serves to pave the way for more substantial discourse. With respect to instrumental interaction, language is used to seek or influence the behavior of others in order to get things done. The addresser may issue commands, make request, and put forward suggestions to direct the addressee's actions or behavior; they may as well offer goods to the addressee, and express their will or wishes. With informational interaction, people give or seek content/factual information. They make statements to impart information and ask questions to seek information. Understood in the way, interaction is simultaneously social, instrumental and informational. Consequently, the exchange of information is inherently social and dialogical.

From the perspective of dialogism (Bakhtin, 1981; 1986), meaning is a dialogue between the addresser and the addressee in that a response is expected. In Volosinov's (2000: 102) words, "meaning is realized only in the process of active, responsive understanding. [...] Meaning is the effect of interaction between speaker and listener [...]". Therefore, in the communicative event instantiated by the text, there holds a dialogic and reciprocal relationship between the interactants. As Bakhtin (1986: 76) states, texts are "oriented towards the response of the other [...]". The implication is that the writer makes efforts to establish via textual means a virtual dialogue with the reader. From the writer's vantage point, it is expected that the reader in turn will engage actively in the dialogue as the text processes. Therefore, the writer must deploy intersubjectivity-boosting devices to secure reader cooperation, to position the reader in ways that explicitly do with the dynamics of the interactive process involving both the writer and the reader.

The viewpoint that the ABR writer is well aware of the reader in text production and that the writer feels it necessary to make special efforts to enhance or boost the intersubjectivity is further verified by Simpson (1993). He argues that communication is a necessarily two-sided act, where meaning is not under the exclusive control of any one side of the interaction.

From the perspective of the writer, certain kind of readings may be encouraged or facilitated, while others may be suppressed or played down. The writer thus has on the reader designs which are manifested in linguistic choices. Therefore, it is fairly important for the writer to employ and develop linguistic strategies/choices to "hook" the reader (Tse & Hyland, 2006), to manipulate the reading direction. From the perspective of the reader, whatever demands expressed by the writer, he may or may not ultimately modify his mental states according to the writer's wish. However, if he engages in the exchange, and understands what is said, he is bound at least to identify the specifics of the claim put on him.

Therefore, the goal of a communicative action is oriented towards establishing norms which reflect reciprocal expectations, and justified and agreed upon by the counterparts in the interaction. In ABR, the writer is required and expected to have an attitude oriented to reaching mutual understanding, and to possess the capacity to establish and reinforce interpersonal relations rather than simply practicing representational purposes. It follows that the writer is concerned to supply as many cues as are needed to secure the reader's understanding and acceptance of the propositional content. These cues exhibit how the writer sees the reader. Therefore, they provide a link between texts and disciplinary, social or professional cultures.

As has been argued, IPC serves as one such clue. Differences in IPC realizations and distributions may therefore prove to be an important means of distinguishing discourse community and accounting for the ways the writer specifies the inference she would like the reader to make. The significance of IPC lies partly in its role in explicating a context for intersubjectivity interpretation and in indicating one way which acts to define communication, to maintain social norms, and to boost interaction. A systematic study of IPC, like the one this present project attempts to make, will definitely provide insights into patterns of interaction and engagement and reveal how the writer, through her texts, understands and construes the values, interests, and assumptions of the community.

3. 5. 2 Intersubjectivity in ABR

As has been argued, intersubjectivity characterizes text, the linguistic manifestation of the communicative event. The writer's writing activity thus presupposes and responds to an active audience (Bakhtin, 1986). It follows that ABR, as one primary academic genre (Swales, 1990), is featured by the reviewer's concern for interactions with the targeted audience. This is based on the assumption that all texts have a social function, and that they have a location in time and space, and have become what they are because the writer and the reader have agreed on the functions the text will have.

However, different genres are featured by different ways of using language to achieve different culturally established tasks. In addition, texts of different genres are texts which are achieving different purpose in culture (Eggins & Martin, 1997). It is thus anticipated that genres are different in terms of their communicative purposes, audience, and the discourse community. The writer's linguistic choices are determined by her consideration of the specific purpose in producing the text, by her anticipation of the potential reader's interpretation and reaction, and by her in-group performance in accordance with the norms and conventions of the community.

With respect to ABR, the reviewer is expected to fulfill her social communicative purposes of being informative as well as evaluative (Hyland, 2000; Motta-Roth, 1998). That is, ABR is there to fulfill the dual social function of the dissemination of knowledge and evaluation of the merits and demerits of the work under review. Taking the audience into consideration, the reviewer is expected to communicate through the writing with disciplinary colleagues, any readers interested, the author[①] of the book, the publisher and even the reviewer who comments on the book in advance of its publication.

With respect to the discourse community, the writer is supposed to cater to the norms and expectations of both the discipline in question

---

[①] Following the convention established by Thompson & Ye (1991), the present study uses "author" to refer to the producer of the book reviewed and "writer" to the producer of the book review. Alternatively, "reviewee" and "reviewer" are seen to be used out of the rhetoric purpose and repetition avoidance.

(e. g. linguistics, physics) and the norms of ABR. For the latter, the reviewer is expected to offer positive as well as negative opinions with relevance to various aspects of the book under review.

It is these contextual parameters that determine the social function of ABR. According to Hyland (2000) and Nicolaisen (2006), ABR carries out the following social functions. First, reviews are informative. They are valuable academic tools by making it feasible for members of the scientific community to keep up with the latest professional progress. Second, reviews are centrally evaluative. They are meant to offer a critical analysis of other people's work, in relation to the strong points as well as the weak ones. Third, the genre is parasitic to the one it critiques. In Hyland's (2000: 45) words, reviews offer "no fresh evidence to the community yet appeal for colleagues' attention". Finally, the genre is public. Reviews are published in academic journals and are accessible in printed and/or electronic versions.

Consequently, it is assumed that ABR is featured by its specific intersubjectivity features. First, in reviews the interpersonal stakes are "much higher" (Hyland, 2000: 41) than in other academic genres, such as research articles. This essentially evaluative genre requires the reviewer to offer her critical opinions on an academic piece of work with respect to its academic quality, clarity, integrity and value to the field. Negative evaluation may provoke controversial reactions from the readership. Consequently, the interpersonal relationships between the interactants may be very sensitive and subtle. It is thus reasonable to assume that reviews are featured by the writer's "strong investment" (Martin & White, 2005) in the intersubjective management.

Second, while criticizing, the writer needs to facilitate a continued sense of solidarity with the reader by appearing in less threatening authorial voice. One strategy she may employ is to resort to certain formulations which give the reviewed author the feeling that the reviewer's comments are not meant as personal offences. Thus, positive and negative judgments are carefully managed in reviews, entailing careful framings that respond to the interpersonal effects while simultaneously addressing the demands of the genre. Therefore, reviews are negotiation of argumentative evaluation.

Third, as a scholarly form of writing, reviews are to be taken seriously by fellow academics in the community. The writer can not avoid attributing the views she criticizes to a particular author, nor can she stake over or ignore weak arguments or unsubstantiated points. However, she can make critical judgments acceptable and identify herself as a reliable and qualified member of the community by deploying reader-winning strategies, inviting the reader to share a certain view, or understand in her perspective, or gain the reader's support, or persuade the reader.

As Thompson (2001) argues, collaboration is a two-way process, and the reader is encouraged to take part in the interaction and to collaborate back by accepting the roles, stances and arguments that are attributed to him. As has been argued, IPC is one intersubjectivity-boosting investment the writer makes to facilitate the reader to easily and clearly identify the writer's alignment endeavor, and to share with the writer her intended position, and accept it as fact that the writer argues reasonably and convincingly.

3.6 Summary

This chapter has proposed a framework for the analysis of IPC, in which four types of IPC are identified. In addition, this chapter has threaded through the theoretical architecture of SFL with the purpose of establishing SFL theoretical foundations for the current empirical analysis of IPC. In relevance to the current study, four systems have been focused upon, i. e. metafunctional systems, projection systems, genre theory, and the concept of intersubjectivity.

According to SFL, natural language functions as a social semiotic in the society and as a unity of three strands of meaning. The ranges of meanings are chosen to create a text in a particular type of context. In Halliday's words,

> The type of symbolic activity (field) tends to determine the range of meaning as content, language in the observer function (ideational); the role relationships (tenor) tend to determine the range of meaning as participation, language in the intruder function (interpersonal); and the rhetorical channel (mode) tends to determine the range of meaning as texture, language in its relevance to the environment (textual). (Halliday, 1978: 117)

While the systems of metafunctions construe the meaning potential for the speaker to choose from in order to achieve her social and communicative purposes, the system of projection finds its manifestations across the metafunctions. The nature of ideational projection is the creation of reality of different orders. That is, through the projection operated by human consciousness, the projected is created as something remote from the reality, or metaphenomenon that is re-represented. Interpersonally, projection is used to construe the relationship between the interactants. When ideational projection is used for interpersonal purposes, IPC is involved. IPC therefore has features of both ideational projection and interpersonal projection. However, it should be pointed out that IPC is not limited to ideational projection. IPC may find its realizations which no longer have the typical features of ideational projection.

IPC works primarily on the interpersonal dimension due to the fact that it co-opts ideational projection to stand for interpersonal meaning. To be specific, interpersonal projection is upranked to the status of clause in IPC. This is a result of the complementarity of projection manifestations of ideation and interpersonality. IPC is of peculiar syntactic characteristics. It tends to appear in the initial position of the clause complex, which enables it to frame, filter, and scope the ensuing clause. Semantically, IPC operates to signal or stress the language user's awareness of the presence of other interactants. In this sense, IPC functions beyond the level of subjectivity in expressing the user's own standpoints to foster intersubjectivity.

The concept of intersubjectivity is used in the sense that it shows the language user's conscious control and regulation of participants' engagement and joint attention as well as social norms and conventions.

Genre is a term for grouping texts together, representing how the writer typically uses language to respond to recurring situations, with respect to the three variables of field, tenor and mode. It is assumed that different genres are different in their GSPs, since they serve different social purposes.

ABR is characterized by intersubjectivity. Intersubjectivity captures the signals the writer provides as to how she expects the reader to respond to the current proposition. It is expected that the ABR writer utilizes a great deal of intersubjectivity boosting devices. This assumption is based on the nature of the particular genre, for particular genres set constraints on language patterns. In ABR, the interpersonal tension is much stronger than that in other academic genres. Therefore, it is reasonable and valuable to examine the discursive features of IPC, the intersubjectivity boosting device in ABR. In fact, an observation of the data has revealed four types of IPC, with respect to the relationship between the interactant and the Projector in IPC.

In the following chapter, the genre of ABR will be given a more systematic and detailed exploration. This will be followed by Chapters 5 and 6 which center on the discursive behavior of IPC in ELBR.

Chapter 4

Genre of ELBR

As was stated in the previous chapter, participants in any communicative act assume certain genre-constituted roles while interacting with one another. That is, they communicate within genres (Bawarshi, 2000). On the one hand, the speaker's speech plan is mediated by her chosen genre. On the other hand, the speaker's very conception of the hearer is mediated by the particular genre, because each genre embodies its own typical conception of the hearer (Bakhtin, 1986: 98). ABR is featured by higher interpersonal risks, or in Hyland's (2000: 61) words, a "potentially threatening genre". Therefore, it is reasonable to expect that the intersubjectivity boosting device IPC behaves more actively in ABR than in other academic genres. In fact, the very linguistic resources are also mediated by the given genre. As Bakhtin (1986: 87) points out, genres correspond to typical situations of speech communication, typical themes, and also to particular contacts between the meanings of words and actual concrete reality under certain circumstances.

This chapter will approach ABR, especially ELBR vis-à-vis their social and communicative purposes, and their generic structural features. In addition, for the purpose of comparison and contrast, a closely related but different genre, i. e. ELJE, will be discussed briefly. This chapter is to pave the way for the analysis of IPC in the following two chapters. This chapter argues that it is the specific nature of the given genre that necessitates the writer's investment in boosting intersubjectivity, which in turn determines her lexicogrammatical choices of IPC.

4.1 Genre of ABR

This section aims to foreground the academic significance of ABR. Meanwhile, social and communicative functions of the genre will be elaborated before the furtherance of its generic identity is conducted. In relevance to the current study, special consideration is assigned to the discourse identities of the ABR writer.

4.1.1 Significance of ABR

The practice of book reviewing is as old as the scientific community itself. According to Nicolaisen (2006), the earliest journals (in the latter part of the 17th century) consisted for the most part book notices. *Journal des Scavans*, the first periodical to provide regular information on scientific matters, was in fact composed entirely of summaries of scholarly or scientific works. In the present academic realm publicly published journals in all fields contain either a section devoted exclusively to ABR or else irregularly publish reviews of interest to those in the field. Some journals even operate exclusively as book reviewing journals.

As a social and purposeful activity, ABR occupies an undeniable position in the academia, considering its practical as well as scholarly significance. In terms of practical significance, ABR helps to estimate the quality and importance of books published in academics; and is thus instrumental in decisions about the individual scholar's hiring, promotion, and salary increases. Institutionally, reviews provide departments, colleges, and universities with a public, external assessment of particular work (Adams, 2007). In addition, the commercial effects of ABR have to be considered. The reviewer's position-taking towards the book in question may guide the purchasing decisions of interested scholars and libraries.

With respect to scholarly importance, the system of evaluation is a necessary portion of the social organization of academic community. Intradisciplinarily, the evaluation system enhances the autonomy of the academic profession, and it facilitates internal control (Adams, 2007). Thus, on the macro-level, ABR as the system of evaluation contributes to shaping the general academic profession. On the micro-level, the review anchors the book in an ongoing conversation about the materials, methods, and values of a specific profession—in the current case, the profession of ABR writing.

For scholars in the field, as has been repeatedly pointed out, ABR is an important vehicle for them for keeping abreast of current development in their field. For the author of the book, the review is important in that it establishes the platform for book recognition and critical feedback from colleagues within the discipline. For the reviewer per se, the appearance of the review in the public publication facilitates to render her visibility to the community.

Therefore, ABR is recognized in the academic community as a necessary vehicle for information, recognition and intellectual dialogue (Champion & Morris, 1973, cited in Lindholm-Romantschuk, 1998: 37). The genre exerts constant considerable influence on a discipline, a community and its members. Accordingly, ABR is an important part of the scholarly communication world.

4. 1. 2 Functions of ABR

Within the sphere of academic research, it is well accepted that ABR primarily functions to evaluate scholarly works of professional peers within the scholarly community (Sanford, 1993; Hyland, 2000; Lindholm-Romantschuk, 1998; Bhatia, 2004; Adams, 2007). In Strong's (1997: 299) words, ABR is basically persuasive, often convincing people to read or not. Nothey & Mckibbin (2005: 37) even state that in reviewing the writer's job is "not to interpret the content but to indicate its strength and weaknesses". Hence the primary function of ABR is to evaluate the book, to provide positive as well as negative comments, in either overt or covert ways or both.

However, ABR is a complex and multifunctional genre (Bhatia, 2004). It serves other important functions as well. According to Lindholm-Romantschuk (1998), ABR has at least the following functions:

A. One of the main purposes of ABR is to announce the publication of a scholarly work, to inform the scholarly community of this new addition to the body of knowledge. This dissemination of information serves the purpose of making the work visible.

B. ABR evaluates the scholarly merits of the book. The evaluation of the work includes placing the work in its scholarly context within the field, assessing the quality, and determining how the book fits in with the existing literature. The evaluation process is unique in two aspects. On the one hand, it is carried out in a public forum, and the identity of both the author and the reviewer is known to the audience. It can be argued that this is the most public form of peer review in existence today. Another important distinction is that book reviewing in scholarly journals is a postpublication review process. The work under review has already gone through a lengthy evaluation process within the publishing house before the review contributed to the journal. It has been reviewed by others for the publication, also accepted by the publisher for publication.

C. ABR serves as a gatekeeping function. The role of the gatekeeper is to accept or reject the innovation she is put to evaluate. A negative review may prevent the ideas in a book from reaching a wider audience, whereas a positive review may facilitate the diffusion of those ideas into the academic community.

D. ABR serves as a forum for disciplinary discourse. It constantly communicates a professional standard for scholarship in a particular field.

E. The reviewing activity reflects the disciplinary background of the reviewer. This is the communities of readers who, because of their common background, read and interpret texts in the same way. Books are therefore evaluated in terms of their value to the scholarly community.

It could be concluded that Lindholm-Romantschuk takes a communicative approach towards the functions ABR performs. Her categorization shows that ABR serves a series of important functions within the discourse community. ABR is regarded as part of the scholarly discourse, as vehicle for promoting innovations, and as part of the peer review system.

4.1.3 Generic Identities of ABR

Considering the fact that ABR is communication-oriented and

multi-functional in nature, it is not easy to pin down its generic identity. To locate the genre within the network of academic genre system requires, on the one hand, the distinction between ABR and other reviewing genres, and the generic nature of ABR on the other hand.

Within the academic genre system, ABR is observed to remain an intermediate between book note and review essay or review article, considering the length and degree of extension (cf. Adams, 2007). The book note provides basic publishing information (author, title, publisher, date of publication, ISBN number, and price), the barest possible summary, and a sentence of recommendation. It is usually of strict word maximum limit. Review articles or "review essay" in Adams's term (2007: 203), are defined as reviews which takes the publication of several books on the same or closely related subjects at nearly the same time as an occasion to survey the field more extensively and forcefully than ABR generally does.

It is not hard to derive from the definition that the book note mainly serves to introduce the book to the disciplinary community. It is not the right place if the reader aims to receive the professional judgment. That is, evaluation is not much favored in the book note as in ABR. Compared with the review article, an ABR text normally covers one single book, or occasionally, two books of fairly close theoretical or methodological affinity. Meanwhile, review articles are usually longer than ABR texts. This is due to the fact that more than one book is dealt with and more background information is expected.

Within the category of reviewing, outside the academia, there are reviews of food and restaurants, software or other products. These reviews, however, are sharply different from ABR in that the former is creating a new appropriated form of reviews, which are increasingly

being used for recommending products and services. As Bhatia (2004:
91) points out, while ABR is essentially balanced evaluations, where
one may find reasonably balanced descriptions of books which may
incorporate positive as well as negative aspects of the product in
question, in the cases of those commercial reviews, a majority of them
are predominantly promotional in character, focusing mainly on
positive description and evaluation.

To account for the complex genre of ABR, the notion of "genre
colony" (Bhatia, 2004) is of significance. According to Bhatia
(2004: 58), a genre colony is a collection of genres within and across
disciplines with a common communicative purpose and also a process
whereby generic resources are exploited and appropriated to create
hybrid (both mixed and embedded) forms. Hence a genre colony
represents groupings of closely related genres serving broadly similar
communicative purposes, but not necessarily all the communicative
purposes in cases where they serve more than one. Bhatia differentiates
between primary and secondary members of genre colonies according to
what he terms "generic values" (i.e. rhetorical acts through which the
communicative purposes of genres are realized, e. g. description,
evaluation, information, explanation). Based on generic theories as
such, he proposes the colony of promotional genres, as is illustrated in
Figure 4.1.

As is shown in Figure 4.1, in accordance with the genre value (i.e.
description and evaluation) of promotional genres, ABR belongs to the
genre colony of promotional genres (Bhatia, 2004: 62). However,
ABR can be considered only a peripheral member of the colony, as
Figure 4.1 demonstrates. It is due to the fact that ABR is a mixed
genre. That is, it is partly promotional, partly information-giving or
opinion-giving. More significant, while the advertisement, as the

Figure 4.1 Colony of Promotional Genres (after Bhatia, 2004: 62)

prototype in the promotional genre colony, serves to offer description and evaluation in a positive manner on the production in question, ABR is, in most cases, a balanced evaluation. In fact, a totally negative evaluation is encouraged if the reviewer can offer sufficient evidence to argue against the book under review, as is illustrated by the following text, retrieved from the current data.

> Bluntly speaking, the authorial descriptions procure insufficient insights that a moderately attentive viewer-reader of the case-study under discussion had not already grasped himself, and that does not make for exciting reading. The disappointment can be at least partially ascribed to the fact that Baldry and Thibault's orientation is too much bottom-up. ...
> A second reason for the limited appeal of the book, alluded to above, is that Baldry and Thibault's expertise is rather heavily language- and social semiotics-oriented, as transpires from their bibliography. Although they admirably produce variables pertinent to the non-language modes, it is a pity they are completely oblivious to fine work done by experts in other disciplines. ...
> For the reasons outlined above, I therefore believe that Baldry and Thibault's is

not the best book to steer students across the vast ocean of multimodal discourse. That best book, to my knowledge, does not yet exist, and is not likely to be written for quite a while. I think the ambitions for the near future should be more modest. [R72]

Another aspect vis-à-vis the generic identity of ABR is its location within the overall system of academic genres. Swales (1990) categorizes academic genres into three groups. The criterion is the kind of audience addressed. Those developed for peer-communication are classed as primary or research-process genres, whereas those serving a didactic purpose are considered secondary or derived genres. The third category of texts is produced for private or semi-private use, defined as interstitial or occluded genres. Taken together, all the academic genres form a spider's web, at whose center stands the research article (Giannoni, 2002). Table 4.1 exhibits the system of academic genre.

Table 4.1 The Academic Genre System (after Swales, 1990)

Primary genres	Secondary genres	Occluded genres
Research abstract	Lecture	Grant proposal
Journal abstract	Textbook	Recommendation letter
Conference abstraction	Introductory text	Request letter for material/advice
Oral presentation	Post-introductory text	Application letter
Thesis	Tutorial	Submission letter
Dissertation	Course description	Cover letter
Book		Research proposal
Monograph		Evaluation letter for tenure/promotion
Chapter		Referee's review of book/article
Case report		Referees' grant proposal review
Review		Memo to book committee
Review article		Editorial correspondence

As Table 4.1 displays, book reviewing is among the primary genres within the academic genre system. Being one member of the primary genre category, ABR is counted as a vital genre in serving the purposes of peer communication. Across the boundaries of discipline, it is observed that ABR is a mixed one, carrying out a combination of multiple social and communicative purposes. Thus, vertically, ABR is grouped under the super-ordinate genre of academic genre system. Horizontally, in the system, ABR co-opts with other sub-genres in a complementary way. Together with other primary sub-genres like thesis and review articles, ABR contributes to the unity and systematicality of the English academic super-ordinate genre.

Beyond the scope of academic genre system, ABR is found to be marginal to the promotional genre colony. In the colony, ABR is far from being prototypical in representing the genre values. One leading cause is that unlike advertisement, which stands at the center of the promotional genre colony, ABR often embraces praises as well as criticisms as it is expected to. In sum, the generic identity of ABR is determined by the social and communicative goals it is assigned to accomplish.

4.1.4 Identities of the ABR Writer

As it is commonly understood, ABR is an academic judging process which is analogous to a conversation which involves multiparties, from the author to the publisher, from the reviewer to the reader. The highly interactive and evaluative nature (Tse & Hyland, 2006: 773) of ABR necessitates not only scrutinized arguments but careful interpersonal considerations. It follows that these genre-specific requirements are imposed on the review writer.

As is argued from the perspective of social constructionists, social roles can be imposed on the writer (cf. Edge & Wharton, 2000). It has been argued that the goals of ABR may be informed by its social purposes. The argument is based on the statement that the relationship between genre and discourse community can be seen as a symbolic one, with each influencing and shaping the other (Swales, 1990). Therefore, genre constructs the identities of its writers. In the present case, it is argued that the complicatedness of ABR assigns specific discourse identities to the reviewer. Meanwhile, the exploration into the reviewer identity is anticipated to throw light upon understanding the inter-interactant relationship within the genre.

The reviewer is, first of all, a community member of the discipline related. As a community member, the reviewer is expected to be familiar with the conventions and norms of the discourse community. Reflected in the process of reviewing, the reviewer needs to portray her ideas as being in a relationship with other ideas and values which belong to the community. The reviewer should therefore be an expert in her specific research areas. Meanwhile, she is supposed to have mastery of the literature of her fields. The reviewer may show this by setting the piece of work in a larger, broader context in relation to previously published works in related areas. To indicate her membership, the reviewer has to, in most cases, balance focus on the book under review with a disciplinary perspective.

The reviewer is also anticipated to be a professional expert in the specific research field. As an expert, she needs to adopt a position of authority in relation to the book and represents herself as qualified to speak both to and for the discipline. On the one hand, she shall provide appropriate discussion of the related literature. This involves comparing research presented in the book with other research in the field vis-à-vis assumptions, methods, and results, etc. On the other hand, the reviewer is expected to express her fresh and thought-provoking opinions with respect to the content, the style, the readership, etc (cf. Hyland, 2000) of the book. A mere summary of the contents will never meet the expectations the reviewer is supposed to take into consideration.

The reviewer is, at the same time, expected to be a reliable assessor. The reviewer writes with attitude (Adams, 2007). She is supposed to be an evaluator occupying the freedom to speculate with sound judgment. The reviewer shall be in possession of the capability of evaluating the quality and integrity of a contribution. Meanwhile, as a judge, the reviewer needs to impress the reader with fairness and with the thoroughness with which the topic is considered.

Furthermore, in presenting evaluative opinions, personal biases can not be avoided. Therefore, a qualified evaluator's trustworthiness is also reflected if the reviewer takes care not to let away preconceived ideas go unsupported (Lunsford & Bridges, 2002). She has to address global features of the book under review, particularly content generalizations, together with the details of the ideas she encounters. In most cases, the reviewee's individual points are picked up in order to raise particular issues for the field and contribute to the sum of knowledge.

The reviewer is also an impressive writer. To begin with, to attract academic attention, the reviewer must make her product significant and interesting. That is, to maintain reader interest, the reviewer needs to make a point, not simply to summarize all the points everyone else has made. To orient and persuade the audience, the reviewer must construct her writing in an incisive and a conversational style (Luukka, 2002) within the limited space. On the one hand, the reviewer strives to minimize the imposition of the arguments on the audience, softening her criticisms, and displaying a fitting affective and disciplinary persona. On the other hand, she must argue clearly and vigorously for her positions. This implies that arguments have to be made with expected procedure and framed to project suitable authority and plausibility (Hyland, 2002a). Therefore, globally the reviewer may turn to text structure for rhetorical strategies (cf. Belcher, 1995). Locally, the reviewer may be observed to employ linguistic devices to achieve impressiveness.

The reviewer is a considerate negotiator as well. According to Belcher (1995), the ability to effectively address a wide audience, even extending beyond the reviewer's field, is valued by professionals across disciplines. The ABR writer is expected to pay attention to "metadisciplinary considerations" (Adams, 2007). That is, the book and the review triangulate with the reader's ruminations. The three parties "sit down" to conversation about the profession. In addition, compared with readers in other genres (e.g. the research article), the ABR reader are more likely to be skeptical about the reviewer's purposes, even disagreeing with the reviewer from the very outset. Therefore, the reviewer not only draws on the reader's familiarity with disciplinary knowledge of the field, but also establishes an interpretive framework that includes a consideration of appropriate social interactions.

In sum, ABR assigns specific discoursal identities to the reviewer, according to which the reviewer positions herself in the community. To verify the positioning, she is expected to turn to both the overall structure and local lexicogrammatical tactics. It is thus worth rementioning here that IPC is a powerful device for the reviewer to forge her supposed identities within the disciplinary community.

4.2 The GSP of ELBR

As has been argued, ABR plays a vital role in the academia. This accounts for the fact that it has recently drawn constant scholarly attention. Some research is devoted to the functions ABR performances whereas others explore the various resources employed by the review writer. However, the literature identifies only a few studies (Belcher, 1995; Motta-Roth, 1998) which primarily work on the text structure of ABR. This section, therefore, launches an exploration into the structural generalization of the specific genre by adopting the SFL genre theory, namely, the theory of GSP.

4.2.1 Requirement/Criteria for ABR Writing

It is shown that the theory of GSP is useful and applicable to a variety of genres. It is reasonable to assume that it also works in the case of ELBR. However, before the conduction of a GSP description of the genre, it is necessary to scrutinize the commonly accepted procedures and requirements for the reviewer to follow. The rationale is that these criteria for review composition guide the reviewer in the process of writing, in terms of content arrangement, structure organization and portion consideration.

According to Sanford (1993: 36-37), in reviewing a book, the reviewer is being asked to follow the five steps:

    A. to provide an overview of what is in consideration;
    B. to decide on specific points or aspects to be evaluated;
    C. to consider the standards (criteria) by which these points will be judged;

D. to determine exactly what judgments the standards lead the reviewer to make about the points she has decided to discern; and

E. to offer reasons, examples and details to support.

Reid (1997: 371-80) concurs with Sanford in stating that evaluative writing such as ABR writing uses techniques of observing and explaining because such writing must both inform and persuade an audience. Different from Sanford, however, Reid orients his proposed procedure more towards the potential audience. Reid (1997) puts forward a six-step procedure for evaluative writing:

A. a description of the product, i.e. providing background information;

B. a statement of an overall claim about the subject (i.e. considering virtues and faults before rendering an overall judgment);

C. use of criteria for the evaluation;

D. separate judgment for each criterion;

E. each judgment supported with evidence; and

F. criteria, style, and format adjusted to the particular audience (i.e. writers should anticipate which criteria are most acceptable for the subject and the audience, and present their claims in an appropriate format and style).

In a similar vein, Lunsford & Bridges (2002) suggest the rhetorical triangle to account for the dynamic relationships between the reviewer, the reviewed subject, and the reader. They argue that evaluation essays present the writer's opinions about her topic and support for that opinion, so that the reader sees something of the process the writer goes through to reach her judgment about the topic. Because the judgment will be a value judgment, evaluation essays are essentially argumentative. That is, the writer makes an assertion a judgment, involving value of her topic. Accordingly she offers an overview of one way to make and support an evaluation, namely, deciding what to evaluate, establishing criteria for the evaluation, making a value judgment, and offering specific support.

However, it is Nothey & Mckibbin (2005: 38-39) who list the most details of evaluation for the reviewer to consider in the process of review conducting:

A. How is the book organized? Does the author force too much on some areas and too little on others? Has anything been left out?

B. How has the author divided the work into chapters? Are the divisions valid? Do the chapter titles accurately reflect each chapter's contents?

C. What kind of assumptions does the author make in presenting the material? Are they stated or implied? Are they valid?

D. Does the author accomplish what she sets out to do? Does the author's position change in the course of the book? Are there any contradictions or weak spots in the arguments? Does the author recognize those weaknesses or omissions?

E. What documentation does the author provide to support the central theme or argument? Is it reliable and current? Is any of the evidence distorted or misinterpreted? Could the same evidence be used to support a different case? Does the author leave out any important evidence that might weaken her case? Is the author's position convincing?

F. Does the author agree or disagree with other writers who have dealt with the same material or problem? In what aspects?

G. Is the book clearly written and interesting to read? Is the writing repetitious? Too detailed? Not detailed enough? Is the style clear? Or is it plodding, jargonish or flippant?

H. Does the book raise issues that need further exploration? Does it present any challenges or leave unfinished business for the author or others to pick up?

I. If the book has an index, how good is it?

J. Are there illustrations? Are they helpful?

K. To what extent would the reviewer recommend the book? What effect has it had on the reviewer?

To summarize, the process of ABR writing is complex and multi-facet. It normally includes the description of the book under review, the overall assessment together with specific judgment, and appropriate style and linguistic choices, etc. It is widely agreed that the genre mainly involves evaluation. Based on the agreement, ABR is supposed to approach the subject from some or all of the six aspects content, style, readership, text, author, and publishing.

However, it must be noted that within ABR, subgenres may vary with regard to the aspects to be foregrounded. In fact, as Hyland (2000) observes, ABR does show disciplinary variations. In another vein, Moreno & Suárez (2008) find that the book reviewer reflects her cultural conventions and identities in her reviewing activities.

Meanwhile, it should be noted that, like instances of other genres, not all ABR texts are alike. Some are short, while others are longer. Some are more focused on outlining the content organization rather than actual evaluation. Some are more scholarly than others. Some reviewer situates the book in the field related while others concentrate on making topic generalizations or informing about the author or potential readership. However, despite the variation with respect to the length, focus, style and reviewer's personal preference, a reliable reviewer is fully aware of the fact that ABR is usually restricted to serving two major generic functions: descriptive and evaluative. In addition, ABR texts share a number of characteristics and social functions as were discussed above. All these make generalizations feasible to some extent.

Bearing all these in mind, it is sensible to speculate that ELBR is featured by its own peculiarities. It is expected that the current corpus-based generic analysis of ELBR will reveal some generic features describing ABR as a whole and meanwhile highlight those facets vis-à-vis structure pattern on the macro-level as well as linguistic choices on the micro-level.

4.2.2 The GSP of ELBR

As was mentioned in the preceding chapter, the theory of GSP captures the structural resources available within a given genre. According to Halliday & Hasan (1989), the power of the theory is further specified as to express the total range of obligatory, optional, and recurring elements and their sequential order. The theory, compared with others, has at least three advantages. First, it is analogical to the functional steps in real-world communicative events by revealing the linearity of the necessary as well as the elaborative steps. Second, it captures the dynamics of the communicative act by offering paradigmatic possibilities. Third, it clarifies the different status (i.e. obligatory or optional) of the steps involved in the social interaction.

Since the theory of GSP was proposed, it has been employed to describe distinctive generic structure features of everyday genres as well as academic genres. With respect to the former, there are Hasan's (1984) generic description of nursery tales and Halliday & Hasan's (1989) analysis of shop transactions in English context. Other scholars show their interest in newspaper Editorials (Ansary & Babaii, 2005). Concerning the latter, the literature identifies several GSP investigations[①] of the Introduction Sections of Research Articles (Paltridge, 1993), Business Letters (Ghadessy, 1993), Introductions and Endings of essays (Henry & Roseberry, 1997). Ghadessy (1993) establishes the GSP of Business Letters by suggesting that it includes an initial

---

[①] Ansary & Babaii (2005) provide a more detailed overview of recent GSP studies.

Reference (R) category followed by the category of Addressing the Issue (AI), and finally a Closing (C) category. The boundaries of this discourse structure are identified as the Initial Greeting (IG) and the final Complimentary Close (CC).

In the same vein, Henry & Roseberry (1997) identify the GSP of the Introductions of essays. According to their observation, there emerge three generic elements in essay introductions, namely, Introducing the Topic (IT), Narrowing the Focus (NF), and stating the Central Idea of the essay (CI). Of the three, only the CI element is obligatory. Their observation results in the GSP of the essay Introductions as (IT)^(NF)^CI.

However, to the knowledge of the present study, there appears no academic attempt to approach ELBR by adopting the theory of GSP. In line with Halliday & Hasan (1989), the present study aims to provide the GSP of ELBR by observing the corpus (see Appendix 1). A close scrutiny of the 100 ELBR texts reveals that the genre is characterized by the following structural elements.

(a) *Headline (H)*

This very first element specifies the book under review vis-à-vis its basic publishing information (author, title, publisher, date of publication, ISBN number, and price). It is indicative of the author and the publisher's presence. As the initial obligatory element of the genre, H informs the reader of the author(s)/editor(s) of the book and the publisher(s) who have invested considerable sums in the book. Furthermore, it establishes the target around which the reviewer centers her evaluations.

Headline (H): Example:

V. K. Bhatia, Worlds of Written Discourse: A Genre-Based View Cornwall, UK

Continuum International Publishing Group Ltd p. 288, Paperback £ 25.00; hardcover £ 75.00, ISBN 0826454461 [R15]

(b) *Reviewer Information (RI)*

This element provides the reader with the name, affiliation and e-mail and/or postal address of the reviewer. The conventions of some journals (e.g. *Journal of Pragmatics*) also prefer the reviewer to give a bibliography note about 50-100 words. The element may appear immediately after the Headline (e.g. *Journal of Sociolinguistics*) or at the very end of the review (e.g. *English for Specific Purposes*). Together with the initial element, RI creates a virtual conversational space involving at least four parties: the reviewer, the author, the publisher, and the reader.

Reviewer Information (RI): Example:

J. R. Stowe
Georgia State University
PO Box 4099, Atlanta, GA
30302-4099, United States
E-mail address: jrstowe@mindspring.com [R15]

(c) *Book Introduction (BI)*

The opening paragraph of most reviews usually specifies the element which provides some general information about the book. It may cover a fairly long "scene setting" (Belcher, 1995) which inserts the book in the broader field relevant. However, the present data reveal that in most cases the element highlights the central topic, purpose and/or motivation, potential readership and/or the background information of the author, etc. In most ELBR texts, the generic element (BI) is keyed to audience needs. That is, they guide their disciplinary audience to the latest literature by concisely and immediately orienting the reader, either by opening with an explicit statement of the reviewer's overall estimate of the work under review, or with an one-or-two-sentence outline of the whole book, or a combination of the two.

Book Introduction (BI): Example

> This book aptly recycles the concepts and systems developed by systemic functional linguistics (SFL) in the work of Halliday (1985) and his followers, particularly Martin (1992), with a focus on 'discourse semantics rather than on lexicogrammar, genre or register' (p. 242) as it is deployed in written texts—and makes such concepts accessible to students and researchers who are starting out with SFL. [R7]

(d) *Summary* (S)

The element is usually the one which occupies the largest portion of the review. It serves the descriptive or informative function of the genre. It typically includes detailed description of the book, content summaries of the chapters. The current sample is indicative of three variations of the element. One is the overall summary of the entire work. Another is composed of a series of chapter summaries. The third type is featured by the overall summary which is elaborated by chapter summaries. As Belcher (1995) stresses, compared with article comments, ABR often contains more summary. The fact reveals that the reviewer is well aware of audience needs by familiarizing the audience with the work under review.

Summary (S): Example

> Chapter 1 being the Introduction, the book has 14 other chapter spread over 4 parts. The order of the chapters is inspired by the metaphor of a student who is supposed to be undertaking a scientific journey. Part I, headed 'General Orientation,' provides information about the basic characteristics of this journey through the diverse landscapes of discourse studies. Part II, titled 'Backpacking for a Scientific Journey,' invites students to fill their backpacks

with some essential travelling material. In Part III, 'Special Modes of Communication,' the different ways of making a scientific journey are presented, while in Part IV, 'Special Interests,' some specific domains of interest can be chosen. The three final chapters in this last part discuss the cognitive, institutional and cultural dimensions of discourse, in that order. [R87]

(e) *Specific Evaluation (SE)*

This element describes the reviewer comment, either positive or negative or both, on specific aspects of the book, and/or sectional evaluations attached to the chapter summaries. The sample shows that the majority of ELBR texts are characterized by this elaborative generic element. Despite the fact that it is not one component of those defining the genre, it is one element commonly deployed by the reviewer to express her position towards some specific points before the general evaluation is conveyed.

Specific Evaluation (SE) : Example

> One particularly nice aspect of these definitions is the neutral stance taken by the authors in the majority of cases. Thus, the entry on 'individual' flags up the debate within sociolinguistics between idiolectal and societal views of language; similarly, the entry on 'critical discourse analysis (abbreviated as CDA)' includes reference to the 'considerable debate' surrounding work within this model of analysis (p. 64). In this way, the reader is able to gain not only an understanding of the term, but to get a sense of contextualisation, in other words to see where each particular approach fits within the bigger picture. [R90]

(f) *Closing Evaluation (CE)*

This compulsory element serves to round up the text by providing a final judgment of the whole work. While Specific Evaluation may be optional and disperse the text, Closing Evaluation ends the text of the review. It is the section where the reviewer declares her assessment of the book as a whole to the potential audience. Therefore, one vital function of this element is for the reviewer, as the organizer of the conversation between the reader, the author, the publisher and herself, to announce her final and overall evaluative decision on the work in question, and to declare the closure of the conversation.

Closing Evaluation (CE): Example

> I strongly recommend this book to scholars in diverse fields, including anthropology, education, English, American history, linguistics, sociology, and urban studies, among the many who truly seek to comprehend the linguistic sophistication and complexity that resulted from the African slave trade in America and elsewhere. W&T use linguistic evidence from the present to provide a vivid multidisciplinary window onto Hyde County's linguistic past. Anyone who plans to teach a course about African American Vernacular English would be well served to assign this book as a required text. [R5]

(g) References (R)

The optional element serves to convey the reviewer's direct references to other researchers. The high frequency of the element is indicative of the reviewer's awareness of the disciplinary community she belongs to. That is, the review writer shows that she is familiar with the well-known scholars and contributions in the field relevant to the book under review. This also demonstrates that the reviewer has read widely and made sufficient preparation for the reviewing.

With respect to the elements discussed above, there are two points worthy of notice. The first is that the element of R appears right before the element of RI or at the very end of the text. If the RI element appears at the beginning of the text, it appears immediately after the H element. However, in terms of R, the present data reveal a marked pattern. That is, in three of the 100 reviews analyzed, the R element appears at the ending position after the RI element. Due to the fact that the three marked cases are from the same single journal (*Applied*

Linguistics), this marked pattern does not disturb the regular generic pattern of ELBR.

The second is that there emerge three optional elements, namely, BI, SE, and R. The element BI appears prior to the element S, setting the scene for the book vis-à-vis its location in the field. The element SE is an iterative element, which functions to elaborate the reviewer's assessments concerning the individual chapters or particular aspects.

A careful examination of all the texts in the corpus of ELBR reveals various generic structure patterns which are exhibited in Table 4.2.

Table 4.2 ELBR Texts by Generic Structure

R1, R2, R18, R37 H^ < S > ^CE^RI	R38, R87 H^BI^S^ < SE > ^CE^RI
R3, R13, R15, R25 H^BI^ < S > ^ < SE > ^CE^ RI	R40 H^RI^BI^ < S > ^CE^R
R4, R6, R9, R22, R23, R31, R43, R53, R72, R76, R79, R83, R100 H^BI^S^ < SE > ^CE^R^RI	R41, R49, R82 H^S^ < SE > ^CE^RI
R5, R96 H^RI^BI^ < S > ^ < SE > ^CE^R	R44, R54, R81 H^BI^S^CE^RI
R7, R19, R59 H^RI^S^ < SE > ^CE^R	R47, R85 H^ < S > ^CE^R^RI
R8, R45, R55, R56, R60, R78, R80, R84 H^ < S > ^ < SE > ^CE^R^RI	R48, R92, R93, R96 H^RI^BI^S^ < SE > ^CE^R
R10, R33 H^BI^ < S > ^SE^CE^RI	R50, R88 H^BI^ < S > ^CE^R RI
R11, R27 H^ < S > ^SE^CE^RI	R57 H^S^SE^CE^R^RI
R12, R16, R17, R26, R28, R30, R32, R36, R39, R61, R64, R65, R66, R69, R70, R71, R73, R74, R75, R77, R86 H^BI^ < S > ^ < SE > ^ CE^R^RI	R58 H^S^SE^CE^RI
R14, R51 H^BI^ < S > ^CE^RI	R61, R67 H^BI^ < S > ^ < SE > ^CE^RI

Continued:

R20 H^RI^ < S >^ < SE >^CE	R89, R90 H^RI^BI^ < S >^ < SE >^CE
R21, R99 H^RI^S^CE	R91 H^RI^BI^S^ < SE >^CE
R24 H^ < S >^SE^CE^R^RI	R94 H^RI^ < S >^ < SE >^CE^R
R30, R42, R52 H^BI^S^SE^CE^R^RI	R95 H^RI^ < S >^SE^CE
R34, R63, R68 H^BI^ < S >^SE^CE^R^RI	R97 H^RI^ < S >^SE^CE^R
R35, R46 H^S^ < SE >^CE^R RI	

As Table 4.2 shows, the texts in the corpus of ELBR display a great variety of generic structures. Taken together, the obligatory and the optional elements of these structures construct the GSP of ELBR as

[H^]RI · [[(BI)^< S >^(< SE >)^CE]^(R)].

In sum, the present corpus of 100 ELBR texts reveals that as an evaluative genre, ELBR is characterized by four obligatory structural components (Headline, Reviewer Information, Summary, and Closing Evaluation). They appear in the order of [H^] RI · [^S^CE]. The order iconicizes the procedure of reviewing. That is, the first step is to introduce to the reader the basic material information of the book. The institutional identity of the reviewer, although necessary, may be presented either at the beginning or end of the reviewing process. The summary has to precede the evaluation because it is rational to familiarize the reader with the content of the book in advance of any comments and judgments.

It should be noted that the GSP catalogued here, taken as a condensed statement of a typical ELBR, is an attempt to abstract ELBR structures. It is clear that the components of the GSP and the order of the components are of close connection with the communicative purposes the reviewer intends to accomplish.

4.3 Genres of ELBR and ELJE: A Comparison

This section will introduce a cousin genre of ELBR, namely, ELJE. The prime purpose is to provide a comparative angle with respect to the understanding of ELBR. The ultimate aim is to pave the way for the study of the discursive behavior of IPC in the subsequent chapters. In a similar vein to the generic analysis of ELBR, the exploration into ELJE will cover the definition issues, the generic identities, and the GSP of the genre. It shall be borne in mind that the study is for the purpose of comparison. Therefore, the analysis is not as detailed as that in the previous section.

4.3.1 Rationale for Comparing ELBR and ELJE

It is within the general area of the humanities and social sciences that ABR appears to be particularly relevant (Moreno & Suárez, 2008: 17). The present study chooses to focus on the particular field of linguistics on the ground that it is only by comparing genres within a single discipline that it is plausible to explore the nature of relations across a set of genres (Samraj, 2005: 153). The present genre-based study necessitates an increased knowledge of genre relations. In fact, as Samraj (2005) argues, disciplinary norms in academic writing may be manifested not just in terms of the genres important to that discipline and variation in generic structure but also in the relationships among related genres. Therefore, a comparative study of ELBR and ELJE will not only shed more light on the discipline of English linguistics, but also increase in delicacy vis-à-vis ELBR as a genre and its intergeneric relationships with other intradisciplinary genres.

Meanwhile, variations have been demonstrated to exist between ABR texts of different disciplines (Hyland, 2000; Tse & Hyland, 2006) and different cultures (Moreno & Suárez, 2008). These relevant explorations have shown that different genres and disciplines make differential use of discursive practices, disciplinary methodologies and pedagogic practices considered effective for individual disciplines (Bhatia, 2004: 46). However, very little research has compared the structures of ELBR and ELJE as related genres produced in academic communities. It is precisely this possibility that the present study aims to investigate.

ELBR and ELJE share the communicative function of being informative. According to Bhatia (2004: 67-70), ABR and the journal editorial have at least one communicative purpose in common, and that is to introduce the book or the article. Nevertheless, they are different with respect to the prime functions. The former primarily functions to evaluate the knowledge claims of other colleague researchers whereas the latter primarily functions to promote (i.e. positively evaluate) new knowledge claims. Hence the social and communicative purposes of ELBR and ELJE overlap while simultaneously showing striking differences in evaluation orientation. Therefore, it will be interesting to compare the couple of genres in terms of generic structures, and the discursive behavior of IPC (as in the subsequent chapters). It is estimated that ELBR and ELJE fulfill different communicative purposes and hence possess different macro-organizations. Considering the dearth of studies on genre sets in general, comparing ELBR and ELJE will be a worthwhile exploration in generic interrelations.

In addition, despite the fact that the journal editorial is an essential section of the journal, there has been, to date, scant study on this common academic genre. As such, a study can inform us on the genre that fills a place in a taxonomy of academic writing. A comparative genre analysis of ELBR and ELJE can shed light on the nature of ELJE, although the focus is primarily on that of ELBR.

4. 3. 2 Definition of ELJE

In defining ELJE, it is worth emphasizing that academic journal editorials are a very different genre from that of newspaper editorials. Academic journal editorials, according to Bhatia (2004: 66), belong to the membership at the level of academic introductions which may include journal article introductions, book introductions, and essay introductions, all of which are used in academic contexts. Therefore, in the present study, journal editorials are defined as journal article introductions. ELJE texts are those article introductions published in international English linguistics journals. In contrast, newspaper editorials, sometimes shortened as editorials, classically comment on recent events which are narrated elsewhere in the newspaper's news stories (Morley, 2004: 239). In a more academic manner, an editorial is defined as an article in a newspaper that gives the opinion of the editor or publisher on a topic or item of news (Sinclair, 1995, cited in Ansary & Babaii, 2008: 278).

Academic journal editorials also differentiate themselves from newspaper editorials in terms of reference. Newspaper editorials are known as leaders (Morley, 2004), newspaper opinion articles (Murphy, 2004), or in Holmgreen & Vwtergaard's (2008) interpretation, include editorial material such as leading articles, opinion letters as well as letters to the editor. In the field of academia, one may find alternative terms for editorials such as overview, about this book, and to the reader (cf. Bhatia, 1997: 186). As will be shown, the current data of ELJE demonstrate a variety of referring terms for this subgenre of academic introduction.

As far as social and communicative purposes are concerned, ELJE is characterized by three main functions, i. e. introducing an academic work (in the present case, an article on linguistics written in English), positively evaluating the academic work for the promotional concern, and attempting to create a consensus of opinions with its readers. However, it should be noted that to an extent the consensus pre-exists in that the reader tends to read or purchase the journal which they know will publish the type of articles they find academic interest in[①]. As will be argued, these communicative purposes are expected to be reflected in its generic identities.

With respect to the writer, or contributors of these academic introductions, ELJE may be contributed to by the author or one of the authors in the current volume, the journal editors (-in-chief), or some other established academics in the field.

4.3.3 Generic Identities of ELJE

As Swales's (1990) academic genre system (cf. Table 4.1) shows, academic introductory texts fall into the category of secondary academic genres, which are mainly instructive in nature. Within the genre set of academic introductions (cf. Bhatia, 2004: 67), related genres could be identified in terms of a general communicative purpose

---

① The consensus is also determined by academic cultures (Bhatia, 2004: 189).

of introducing a written or spoken academic action.

It must be mentioned, however, that academic introduction is different from research article introductions (henceforth abbreviated as RAIs). RAIs are indirectly promoting research in that promotional input is rather subtle. In academic introductions, however, the promotional input is increasingly becoming transparent and more direct and dominant in some cases (Bhatia, 2004). In fact, it is not rare to find academic introductions with a clearly dominant promotional input, so much so that even the main purpose of introduction becomes secondary to this selling effort. It is pointed out (ibid) that academic introductions are instantiations of increasing use of promotional strategies in genres which are traditionally considered non-promotional in their communicative purposes. A scrutiny of observation will be indicative of the fact that it is often the case that informative functions are more likely to be colonized by promotional functions than any other. Figure 4.2 displays the colonization.

As Figure 4.2 displays, academic introductions are undertaking the colonizing process of from being informative to promotional. This process of genre mixing, in Bhatia's (1997; 2004) interpretation, is a striking property of academic introductions. The motivation behind is essentially the expression of private intentions within the socially recognized communicative purposes. In fact, as a subgenre of academic discourse, academic introduction is seen as a deliberate, non-conventional use of generic resources for promotional purposes.

Through the process of genre mixing, therefore, the two functions of academic introductions (again in the present case, ELJE), i.e. informational and promotional, are unlikely to create functional tension (Bhatia, 2004: 88), even if they may not be entirely complementary to each other. Such instances of mixed genres are termed "advertorials" by

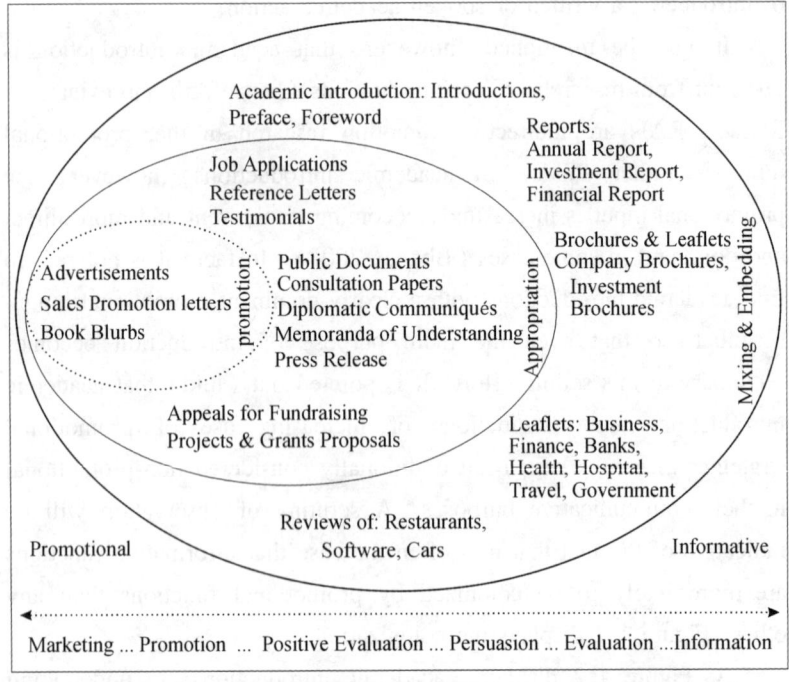

Figure 4.2 Colonization of Academic, Professional and Other Institutionalized Genres (after Bhatia, 2004: 90)

Bhatia (2004), a hybrid of editorial and advertisement. Accordingly, advertorials do not fulfill the typical expectations one may have from an advertisement. Instead, advertorials appear to incorporate a number of typical features of editorials (e. g. arguing for positive aspects of the articles). It should be noted that unlike typical editorials, advertorials do not incorporate any of the negative aspects. In a word, as Fairclough (1992) argues, the academia is becoming increasingly promotional. Consequently, academic introductions are becoming increasingly promotional in practice, so that promotional elements are dominant in these essentially informative genres.

4.3.4 The GSP of ELJE

Applying the GSP methodology to the present data of ELJE, it is revealed that the following elements characterize the genre, either obligatory or optional.

(a) *Headline* (*H*)

This very first compulsory element identified serves as the generic title and in most cases functions to highlight the theme of the current issue. Different from the H element in ELBR, the ELJE corpus demonstrates a variety of title names: Editorials (n = 59), Introduction (n = 24), Guest Editorial (n = 8), Editor's Preface (n = 1), Editor's Note (n = 1) and Editor's Introduction (n = 1). In more than half of the cases, the genre title is modified with a specifying subtitle. In the rest 6 cases there are specifying subtitle without direct genre titles. In such cases, however, the initiating words of the text are usually of genre indexing function, such as "*The articles in this special issue...*".

Headline (H): Example:

> Editorial
> Functional approaches to discourse: Perspectives, interactions and recent Development [E47]

(b) *Editor Information* (*EI*)

One particular feature of this obligatory ingredient is that in some cases there is information about the editor's professional position (e.g. Editor-in-Chief).

(c) *Article Introduction* (*AI*)

The third obligatory element identified in ELJE is indicative of the content gist of contributing articles.

Besides the three compulsory elements, five optional elements are identified: Background Information (BI), Volume Preview (VP), Closing Summary (CS), Journal Announcement and Acknowledgement (JA&A) and References (R). It is surprising to find that there is no generic element which serves promotional function. However, a closer observation is indicative of the fact that promotion penetrates most generic elements. The process of genre colonization has made it possible for the informational function to simultaneously perform promotional functions. The following examples represent the elements of VP and CS respectively.

Volume Preview (VP):

> In this issue of JEAP, we bring you a fairly wide-ranging collection of articles, that nevertheless displays the growing awareness of and concern with genre analysis/study in EAP, and also strongly demonstrates the practical concerns of readers—and authors—of this journal. We also bring you a selection of ABRs that are similarly diverse. [E34]

Closing Summary (CS)

> As a whole, this collection of papers advances our understanding of family interaction based on two related but distinct research projects, both of which afford unique access to actual interaction among family members. Together, the findings of these two projects, juxtaposed and interspersed here, represent a new level of insight into the everyday lives of families at the same time that they afford a uniquely broad view of theoretical and methodological approaches to ethnographic microanalysis of interaction. [E8]

A scrutinizing examination of all the texts in the corpus of ELJE reveals that they are of various generic structure patterns, as is exhibited in Table 4.3 below.

Table 4.3 ELJE Texts by Generic Structure

E1, E10, E19, E35, E55, E58, E64, E73, E82, E97, E98, E100 H^BI^VP^ < AI > ^CS^JA&A^R^EI	E30, E75 H^VP^ < AI > ^JA&A^R^EI
E2, E16, E23, E24, E36 H^BI^ < AI > ^JA&A^EI	E32, E41 H^BI^ < AI > ^CS^JA&A^EI
E3, E11, E13, E48, E49, E59, E63, E65, E68, E74 H^BI^VP^ < AI > ^CS^R^EI	E39, E42 H^BI^ < AI > ^EI
E4, E66, E67, E69, E76, E78 H^VP^ < AI > ^CS^R^EI	E43, E44 H^BI^VP^ < AI > ^CS^JA&A^EI
E5, E8 H^EI^BI^ < AI > ^CS^JA&A^R	E45 H^BI^VP^ < AI > ^EI
E6, E7, E51, E86, E87, E88 H^EI^BI^VP^ < AI > ^CS^R	E46, E57, E95 H^EI^BI^ < AI > ^CS^R
E9, E31, E54, E62, E70, E80 H^BI^ < AI > ^CS^R^EI	E47, E83, E84, E89, E91, E96 H^EI^BI^VP^ < AI > ^CS^JA&A^R
E12, E26, E71, E72 H^VP^ < AI > ^EI	E50 H^EI^BI^VP^ < AI > ^R
E14, E15, E38, E99 H^ < AI > ^EI	E53 H^BI^ < AI > ^CS^JA&A^R^EI
E17 H^ < AI > ^JA&A^EI	E56, E85 H^EI^BI^ < AI > ^JA&A^R
E18, E21 H^BI^VP^ < AI > ^CS^EI	E60, E61 H^BI^VP^ < AI > ^R^EI
E20 H^BI^ < AI > ^R^EI	E77 H^BI^VP^ < AI > ^JA&A^EI
E22 H^BI^VP^ < AI > ^JA&A^R^EI	E79, E81 H^VP^ < AI > ^CS^EI
E25 H^VP^ < AI > ^R^EI	E90 H^EI^BI^VP^ < AI > ^CS
E27, E40 H^VP^ < AI > ^JA&A^EI	E92 H^EI^BI^ < AI > ^R
E28, E33, E34 H^ < AI > ^CS^JA&A^EI	E93 H^EI^VP^ < AI > ^CS^R
E29 H^VP^ < AI > ^JA&A^EI	E94 H^EI^BI^ < AI > ^JA&A

As Table 4.3 shows, the texts in the corpus of ELJE display a variety of generic structures. Taken together, these generic structure variations construct the GSP of ELJE as

[H^]El · [[(BI)^(VP)^<AI>^(CS)]^(JA&A)^(R)].

As with the GSP analysis of ELBR, the GSP of ELJE is based on the observation of the current data. It seems advisable to consolidate the findings of exploratory genre analysis, inclusive of the one under discussion, through more larger-corpus-based research.

4.4 Summary

Genre, as Eggins & Slade (1997: 231) stress, is an institutionalized language activity and has its particular text structure. The unfolding structure serves to achieve the social purposes of the genre. With respect to ABR, the purposes are complex and multiple (Swales, 2004). As far as ELBR is concerned, its major purpose is not only to inform the reader about new books in the academic discipline of linguistics, but also, and mainly, to evaluate the work written by a professional peer within the discourse community. As ABR is a highly charged genre (Tse & Hyland, 2006: 788) due to this evaluative function, the reviewer must respond to interpersonal management while simultaneously addressing the demands of the genre. Therefore, it is reasonable to assume that the reviewer has to resort to specific lexicogrammatical devices to boost intersubjectivity. As the coming chapters will prove, IPC helps reveal how the writer handles the complex interpersonal relationships that the expression of ideational judgments necessitates.

This chapter explores ELBR as a genre. On the one hand, the generic investigation reveals the social and communicative functions of the genre. On the other hand, the study paves the way for the subsequent scrutiny of the discursive behavior of IPC. In addition, this chapter conducts a comparative generic study of ELBR and ELJE, with special consideration on social and communicative functions, generic identities, and GSP features of the genres. The motivation behind is relevant to the subsequent investigation of IPC within ELBR. On the one hand, the two genres share certain degree of similarity in social and communicative purposes (i. e. informative). On the other hand, each tends to have its distinct communicative purpose (evaluative or promotional). These purpose differences have been, to some extent, reflected in their respective GSPs. The comparative generic study has suggested that different genres within one discipline are differential in terms of GSP features, generic identities, etc.

The preliminary comparison of the two genres has offered us some understanding of ELBR. This study has also indicated that it is possible to analyze IPC as an intersubjectivity booster. It can be predicted that the frequency and distribution of IPC are determined by its purposes in the social and situational context. Due to the differences vis-à-vis social purposes, the discursive behavior of IPC in ELBR must vary in interesting ways from that in ELJE. Hence the findings in the current chapter can be employed in the analysis in the following chapters of IPC in terms of its discursive behavior.

Chapter 5

I-IPCs and *we*-IPCs in ELBR

The previous chapter focuses upon ELBR vis-à-vis its social and communicative functions, generic identities, the discoursal identities of the reviewer, and the GSP features. It is argued that in ELBR the reviewer's investment in boosting intersubjectivity is reflected in the discursive behavior of IPC.

Within the framework established in Chapter 3, this chapter and the following one will examine the types of IPC operating as intersubjectivity boosters within ELBR. The emphasis is on the analysis of each type in terms of its lexicogrammatical realizations in delicacy, its semantic features relating to projection, comparative cross-genre studies, and how it functions to boost intersubjectivity. The immediate goal of the analysis is to examine the discursive behavior of IPC. The ultimate goal is to bring out the functional choices the reviewer makes, which are closely related to the requirement of different identities in her texts.

As was outlined in Chapter 3, the criterion adopted for categorizing IPC in ELBR is the relationship between the interactant and the Projector in an IPC. In the current chapter, a scrutinizing examination will be conducted with respect to two types of IPC, namely, *I*-IPCs in which the Projector is the interactant, and *we*-IPCs in which the Projector includes the interactant.

5.1 *I* -IPCs

In this type of IPC, the Projector① is the interactant herself. That is, in such IPC resources, the reviewer resorts to self-mention or self-reference via *I* and its variations *me* and *my*. This section unfolds with an elaboration on the social interactional nature of *I*, which is followed by a detailed exploration into the resources presented in the current corpus in terms of metafunction, projection, generic consideration and its functions vis-à-vis intersubjectivity. It is argued that *I*-IPCs are powerful devices employed by the reviewer to fulfill her intended goals. Meanwhile, it is expected that the discursive performance of *I*-IPCs will display genre-specific features.

5.1.1 The Social-Interactional Approach to *I*

The personal pronoun *I* has been drawing constant academic

---

① It should be borne in mind that in English the interactant involved in a communicative event refers to both the producer and the receiver of the information (in the present case, the reviewer and the reader respectively). However, the present data do not show any presence of *you*, the second person pronoun indicating the receiver, in constructions of IPCs. The rare occurrence of *you* IPCs is, as Hyland (2004: 20) speculates, probably due to the fact that they imply a detachment between the writer and the reader, emphasizing a counter-productive lack of involvement. Meanwhile, the data shows no IPC use of *me*, *my*, *the reviewer* and other variations of *I*. Therefore, the current discussion is on the discursive behavior of *I*, the first person pronoun indicative of the writer as the interactant.

interest because of its vital role within and outside the academic writing. In the field of academia, *I* is assigned multiple functions, as illustrated by the following comments.

> The personal pronoun 'I' is very important in philosophy. It not only tells people that it is your own unique point of view, but that you believe what you are saying. It shows your colleagues where you stand in relation to the issues and in relation to where you stand on them. It marks out the differences. (Interview with Philosophy researcher) (Hyland, 2001: 217)

Traditionally, the first person pronoun *I* is approached from the subjective perspective. It is perceived as a person deixis which maintains the primacy of writer-centering (cf. Jacobs, 1999). Recently the egocentric viewpoint is challenged by scholars who are exponents of social interaction researches (cf. Verhagen, 2005; Hyland, 2000; 2005; Martin & White, 2005). All of the studies point to the social-interactional nature of the deictic field. To them, and to the present study, interaction is a negotiation process in which joint, goal-oriented activities are mediated by language. In fact, as Jones (1995, cited in Jacobs, 1999) argues, the subjective perspective in essence departures from the default harmonious situation which orients to both the reader and the writer.

This intersubjective communicative dynamic implies that the writer will present herself in a specific way in order to define and control the communicative situation according to her goals. It has been argued that in the case of written academic discourse the degree of control is indeed relatively high (cf. Cecchetto & Stroińska, 1996). In ELBR, the reviewer usually presents herself as an expert and accordingly delivers expert assessment on a particular book to the interested audience. Thus, as has been discussed in the previous chapter, the reviewer appears to be assigned multiple discourse roles. All of the roles necessitate her constant contacts with the reader. Therefore, it is reasonable to estimate that *I*, as the most explicit signal of authorial presence, contributes to the building and strengthening of writer-reader relationship. With respect to the present study, *I* will be examined within IPC constructions.

5.1.2 Metafunctional Features of *I*-IPCs

This subsection will present corpus findings with respect to the functional features of *I*-IPCs. In the corpus of ELBR, there are 213 instances of *I*-IPCs identified. These instances will be statistically investigated in terms of process types and tense within the ideational metafunction, modalization within the interpersonal metafunction, and the Thematic position within the textual metafunction.

From the perspective of ideational macrofunction, three types of processes (i.e. mental, verbal and relational) are found in the corpus. Figure 5.1 displays the distribution of the process types in the *I*-IPCs.

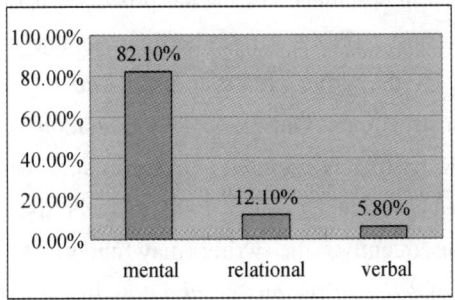

Figure 5.1 *I*-IPCs in ELBR by Process Type

As can be seen in Figure 5.1, the processes of sensing, being and saying distribute unevenly across the *I*-IPCs, with respective percentages of 82.10%, 12.10% and 5.8%. Of the three processes that human beings commonly employ to construe their experience of the world, either the external or the internal, the mental ones dominate. One important implication of the findings is that, in ELBR, the reviewer tends to select a combination of first person singular with a mental verb to form an *I*-IPC to achieve specific desired goals. The findings are of particular significance in the following aspects.

First, the predominance of mental processes suggests that by using *I*-IPCs the reviewer tends to portray herself as an active as well as capable thinker. In the academic activity of book reviewing, the reviewer is anticipated to express her judgment and standpoint. Another factor that accounts for the dominance of mental processes is that the writer may turn to the processes of sensing to convey her personal wishes and emotions directly to the reader. This reflects the generic features of ELBR. It is natural to expect that the writer will employ mainly processes that display her mental activities and value orientation when she is supposed to express publicly her evaluation and judgment.

Second, the predominance of mental processes over relational ones indicates that in most *I*-IPCs a verb rather than an adjective is deployed. That is, in EBLR, the writer prefers to use "*I do...*" constructions to "*I am...*" constructions. One possible explanation is the tight space constraint. ABR writing is required, in accordance with most journal conventions, to be succinct enough so as to meet space constraints of the genre. Consequently, the writer may choose *I*-IPCs such as *I suspect* instead of *I am suspicious of/about* as in the example below.

> (104) *I suspect that* these analyses are only the tip of the iceberg in terms of what adolescent girls are communicating about, how they are presenting themselves online, and what we can learn about them through their conversations in places they often believe to be private. [R39]

Finally, a closer observation reveals that within each process, the portions of different subtypes are out of balance. This is conspicuous with respect to mental processes. The results are shown in Table 5.1.

Table 5.1 *I*-IPCs in ELBR by Process Type and Subtype

Process	Subtype	Number of Occurrences	Frequency
Mental	Perceptive	8	3.8%
	Cognitive	119	56.1%
	Desiderative	41	19.3%
	Emotive	6	2.9%
Verbal		12	5.8%
Relational	Emotive	16	7.7%
	Cognitive	9	4.4%
Total		213	100%

The findings shown in Table 5.1 indicate that of all the processes, cognitive mental ones are dominant, occupying 56.1% of the total. Desiderative mental processes rank the second, occupying 19.3% of all the processes. Perceptive and emotive processes are also found, though of fairly low frequencies, 3.8% and 2.9% of the total respectively. Outside mental processes, verbal processes (5.8%) and the two relational processes, namely emotive (7.7%) and cognitive (4.4%), all show their low frequencies.

Of all the cognitive processes, the five most frequently used items are: *believe* (n = 24), *find/found* (n = 16), *think/thought* (n = 13), *feel/felt* (n = 13), *wonder* (n = 9). Taken together, the five items account for 63% of all *I*-IPCs in cognitive processes. These numbers indicate that the largest portion of *I*-IPCs is constructed through conscious-verbs (*find/found*, *feel/felt* and *wonder* in particular). These *I*-IPCs are employed when the writer is to propose a disagreement or controversial opinion vis-à-vis the author's viewpoints. The finding can be explained by the writer's strong awareness of the reader and the potential objection against her ensuing opinions. Consider the following examples.

(105) *I find that* the different chapters and sections are not well differentiated. [R16]

(106) Also, *I wonder if* the unit on corpus linguistics could not have been integrated into other units in some way since the information included is really about a research methodology that lies behind some of the approaches to language analysis presented in the other units. [R66]

The examples above illustrate the evaluation-orienting function of these constructions. By using such *I*-IPCs, the writer shows her effort to enhance the social negotiation of knowledge and to persuade the reader of the correctness of her claims. *I*-IPCs in this sense help the reviewer to gain community acceptance for her judgments.

Similarly, of all the desiderative mental processes, there emerge some special *I*-IPCs which allow the writer to foreground and the reader to perceive with least effort her unfavorable comments. Of the total 41 instances of desiderativeness, the *would like to* type ranks the first in terms of frequency (n = 16), with *wish/wished* ranking the second (n = 11). One striking feature of these *I*-IPCs which indicate "wanting" (Halliday & Matthiessen, 2004: 207) is that in most cases they are predictors of negative or disagreeing suggestions on the part of the reviewer. Consider the following examples.

(107) However, *I would have preferred to* see Bhatia's definition of interdiscursivity as well as a more detailed justification for his division of genre into genre sets, genre systems, and disciplinary genres. [R15]

(108) *I wished that* I could read more about these recent and very important domains of writing assessment, but Casanave leaves it to us to explore these areas in greater depth on our own. [R64]

In Examples (107) and (108), modalized interpersonal projections (as will be discussed right below) are chosen out of the writer's sensitivity to the views of the reader and to strategically creating a "space of possibilities" (Hanks, 1996: 196-97), which encompasses both interactive roles and the positional arrays in which they are realized. As Hanks (1996: 161) rightly points out, this space facilitates co-engagement of social actors in an ongoing activity.

Regarding verbal processes, the use revolves around the verb *say* (n = 6). On close examination, the study finds that these instances of *I*-IPCs are mostly employed as digressions or personal asides to remind the reader of the friendly, conversational overtone of the academic interaction. Consider Example (109).

(109) I am certainly with him on that—aggressively so, *I would say*. [R73]

As is illustrated in Example (109), the IPC *I would say* appears at the end of the sentence. It appears as an afterthought which is often used in casual conversation (cf. Halliday & Matthiessen, 2004; Schiffrin, 1987). Therefore, the deployment of IPC strongly suggests that the writer and her audience are in a simultaneous informal conversation. The purpose of doing so is to shorten the distance between the writer and the reader.

The findings also reveal some interest-provoking features vis-à-vis tense. It is worth rementioning that in IPC, according to Halliday & Matthiessen (2004) and Matthiessen (2004), the unmarked constructions are "either first person + present tense or modal". Accordingly, it is suggested that instances like *I think that* and *I would say* are the prototypes, with the former in present tense and the latter modalized. On close examination of the present corpus of ELBR, however, the study finds that the corpus consists of prototypical as well as marked options, as is shown in Table 5.2 numerically and Figure 5.2 visually.

Table 5.2 *I*-IPCs in ELBR by Tense and Modalization

Tense	Number of Occurrences	Frequency
Simple present	103	48.4%
Simple past	29	13.6%
Modalized	58	27.2%
Others	23	10.8%
Total	213	100%

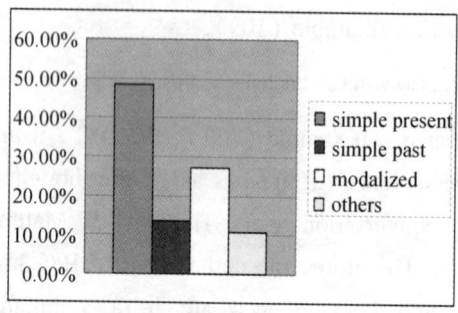

Figure 5.2 *I*-IPCs in ELBR by Tense and Modalization

As has been shown in Table 5.2 and Figure 5.2, *I*-IPCs in the present data tend to be realized by the tenses of simple present (48.4%), modalization (27.2%) and simple past (13.6%). The figures indicate that while prototypical simple present IPC expressions and modalized ones enjoy 75.6% of the whole share, instances in past tense and miscellaneous cases taken altogether take 24.4% of the total. It is an alerting result because the marked option carries a special interpretation (Halliday & Matthiessen, 2004: 207). Therefore, these marked instances deserve a careful investigation.

To begin with, the inclusion of these atypical cases into the scope of IPC has to be verified. As was argued in Chapter 3 (cf. Section 3.3.2), IPC maps onto ideational projection. This re-mapping of meaning may result in the resetting of its lexicogrammatical realizations (cf. Thompson, 2007) under the influence of particular situations of communication. Therefore, it is possible that in certain genres, IPC may evolve to favor some particular construing ways. In practice, there is evidence as well for their being counted as IPC cases. Consider the following example.

(110)... *I was disappointed that* major voices in the discussion of language in use are not included. [R66]

As Example (110) suggests, while the use of the past tense *I was disappointed* pushes the interpretation toward experiential projection, the presence of *I* as Subject and the tag question test (the most likely tag question is *are they*?) push the reading toward interpersonal projection. These interesting cases, according to Thompson (2005), are intermediate ones. They are chosen out of the meaning potential for the purpose of multifunctionality. In the case of Example (110), the writer construes her negative evaluation as being further removed, than projection in present tense, from experience that is shared. In this strategic use of interpersonalized experiential projection, the writer softens her interpersonal criticism and therefore solicits acceptance.

While the verbs appearing in simple past tense are similar to those in simple present tense and thus do not show particular lexical preference, the category of modalized *I*-IPCs is featured by two strong tendencies with respect to their lexicogrammatical resources. On the one hand, the category sees a high frequency (89.6% of the total) of modal operators of medium value (e.g. *should*) and low value (e.g.

can, and *would*). On the other hand, the following constructions are found to appear in more cases than other modalized *I*-IPCs.

(111)... *I would have expected the compilers to* discuss the implications of their choice and warn readers, who will be unaware of the similarities unless they scan the multiple copies of the text. [R22]

(112) *I would have liked to* know more about how the author interacted with the particular groups in their school and the community, particularly the parents, teachers, and administrators, and how her role as university researchers was negotiated in the field. [R21]

As the two examples display, one dominant type of modalized *I*-IPCs found in the current data are modalized past in present. The fact that this specific construction is favored by the book reviewer can be accounted for in the following aspects. First, the hypotactic projection makes it possible for the *I*-IPC to hold the projected clause within its scope so as to modify it interpersonally by positing a particular modalized stance on it. Second, the selection of the tense and modalization grounds the projected clause as an arguable proposition to the here-now of the writer and simultaneously sets a particular modal value on the discursive negotiation. Third, the hypotactically projected status of the non-finite clause means that the deictic and mood center of the clause complex as a whole is transferred to that of the projecting clause, i.e. the *I*-IPC. Therefore, the non-finite clause is assigned a non-negotiable status in the structure of the complex as a whole. That is, in plain words, one can argue with the writer by asking *would you*? but not *do they*? (in Example (111) above). Thus, the *I*-IPC operates to realize the writer's communicative goals by on the one hand providing semantic space for delicacy increases (e.g. delicacy in tense and modalization) and on the other hand creating discursive space in which the reader can dispute their interpretations by directly engaging in the disciplinary forum with the writer.

Thematically seen, 89% of the *I*-IPCs in the corpus are thematized while the rest 11% appear in non-Thematic positions. The high frequency of thematized *I*-IPCs is not beyond anyone's expectation. It should be rementioned that one leading function of IPC is to set an interpretation frame for the projected clause. Naturally, the choice of initial position can contextualize the sentence in this way. In fact, fronting the *I*-IPC suggests a strong persuasive impact upon the ensuing discourse by highlighting the writer's heavy investment into the discursive negotiation. A searching examination reveals that thematized *I*-IPCs have a powerful impact in texts where the thematic selection of the writer represents an important departure and signals a more authoritative stance. Consider Example (113) below.

> (113) *I do wish that* the authors had decided not to include the, admittedly important in other settings, topic of standard English and varieties of English so that they could have had more space for additional discussions and readings on language used in more discourse settings than they were able to include. [R66]

In Example (113), the writer chooses to thematize the *I*-IPC whose domain covers all the rest of the sentence. Through thematization, therefore, the reviewer is able to pre-set an understanding frame for the reader's interpretation of the subsequent meaning unit. The Thematic position enables the writer to alert the reader to the shift of opinion and to foreground her explicit intervention into the ongoing text. Thus, the *I*-IPC serves actively to engage the reader in the writer's train of thought. In this context, it should be seen as an invitation rather than an injunction to the reader.

However, as the corpus shows, sometimes the writer does choose to unthematize the *I*-IPC, as in the following split projections.

(114) This task, *I suggest*, is an ongoing one, never finished, always being revised. [R23]

(115) Robinson's text, *I should note*, does not indulge in such rosy imaginings; whimsical, he is not. [R38]

The presence of split projection as in Examples (114) and (115) in ELBR, although of low frequency, suggests the process of conversationalization of academic discourse① (Fairclough, 1992). In essence, the process moves the discourse away from an objective stance towards a more contingent, interpersonal one. In book reviewing which involves higher interpersonal risks and more complex interpersonal relationships (Hyland, 2000), the writer may use split projection to create a pause after the semantic units (in the cases above, *this task* and *Robinson's text* respectively) before emphasizing them. Meanwhile, in using split projection, the writer deliberately creates a mock dialogue by addressing the reader in a colloquial style. Thus, a dialogic overtone is disseminated into the academic discourse. In this way, the writer reminds the reader that they are engaged in an academic forum.

5.1.3 A Cross-Genre Analysis of *I*-IPCs

So far the study has conducted a quantitative research on the discursive features of *I*-IPCs in terms of their lexicogrammatical realizations. This subsection will, based on the findings in Chapter 4 and a further observation of the current corpora, explore the behavior

---

① It is worth exploration whether other academic discourse also shows the tendency of conversationalization, although it is beyond the scope of the present study.

of *I*-IPCS across ELBR and ELJE. The study is of two folds. First, the discursive features of *I*-IPCs will be compared. The aim is to highlight striking differences, if there is any, as well as similarities, if there is any. Second, the differences and/or similarities will be discussed and accounted for.

Globally, the corpus of ELJE is found to have *I*-IPCs which amount to less than half of those in ELBR, despite the fact that both corpora are of almost the same word number and sentence number (cf. Section 1.4). *I*-IPC frequencies against word number and sentence number are shown in Table 5.3.

Table 5.3 Cross-Genre Comparison of *I*-IPCs by Frequency

Genre type	Number of occurrences	Frequency/10,000 words	Frequency/100 sentences
ELBR	213	10.4	3.3
ELJE	97	4.2	1.4

As is displayed in Table 5.3, there emerge in ELJE only 97 instances of *I*-IPCs. This forms a stark contrast with the frequency in ELBR. In addition, the comparison in terms of frequency shows that *I*-IPCs in ELBR are roughly three times as many as those in ELJE. The findings indicate that the reviewer shows a much stronger tendency to signal to the reader her personal presence in the discourse than the editor does. The interesting results may attribute to several factors.

First, in the present data, all the reviews are single authored. In contrast, 42% of ELJE texts are co-authored. This fact may decrease the chances for the editor to use *I*-IPCs for self-reference.

Second, the contrasting frequencies may be due to the different generic identities of the editor and the reviewer. The editor represents the editorial board of the journal whereas the reviewer stands in most cases as a single individual identity.

Third, the reviewer seems impelled to set a public persona for herself and to establish her voice in the community by showing her presence in the discourse while for the editor such impel is not that strong. As has been argued in the previous chapter, the editor is usually of established status and position in the disciplinary community.

Fourth, the expected communicative purposes of different genres play a vital role. In book reviewing, the reviewer is anticipated to offer balanced evaluation. This might contribute to the higher frequency of *I*-IPCs. That is, when putting forward negative assessment, the reviewer may turn to *I*-IPCs to make it explicit that it is only personal judgment, and thus creates space for negotiation. In contrast, ELJE is a promotional genre, fraught with positive evaluations. The editor therefore does not need to make any special effort to stress personal opinions.

Locally, the corpora display differences as well. In terms of process types, the difference lies in the processes of cognitive and desiderative processes. The occurrence differentials by process are made salient in Figure 5.3.

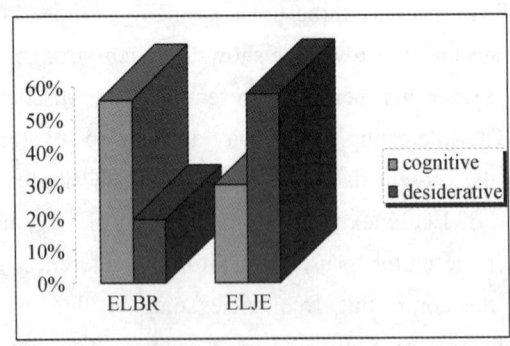

Figure 5.3   Cross-Genre Comparison of *I*-IPCs by Cognitive and Desiderative Processes

As the figure above exhibits, in percentage terms, the number of desiderative processes in ELJE vis-à-vis *I*-IPCs is nearly the same with that of cognitive processes in ELBR. Interestingly, a similar relation holds between cognitive processes in ELJE and desiderative processes in ELBR. Despite the fact that the ratio of *I*-IPCs in ELJE to those in ELBR is only 1:3, the contrasting prominence of the two processes across the genres deserves further exploration and explanation.

In ELBR, the overwhelming predominance of cognitive processes suggests that the reviewer tends to forge a self image of thinker and researcher by selecting options indicating mental activities. In addition, of all the cognitive processes, the percentage of instances in which the reviewer construes herself as a Projector is fairly high (75%) while only 25% of them construe the reviewer as a Senser. This further indicates that the reviewer prefers to portray herself as an active thinking Projector to a passive Senser, whose thinking brings thought-provoking ideas and penetrating assessments into existence.

As was mentioned in Chapter 3, the bidirectional feature of cognitive processes offers the writer alternatives to construe either conscious processing as the phenomenon impinging on the Senser's consciousness or as the Senser's consciousness having the phenomenon as its domain. Considering the feature of cognitive processes, the reviewer's preference for Projector over Senser in a particular process shows that she prefers to present herself in the academic conversation as an active thinker and idea-producer rather than a passive Senser and receiver. In ELJE, however, the cognitive processes do not show any noteworthy features.

In terms of desiderative processes, a preliminary observation of the corpora shows that ELJE shares with ELBR a majority of desiderative-type *I*-IPCs. As was discussed in 5.2.2, *I*-IPCs in ELBR are often used to forecast the writer's opposing opinions or shifts in evaluation orientation (usually towards unfavorable evaluation). In terms of frequency, the top three are *I would like*, *I hope* and *I wish*. However, by locating the resources in their contextual surroundings instead of in isolation, the present research brings into vision a different picture. It turns out that in ELJE, nearly all of the desiderative *I*-IPCs are used for the purpose of positive evaluation or acknowledgement expression. The fact has at least two implications. First, meanings do not reside in the items themselves but are assigned to sentences that contain them. Second, the social and communicative goals of a given genre determine the semantic nature of *I*-IPCs. With regard to ELJE, the primary goal is to promote (cf. Section 3.4). The editorial writer is expected to act as a journal advertiser, article promoter and advocate of the academic opinions represented in the volume. Consequently, her evaluation is of favorable orientation. The stark contrast in orientation is best illustrated by the following examples.

(116) Nonetheless, *I would like to* mention two tiny shortcomings. [R5]

(117) As a third syntactic phenomenon, *I would like to* draw attention to one of the points discussed by Hewitt in his contribution concerning relativization in North West Caucasian, and more specifically in Abkhaz. [E59]

As can be seen, the desiderative processes are exactly the same in Examples (116) and (117). The difference lies in the fact that in Example (116), the *I*-IPC serves as an indicator of the reviewer's upcoming negative comment on the book under review whereas in Example (117) the *I*-IPC functions to highlight the new value of a particular contribution. Both examples show that while *I*-IPCs are tactically used to express interpersonal meanings and to engage the audience in appropriate ways, their functions display strong conformity to interactional norms valued in different genres.

The second notable cross-genre difference lies in the distribution and allocation of tense and modalization. This is demonstrated in Figure 5.4.

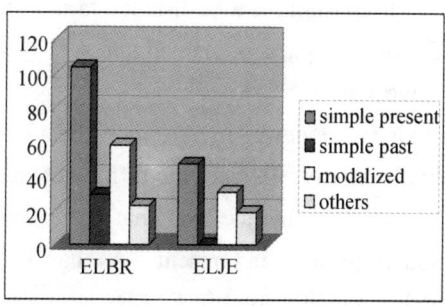

Figure 5.4 Cross-Genre Comparison of *I*-IPCs by Tense and Modalization

Figure 5.4 shows two important facts in terms of tense and modalization distribution. On the one hand, both genres give priority to simple present tense, which reflects the unmarked feature of IPC. On the other hand, the genres show a contrasting difference with respect to the deployment of simple past tense. As has been shown in Table 5.2 and Figure 5.2, 13.6% of the total *I*-IPCs are in simple past tense. Nonetheless, the corpus of ELJE shows no occurrence of *I*-IPCs in simple past tense.

This finding implies that in ELJE texts, past tense avoidance tends to be the norm as far as the deployment of *I*-IPCs is concerned. It is obvious that concerning *I*-IPCs, ELBR witnesses a higher degree of departure from unmarked expressions. This may be attributed to the "principle of interpersonal iconicity" (Halliday & Matthiessen, 2004: 631). According to the principle, the greater the semiotic distance between meaning and wording, the greater the social distance between the interactants involved. In the case of past tense in *I*-IPCs, a greater distance is created between the statement and the here-now writer. That is, the *I*-IPC (e. g. *I thought*) appears as if it resided in the past thought of the writer. In this marked way, the reviewer makes her evaluation tentative by pushing it to a distance farther than the present. Thus, a larger discursive space is created for the interactants, which allows for alternative voices.

This shows that the reviewer invests more heavily than the editor in managing intersubjectivity. In fact, the difference in intersubjectivity investment is also reflected by the fact that there emerge no *I*-IPCs manifested in modalized past in present. As has been noted, such instances are found commonly used in ELBR.

In sum, the writer's preference for and avoidance of past tense and modalized past in present is not a matter of personal choices. Instead, it reflects the norms and social purposes of a particular genre. In ELBR, which requires a balanced and sometimes even negative evaluation, the reviewer has to resort to marked realizations of *I*-IPCs, aiming at conveying special connotation to the reader. In ELJE, which is primarily a promotional genre, the writer aims to promote the journal and articles contributed. Since no negative assessment is anticipated, it is of no necessity to employ marked expressions. It is therefore reasonable to conclude that within a particular genre, the expert writer shows her awareness of and respect to the preferred interpersonal conventions of the community.

Finally, the behavior of *I*-IPCs will be compared from the generic structural perspective. Figure 5.5 and Figure 5.6 illustrate respectively the allocation patterns of *I*-IPCs in different elements of the GSPs of ELBR and ELJE.

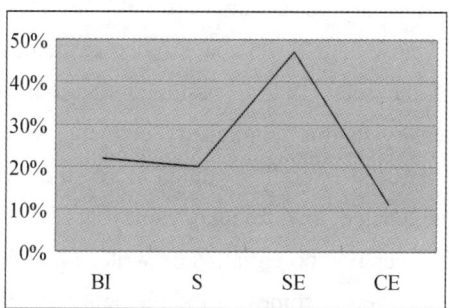

Figure 5. 5 Generic Structural Distribution of *I*-IPCs in ELBR

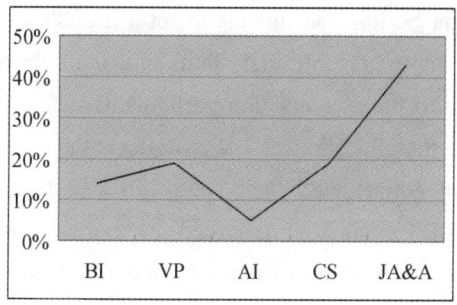

Figure 5. 6 Generic Structural Distribution of *I*-IPCs in ELJE

Figure 5. 5 displays an interesting overall allocation of *I*-IPCs in ELBR. It is within expectation that the element of SE is marked by the highest *I*-IPC intensity (48% of the total *I*-IPCs). The element functions to convey the reviewer's evaluative assessment of specific or detailed information of the academic product. In many cases it is this element which sees particular problematic issues for the discipline be raised. It is thus reasonable to predict that the writer constantly resorts to IPC in this element to foster intersubjectivity. *I*-IPCs are therefore selected to manage communicative intentions and to establish a reader-friendly atmosphere by directly engaging the reader in a talk.

In contradiction to the assumption held by the present study, however, *I*-IPCs show their lowest occurrence frequency in the element of CE (11% of the total). It is assumed that *I*-IPCs would be of relative high intensity in this compulsory element, which functions to express the reviewer's overall evaluation of the whole academic product. The unexpected low frequency may attribute to the writer's tactic allocation of her IPC potential. The writer may probably resort to other types of IPC when it comes to the element CE. It seems that the reviewer avoids much self-presence in CE. On the contrary, the reviewer chooses more *I*-IPCs in the element BI. The possible explanation might be that she intends to set a friendly overtone as early as possible, to make her authorial status and the role of conversation organizer visible to the conversation participants.

In essence, the allocation of *I*-IPCs reflects the insider's perception of how best to negotiate with their peers. In a particular community, the choice of *I*-IPCs may be regarded as a clear indication of the academics' aim to balance evaluation and a sense of disciplinary solidarity while influencing the perspective from which their texts are expected to be interpreted.

Figure 5.6 indicates how *I*-IPCs distribute across the generic structural elements of ELJE. The figure has two important implications. First, the overwhelming portion of *I*-IPCs appears in the element JA&A (42% of the total). The prominence is of close relevance to the conventions and norms of the genre. As was shown in Section 4.3, although JA&A is not an obligatory element, it is one of fairly high frequency. In this element, the editor feels obliged to express her or the journal's gratitude to contributors, to other editors, or others, as is shown by Example (118) below. Also in this element, the editor may deliver some announcement as in Example (119) below.

(118) *I wish to* thank all the Contributors to this volume, who have undertaken this task with enthusiasm and generosity. *I would also like to* thank J. Rooryck, N. Smith, the various anonymous reviewers who devoted some of their time and energy to this volume. [E55]

(119) Finally *I would like to* announce some changes to the Editorial Board. [E23]

Second, while JA&A sees 42% of all *I*-IPCs, the rest *I*-IPCs are seen to disperse over the other four elements (i.e. BI, VP, AI and CS, respectively 13%, 19%, 7% and 19% of the total) in a roughly balanced way. This balanced distribution partly attributes to the generic identity of ELJE. As was stated in the previous chapter, there is little functional tension in the genre. Consequently, the editor may choose to intrude into the text at any point to make a promotional endeavor. Generally speaking, the *I*-IPCs in ELJE convey the writer's active membership in the discourse community. In particular, a harmonious microcosm of intellectual harmony and empathy is constructed (cf. Giannoni, 2002: 16).

5.1.4 *I*-IPCs as Intersubjectivity Boosters

So far, the study has conducted considerable quantitative analysis in the extent to which *I*-IPCs manifest across three macro-functions within ELBR and across the two genres of ELBR and ELJE. This subsection will elucidate what intersubjectivity-oriented functions or discourse acts *I*-IPCs perform. The research will present a categorization of intersubjectivity boosting functions that *I*-IPCs carry out. The taxonomy is based on the observation of the present corpora with specific consideration on the immediate discourse context of the instances.

Before a detailed probe into the intersubjective use of *I*-IPCs in

ELBR, however, it is worth mentioning previous studies with respect to the functions of *I* in academic discourse. A number of studies (cf. Kuo, 1999; Harwood, 2005) have specified a range of functions that *I* plays in academic discourse. A majority of the research anchors their interest in research articles and identities some discourse functions of *I*.

One of the most detailed taxonomies of the discourse functions of the first person singular *I* is attributed to Vassileva (1998) who identifies ten functions for which *I* is to be employed. Based on research articles in linguistics in English, German, French, Russian and Bulgarian, Vassileva categorizes the functions of *I* into describing aims/procedures/data; self-reference; referring to personal experience; introducing terms; focusing on goals purposes or expectations; expressing personal view; citing examples; concluding the article; referring to other researchers' work; and asking for permission (e.g. *let me*). It can be concluded that Vassileva's classification is, as Ädel (2006: 58) points out, mainly concerned with the textual organizing function of *I*. In fact, for these investigations, the focus of interest is primarily on the content or the information per se in the text.

In another vein (Tang & John, 1999; Hyland, 2002; Hewings & Coffin, 2007), *I* is observed to facilitate to reveal how the academic writer constructs her relationship with the reader and with her discourse community. Gragson & Selzer (1990) argue that the relatively high frequency of *I* is indicative of the writer's intention to establish herself as the authority and the imagined reader as the novice in need of direction. In this trend, researchers' prime concern is whether the authorial presence realizes the writer's textual intervention or her exposure to face-threatening (i.e. the potential to be attacked by the audience). In essence, the second trend is a writer-oriented approach to the study of *I*.

Hyland (2004a), Samson (2004) and Ädel (2006) concur with the writer-oriented trend in extending the study to writer-reader interactions. The main motivation behind is to draw attention to how the writer builds connections with the reader. The present study, in this sense, is a furtherance of the discoursal interaction study by scrutinizing *I*s in one special linguistic construction (i.e. IPC). A close data observation reveals the following functions that *I*-IPCs perform with respect to intersubjectivity boosting.

1. Conversational Involvement

It is a conscious choice that contributes to ego involvement, to the degree of intimacy and remoteness, and to the ways the writer wishes to be represented in the text. The present data sees in many cases *I*-IPCs are adopted by the reviewer to create conversational atmosphere. As has been stated, book reviewing is analogical to a conversation involving multiple parties, from the reviewer to the reader interested, from the author to the publisher. As the organizer of the conversation, the reviewer is constantly aware of the presence of the potential reader. To attract the reader and focus the reader's attention on the ongoing conversation, the reviewer may resort to *I*- IPCs, as in the following examples.

> (120) Given this title, *I was surprised that* this book starts by posing the question why 30 many Germans could be persuaded to back the Nazis. [R11]
> (121) All in all, *I would say that* the strength of the book—that it provides a general introduction to the main areas of sociolinguistics in only fifteen pages per area—is also its weakness. [R20]

Example (120) appears as the initiative sentence of the text. It is indicative explicitly of the fact that the reviewer's claim of personal involvement is also a way of claiming recognition for the contribution she has made herself. By declaring the opening of an academic dialogue, the reviewer positions herself immediately in the conversation as the organizer. In addition, by referring directly to herself through the *I*-IPC construction *I was surprised* which shows not only the authorial presence but also her emotive reaction to the book under discussion, the reviewer creates an impression of a direct contact with the audience. In this way, the reader is invited into the conversation. In a similar vein, the reviewer in Example (121) creates a dialogic space for herself and the audience by directly addressing the reader. In choosing the fairly direct personal style of delivery, the writer is able to acknowledge and respond to an active audience, often to initiate a brief dialogue that is largely interpersonal.

It is also observed that *I*-IPCs may be used to bring the reader into argument through asides and interruptions to the ongoing discussion. These are termed by Hyland (2004) as "digressions", which directly address the audience. In such cases, the reviewer briefly breaks off the argument to offer a personal comment or opinion on what has been said. Consider the following examples.

(122) Dancygier and Sweeter's, *dare I say*, West Coast Isolationism, is rather extraordinary on a plane where the rest of human activity is marked by an increasing internationalism and intergrationalism, and their analysis, for all of its interest, is the poorer for it. [R71]

(123) But if what Shotter argues in *Conversational Realities* is reasonable, *I thought*, my intellectual and disciplinary experiences could be an asset rather than a liability. [R23]

As these examples indicate, by turning to the reader in mid-flow, the reviewer maintains a colloquial style by expressing a personal view on the reviewees' opinions under question. As the examples illustrate, this type of *I*-IPCs are often realized by split projections (as in the present cases, *dare I say* and *I thought*). The fact that both *I*-IPCs are interpolated rather than postponed iconically reflects the reviewer's desire to establish the interruptions as early as possible in terms of sequential placement (cf. Vandelanotte, 2004). In this way, the reviewer demonstrates her constant awareness of how to employ appropriate linguistic resources to keep the reader online, so as to actively participate in the academic conversation of book reviewing.

2. Appealing to the Reader

I-IPCs are also utilized by the reviewer to influence the reader by appealing for sharing private experience or emotions. The reviewer appears in the text to ask the reader to be in sympathy with her. Barnes & Moss (2007) have noticed how in both everyday and institutional interaction private feelings and thought are communicated publicly. Based on their corpus, they identify three different formats which report private thought, namely, *I thought*, *most of the time I think*, and *I might think*. According to them, by resorting to constructions as such, the interactant within a communicative event appeals for an overhearing audience to shared experience.

Similarly, Fetzer (2008a) argues that constructions composed of cognitive verbs (e.g. *think*, *suppose*, and *guess*) allow the speaker to express epistemic, emotive, and social commitment. Thus, through signifying solidarity and social commitment via *I*-IPCs, the discourse identity of the reviewer gets intersubjectified. This is because as soon as reference to the subjective world is communicated, it is no longer part of the subjective world, but assigned an intersubjective status. As in Du Bois's (2007: 159) words, intersubjectivity presupposes subjectivity. In plain expressions, it implies that such *I*-IPCs convey the writer's attitudes with the reader in mind. Consider the following examples.

(124) Personally, *I believe that* students (and even parents) could benefit from the explicit identification of these two models, since they would be furnished with a top-down framework to help them understand better the various arguments. [R44]

(125) Overall, however, *I feel that* the book was written with the researcher rather than the student in mind. [R13]

In Example (124), the writer exchanges personal opinions (reinforced by *Personally*) with the reader by inviting the reader to share her private thought. The use of *I believe* is persuasive since the writer seems to encourage the reader to do something. Example (125) explicitly displays the reviewer's private feelings to the reader. In both cases, intersubjectivity arises to focal prominence in that the writer stresses disciplinary solidarity by being on intimate terms with the reader so as to let her private mental activities be shared. In fact, the *I*-IPCs in the two examples are typically used in situations in which the writer announces that she is about to say, claim, or suggest something. They are usually interpreted as a sign of weakness or of unassertativeness on the part of the user (in the present case, the reviewer). Halliday (1994) regards them as interpersonal grammatical expressions, which denote the concept of possibility on the part of the subject. Similarly, Hewings & Coffin (2007) suggest that such expressions convey opinions in a tentative way. However, seen from an interactive perspective, such *I*-IPCs are in fact "a resource of doing friendship" (Coates, 2003: 346). Besides appealing to the audience for internal experience sharing, the writer may resort to emotional appeal in order to foreground intersubjectivity. Here is one representative example.

(126) *I hope that Assessing Writing* may see the outcomes of such research in these pages before too many years and test administrations have elapsed. [E20]

As is shown in Example (126), the writer expresses her wish that the reader, while reading the text, will be impressed by the journal's publication orientation and calls for relevant articles. In this way, the reader is appealed indirectly to focus particular attention on the articles under discussion. The foregrounding of this dialogic relation potentially invites the reader to read on and to contribute to the journal either by academic activities or immediate purchases. In sum, as Hyland (2005b) argues, the writer's personality and willingness to explicitly intervene to offer a view is a key reader-oriented strategy.

3. Perspective Alerting

The current corpora also demonstrate a large portion of *I*-IPC constructions which function to alert the reader to the writer's perspective towards the propositional information and to the reader himself (Hyland, 1998: 5). The motivation is to prepare the audience for a change of state or to hint at a stance with respect to what is to be projected.

In the genre of academic reviewing, the writer is expected to encounter more potential unfavorable reactions from the audience due to the evaluative nature of the genre. In fact, the reader can always refute claims and this gives him an active and constitutive role in how the writer constructs her arguments. Thus, the reviewer is located intertexually within a large web of opinions, and within a community whose members are likely to recognize only certain forms of argument as valid and effective. It is easy to imagine that blank expressions in direct and abrupt manner might evoke unpleasant or even negative reactions on the part of the audience. Consequently, interpretations and assessments need to be presented in ways that the reader is likely to find persuasive. Hence the writer must draw on linguistic devices such as *I*-IPCs to frame her subsequent opinions. Meanwhile, alerting *I*-

IPCs propose that the writer has undergone some kind of change in her current state of knowledge, information, orientation or awareness. In the present collection, such IPC resources are very common and of a canonical ordering. That is, when they occur, they always occupy the first position of the projection construction, as is shown in the following examples.

(127) *I think* there are some mechanisms at work that do not get discussed. [R39]

(128) Although she rejects the use of statistical data as irrelevant for her purposes, *I would have liked to* see data on frequencies here and check to what extent the examples presented can be said to constitute a significant pattern or not. [R46]

In Example (127), depending on its sequential position, *I think* displays that the current writer adopts a new stance. Such alerting constructions often occur at crucial points, aiming to invite the audience to join in the evaluating activity. Thus, the use of the *I*-IPC draws the co-participant's attention to the reviewer's assessment orientation. In this way, the projection construction operates to increase and facilitate the reader's understanding and acceptance of the framed viewpoint. The alerting function performed by *I would have liked to* in Example (128) is made salient in two ways. First, the preceding *although* clause predicts a shift in the reviewer's attitude conveyed in the subsequent dominant clause. This concessive syntagmatic structure prepares the audience for the following stancetaking by the writer towards the reviewed. Second, the *I*-IPC itself strongly signals a preferred viewpoint of the writer. As the example indicates, the IPC denotes negative evaluation towards the object.

Also covered by this function is perspective clarifying. It is motivated by a wish to avoid being misinterpreted by the reader. In a persuasive discourse such as ELBR, it is particularly important to be clear about what one's arguments imply and what they do not imply. In this sense, it is important to assure felicitous communication between the interactants. In adopting perspective-clarifying *I*-IPCs, the writer may aim to monitor the reader's possible responses by explicitly stating her intentions for the benefit of the audience and thus avoids misinterpretation. Negative statements such as *I am not saying* ... are commonly used in conversational environments to achieve a clarifying effect (cf. Ädel, 2006).

Concerning perspective clarifying, the present data of ELBR reveal an interesting *I*-IPC pattern which is identified by Haddington (2007) as a recurrent and routinized pattern in political news interviews. The pattern is composed of two parts: NEG + POS. The first part doing the denial contains an *I*-IPC which is characterized by negated mental or verbal processes. The second part doing the account is similar in structure except that it does not appear in negation. Consider the following example.

(129) IE: Well *I don't know* about taking him out Larry
But *I think* we have a lot of options. (Haddington, 2007: 304)

According to Haddington, this pattern is used for displaying engagement with the preceding question, but also for denying a presupposition or a position set up in the question. Meanwhile, denials do not occur alone. It is claimed that in everyday conversation a denial is actually only one part of a combination of two actions. The second action, which follows the denial, is a correction or an account by the same speaker that gives an alternative interpretation to what has been denied. Here is an example from the current corpus:

(130) *I disagree that* Austin and Searle are guilty of all the shortcomings Derrida

> lays at their feet, but *I agree that* neither adequately attends to the profoundly social and interactive nature of communication. [R75]

As Example (130) shows, this particular *I*-IPC pattern is used to perform an aligning activity by which the writer attempts to find a place to carefully word her stance orientation that not only takes into account some evoked or presupposed point of view, but also reflects her own aims. Thus, the writer uses it to vitiate preferred stance in the audience. It seems that in such instances, the choice of *I*-IPCs relies on prior beliefs or disciplinary values that are bound to the viewpoints assumed by all the participants.

4. Interpersonal Coherence

A fourth intersubjectivity boosting function of *I*-IPCs should be examined in a wider context in which the *I*-IPC occurs. In most cases, this has to do with interpersonal coherence or interpersonal conjunction (cf. Hoey, 2000; Thompson & Zhou, 2000; Thompson, 2005) which is in nature a matter of negotiation between the writer and the reader. The motivation behind may be that the writer feels that she needs to signal to the reader the intended relationship by including personal comment at precisely this point in the text. It is usually the case that the writer attempts explicitly to forge alignment with the reader. It is expected that such interpersonal conjunctions occur in the context in which intense arguments or controversial viewpoints are unfolding. It should be noted that interpersonal conjunctions have a cohesive function in themselves, and one which is innately connected with their interpersonal meaning.

The functions of the *I*-IPC, in this sense, can be interpreted as signaling a particular interpersonal coherence. That is, by overtly appealing to the reader, it invokes negotiation and the reader's cooperation in constructing coherence within a particular part of the discourse. In addition, it guides the reader towards the type of interpersonal conjunction which the writer has already decided on. Example (131) is given by Thompson (2005) when he discusses the interpersonal aspect of conjunction.

(131) Further retributive justice... is not   ↓ *denial of expectation*
the only form of justice.
I contend that
there is another kind of justice,   ↑ *counter*
restorative justice...   (Thompson, 2005: 781)

As is shown in the example above, the *I*-IPC *I contend that* is used to signal the relation of denial-counter. It should be acknowledged that without the *I*-IPC, a cohesive relation still holds between the two semantic units. In fact, as Thompson (2005) and others have rightly observed, it is not the IPC that enters into Thematic progression. The adding of the *I*-IPC may well derive mainly from the fact that an adequate picture of interpersonal coherence has not yet been built up. In Fetzer's (2008a) interpretation, such IPC constructions add intersubjective corrections to plain texts. In the current case, the *I*-IPC modified by a verbal process renders precisely the writer's intention to the reader. In this way, it bears directly on the interaction by encoding the writer's illocutionary directions. The present study reveals similar examples of interpersonal coherence, as Example (132) shows.

(132) *That is not to say that* in MCA studies analysts always leave their own cultural assumptions at the door, but *I do not think* Stokoe and Smithson establish that making sense—even 'feminist' sense—of how participants use categories to do social work requires appeal to the analyst's 'orientation'. [R75]

Example (132) is an illustration of how *I*-IPCs work in terms of the denial-counter type of interpersonal coherence. As was seen, the denial part is itself an IPC which clarifies the writer's assessment orientation. The motivation behind is perhaps the writer's prediction that others may misinterpret her preceding comments and have opposing views. In addition, the use of the *I*-IPC strongly suggests the reviewer's familiarity with the topic under discussion. While the IPC in the denial part clarifies her viewpoint, the second *I*-IPC reinforces the reviewer's attitudes towards the reviewees' contribution. It is obvious that in Example (132), the reviewer invests heavily in boosting intersubjectivity by employing the two IPCs. Two factors account for the heavy investment. The first is that the writer predicts that her previous views may cause negative reactions from other members (i. e. those devoted to MCA studies) of the community. The second is that the writer attempts to maintain her specific evaluation orientation. Consequently, the writer resorts to IPC to invoke both her presence and her awareness of the reader. In fact, the writer often exploits IPCs to achieve a reader-friendly tone by making what is in fact a monologue sound like a dialogue.

Besides the denial-counter type, the current data sees other types of interpersonal coherence as well. Consider the following examples.

(133) These processes may deserve to be called inferences, but *I am doubtful about whether* they can count as instances of reasoning. [R29]

(134) *I am aware that* O'Grady's work consciously avoids academic references within the main text, but perhaps the identification of certain crucial principles and theories could facilitate readers' understanding of different approaches to first language acquisition. [R44]

Example (133) represents an affirmation-counter type of interpersonal coherence while Example (134) an alternation type. In Example (133), the writer chooses an emotive *I*-IPC to report her response to perceived truth of somebody else's statement. The desired interpersonal coherence is achieved through two steps. First, the writer states her familiarity with the disciplinary knowledge and thus foregrounds her status of being a qualified expert to conduct the review. By acknowledging others' viewpoints, she shows her respect to members of the particular community. Second, she uses an *I*-IPC to decrease the writer-reader distance by drawing the reader into a direct person-to-person conversation. This *I*-IPC forecasts that the writer is going to express some challenging views and thus prepares the reader for the views. The example shows that by turning to *I*-IPCs, the writer could produce a text that feels purposeful but does not appear overtly directive. In Example (134), the *I*-IPC highlights the writer's endeavor to balance between an established fact and her alternative viewpoint. The interpersonal stake is high in that her view challenges the contribution under review. However, the writer achieves her expected communicative purposes by initiating her argument with an *I*-IPC and by coating the alternative with double modalization (*perhaps*, *could*).

These examples indicate that the primary motivation for employing the *I*-IPC is to align the reader. It suggests the possibility that within general generic constraints, an expert writer may aim at a balance between telling the reader where to go next and asking for reader cooperation.

To summarize, *I*-IPCs are employed by the reviewer to fulfill a variety of functions vis-à-vis intersubjectivity management. However, it should be mentioned that *I*-IPCs only occupy a portion, and perhaps a small portion of all the IPC resources that operate within the genre of book reviewing. Therefore, it is necessary to examine other types of IPC. On the one hand, this furtherance will bring into vision a general picture of the discursive behavior of IPC. On the other hand, it will shed more light upon the understanding of individual types of IPC and their interrelationships.

5.2 *We* -IPCs

As was noted in Section 5.1, *I*-IPCs have been investigated with respect to their manifestations and functions in ELBR. This section will further the examination by probing into a second type of IPC which is of close connection with *I*-IPCs, namely, *we*-IPCs. Similarly, this type of IPC is featured by the Projector. Different from the Projector in the *I*-IPC, which indicates the interactant in the direct and explicit form, the Projector in the *we*-IPC is a generalizing concept, or a collective notion. This can be interpreted on two dimensions. On the one hand, it may refer solely to the interactant. On the other, it may refer to a group in which the interactant is included. It should be highlighted that the scope of reference is largely determined by the particular genre in which the collective concept is interpreted. It should also be borne in mind that *we* is only one possible, and typical, realization of the Projector in *we*-IPCs. In a similar vein to the analysis of *I*-IPCs, this section will explore *we*-IPCs by examining their lexicogrammatical realization resources, up to the generic features, and end with a discussion on its discoursal functions with regard to intersubjectivity management.

5.2.1 The Concept of Generality

As is commonly held and repeated in the present study, intellectual discourse is an instance of social interaction between the writer and the audience (cf. Cecchetto & Stroińska, 1996). In fact, the writer and the audience in academic communication shall be understood as social agents, located in a network of social relations, in specific places in a social structure. In this sense, the awareness on the part of the academic writer of how to employ appropriate devices to increase or decrease the reader's inclusion in the text reflects in essence an insider's constant attention to the interactive aspects of a particular disciplinary community.

From this interactive perspective, generality is adopted as a general term in this study to refer to the writer's purposeful choice of linguistic expressions which are inclusive of the interactant and, sometimes, others. Scheibman (2007: 113-14) highlights two distinct characteristics of generality. First, it is referentially general. Second, it serves broadening or inclusive functions in discourse. The two features enable participants to elaborate the meanings of expressions of generality by making reference to shared knowledge and to interactive contexts. In this sense, generality is of close connection with intersubjectivity. According to Scheibman (2007), generality can be used to express solidarity which contributes to the collaborative construction of intersubjectivity.

Due to the fact that generality is socially situated, its meaning varies according to genre and discipline. In the academic field, generality is seen to be approached by studies on *we* and its variations *our* and *us* (cf. Kuo, 1999; Hyland, 2002c), particularly in research articles. In academic writing, *we* is considered the most frequently used engagement device (Hyland, 2004: 20). It identifies the reader as someone who shares similar understandings and goals with the writer. The significance and function of this general reference term is foregrounded in the following statement.

I often use 'we' to include readers. I suppose it brings out something of the collective endeavor, what we all know and want to accomplish. I've never thought of it as a strategy, but I suppose I am trying to lead readers along with me. (ME interview) (Hyland, 2004: 21)

Occasionally, the literature sees researches into another general term *one* (cf. Ädel, 2006). However, there has been no attempt to examine generality within the construction of IPC. In addition, while much interest is assigned to generality and its expressions in research articles, the genre of ABR is simply neglected. Therefore, the present study focuses on generality by anchoring it in IPC constructions in the particular genre of ELBR.

5.2.2 Metafunctional Features of *we*-IPCs

This subsection scrutinizes lexicogrammatical realizations of *we*-IPCs with respect to Projector realizations, process types involved, favored tense types and Thematic positions. Statistics will be provided, examples offered, and interpretation suggested.

In terms of Projector expressions, Table 5.4 summarizes the *we*-IPCs identified, which see a greater variety of realization forms, compared with *I*-IPC realizations.

As Table 5.4 displays, there are 134 instances of *we*-IPCs in total. It is clear that *one* (55.2%) and *we* (29.1%) are the most commonly used Projector-realizing resources. *Reader(s)* (7.5%) is also observed to be used in a general sense. Miscellaneous items (8.2%) are identified as well, such as *us*, *many*, *some*, *someone*, *anybody*, and *more critical voice*. The findings are interesting in that to the analyst's surprise, it is *one* rather than *we* that is most frequently used in these *we*-IPCs.

Table 5.4 We-IPCs in ELBR by Projector Realization

Projector realization	Number of occurrence	Frequency
we①	39	29.1%
one	74	55.2%
reader(s)②	10	7.5%
others	11	8.2%
Total	134	100%

In fact, the findings contradict other researchers' (Samson, 2004; Charles, 2006b) conclusion that of all inclusive pronouns, the dominant form is inclusive *we*. However, it should be noted that most of these studies base their conclusions on observations of research articles. Tentatively, one might suggest that genre must play a vital role in determining the allocation of *one* and *we*. It should also be noted that it is *we*-IPC constructions but *we* in isolation that the present study focuses on. It seems that in ELBR the writer inclines to deploy *one* to construct interactant-inclusive IPC expressions. The findings

---

① As is well recognized, *we* can be further divided into exclusive *we* and inclusive *we*, depending on whether it refers to the writer(s) exclusively or co-participants in the communication. The present corpus of ELBR does not identify any IIPC instance in which *we* is used in its exclusive sense.

② Some may argue that "reader(s)" refers to *you*, the direct interactant of a communication. To include "reader(s)" in *we*-IPCs is out of two considerations. First, in all the *we*-IPC constructions identified in ELBR, "reader(s)" refers to the reader of the book under review, rather than the reader of the review. That is, it does not refer solely to *you*. Thus, "reader(s)" might be inclusive of both interactants. Of course, this inclusiveness is defined in accordance within the particular genre of book reviews.

may attribute to several factors.

First, as was stated in Section 5.1.2 above, all the reviews are single authored. This may contribute to some extent to the obviously low scores of *we*. Second, it seems that the reviewer deliberately avoids the dichotomy between *we* and others. In the context, it is conspicuous that when *we* is used, the author of the book is excluded. This perhaps shows the writer's sensitivity of the disciplinary community. Third, the avoidance of *we* can be accounted for by the fact that in the present corpus, the presence of *we* is not of significance. It seems that it is there mainly for the purpose of avoiding rhetoric repetition, that is, as an alternative of *one*. On a closer scrutiny, it is found that when *we* is used, the primary function is to guide the reader through the argument as in *now we understand*, *we can see*, and *we learn*.

The reviewer's preference for *one* in constructing *we*-IPCs could be linked to the indeterminate nature of *one* as a general referent. *One* always has generic reference as its default interpretation. According to Kuo (1999), *one* can refer to researchers in general, the writer exclusively, or writer-and-reader together. Ädel (2006: 82-83) concurs with Kuo (1999) in stating that *one*, although indefinite and faceless, can make reference to the writer, and in fact, even to the imagined reader. In many other cases, it can serve as a signal of the presence of current discourse participants. Thus, *one* is empowered to have double-layered primary and secondary referents.

However, in some contexts, there may be an additional referent, in which case the reader or someone in the audience will have to do some inferencing. In this way, *one* opens the possibility for anyone to think that the writer is considering his potential view. In this sense, the writer tends to depict the reader as an individual academic identity who is capable of quick thinking and shrewd reasoning. It is likely that the secondary referent is the reader, in that his thoughts and objections are likely to be the focus of the writer's argumentation. Overall, the use of *one* in the *we*-IPCs seems to either bring in different but unspecified voices that the reviewer does not necessarily agree with (as in Example (135) below) or to align the reader by presuming shared opinions between the writer and the reader (as in Example (136) below).

> (135) However, even if *one agrees that* a meaningful distinction can be made between language use for communication and symbolic language use (as I don't), there is a crucial difference between these two texts. [R19]
>
> (136) *One wonders why* the author should have felt it necessary at all to rehearse these ancient and well-known truths about the reach of Scandinavian speech and the Scandinavian form of the runic alphabet. [R76]

As can be seen in the examples above, *we*-IPCs initiated by *one* create more referent options due to their indefiniteness and indeterminacy. Consequently, they are favored especially in contexts where alternative views are expected to be attended to, or the writer feels necessary to take the position without appearing imposingly authoritative. Therefore, it is reasonable to argue that the reviewer's IPC choices vis-à-vis *one* are deliberate, conscious processes. On the one hand, the reviewer establishes her discourse identity as an expert, knowledgeable about the disciplinary information by presuming potential objections or alternative views held by individuals or a group within the community. On the other hand, she shows her intersubjectivity consideration by creating a mock dialogue in which her own voice is disguised in the general *one* or the unspecified *one*.

Reader(s) occupies the third place in terms of frequency of occurrence (7.5% of the total). On closer examination, the study reveals that in all instances it serves as an alternative of *one*. Due to the fact that such *we*-IPCs are small in number, and that in particular, they do not show any specific discourse features, it is suggested that the presence of these *we*-IPCs are not of significance. They are better seen as the writer's expression choices out of rhetorical consideration.

In terms of process types and subtypes emerging in *we*-IPCs, Table 5.5 displays a clear picture in terms of token number and frequency of occurrence.

Table 5.5 *We*-IPCs in ELBR by Process Type

Process	Subtype	Number of occurrences	Frequency
Mental	Cognitive	63	47.0%
	Desiderative	38	28.4%
Verbal		27	20.1%
Others		6	4.5%
Total		134	100%

As is shown in Table 5.5, with respect to *we*-IPCs, findings disclose that cognitive processes are the most frequently used category, accounting for 63 tokens of the total number of *we*-IPCs, with a frequency as high as 47%. The figures indicate that the process type is most preferred by the review writer to construct *we*-IPCs. Specifically, epistemic verbs are the most frequently used to express doubt or uncertainty, represented by *wonder* (n = 18). In diminishing order, desiderative processes follow this list of *we*-IPCs, with 38 instances, occupying nearly one third of the total *we*-IPC constructions. Linguistically speaking, the findings reveal that the reviewer alternates the use of *expect* (n = 9) with *wish* (n = 8).

A careful scrutiny shows that these "wanting" processes function to alert the reader to the demerits of the book under review and thus signal the reviewer's negative evaluation. This finding confirms the crucial importance of prefacing unfavorable assessment with *we*-IPCs in ABR in order to attain effective persuasion and communal intimacy. Verbal processes are also found in the data, with a total of 27 instances, sharing one fifth of all *we*-IPCs, mostly grouped under three verbs: *argue*, *say* and *ask*. By such verbal processes, the writer states the ensuing opinion as a discourse act rather than views, as in Example (137) below.

(137)... *one could argue that* this is a matter of convergence to English, which does not overtly mark accusative case. [R5]

It is noteworthy that verbal processes show their different discursive behavior across *I*-IPCs and *we*-IPCs. As was observed in Section 5.1.2, in *I*-IPCs, verbal processes mainly appear in split projection, functioning as personal digressions. In *we*-IPCs, however, verbal processes are employed to convey the writer's intention of arguing for or against the upcoming proposition, a finding concurrent with Ädel's (2006: 85).

Figure 5.7 summarizes *we*-IPCs by mental and verbal processes.

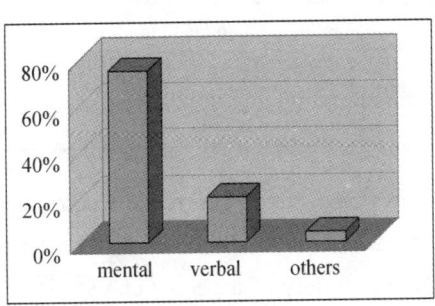

Figure 5.7 *We*-IPCs in ELBR by Process Type

As the figure above shows, mental and verbal processes taken together occupy 95.5% of all instances. As is shown, mental processes dominate with a frequency of occurrence of 75.4% of the total. This finding, similar to that with respect to *I*-IPCs, suggests that in reviewing, the writer seems to prefer processes of "thinking" to other processes, as far as IPC constructions are concerned. This suggestion is supported by the fact that the majority of *we*-IPCs are non-fact projections. One possible attributive factor is that the writer chooses to construe herself and the reader as reasonable and capable thinkers and idea-producers qualified to offer valuable judgments concerning the academic product. Thus, the writer augments her professional credibility and simultaneously brings the reader into the current academic forum by positioning him in the discourse as an active and knowledgeable in-group member of the disciplinary community.

With regard to tense and modalization, Table 5.6 demonstrates the discursive behavior of *we*-IPCs in ELBR.

Table 5.6 *We*-IPCs in ELBR by Tense and Modalization

Tense	Number of Occurrences	Frequency
Simple present	31	23.1%
Modalized	89	66.4%
Non-finite	14	10.5%
Total	134	100%

Table 5.6 shows respective occurrence frequencies of *we*-IPCs in simple present, modalization and non-finite constructions. *We*-IPCs differ from *I*-IPCs in a variety of aspects (cf. Section 5.1.2). As was noted, 48.4% of all *I*-IPCs appear in simple present tense whereas only 27.2% of them are modalized. In the case of *we*-IPCs, the findings show that modalization is overwhelmingly predominant.

A scrutinizing examination reveals a total of 89 cases of modalized *we*-IPC constructions in the corpus of ELBR. The percentage of modalized instances is predominantly high, around 66% of the total. Considering the predominance of *one* in *we*-IPC constructions, the finding partly confirms the findings of other studies which take *one* as a signal of general attribution (Charles, 2006b). According to Charles (ibid), her data consisting of 16 theses shows that all instances of *one* occur with a modal verb. The present corpus reveals that 80% of all *one* cases are modalized, an interesting finding suggesting that the discrepancy may be accounted for from the perspective of genre variation. On searching examination, the study displays that there is quite a numerous representation of low modal value (n = 58) in the data. These modal verbs are mostly categorized under *may/might* (n = 30), *can/could* (n = 17) and *would* (n = 11), suggesting tentativeness or possibilities. Consider the following example.

(138) *One can anticipate that* much would be gained from a more explicit connection between these approaches and, in general, between theories of structural syntactic analysis and those connected with parsing problems. [R48]

As Example (138) shows, the IPC *one can anticipate* indicates that the ensuing proposition is a possible alternative viewpoint that might derive from the readership.

Regarding present tense, there are merely 31 instances. The percentage of tokens of present tense is slightly over 20%. The distribution is found to be linked to Projector types. With *we*, instances of present tense mainly function to guide the reader through the argument (e.g. *we learn now how*); with *one*, they are observed to express possible viewpoints as is shown in Example (138).

At a considerable distance, there are non-finite constructions with

14 examples in the corpus, occupying slightly over 10% of the total, as is exhibited in Table 5.6. Example (139) below is an illustration.

> (139) The book inspires sufficient confidence for *the reader to assume that* such evidence is available so its absence here serves to underline the particular challenge that linguistic ethnography faces. [R3]

On the surface, these non-finite constructions such as the italicized part in Example (139) are devoid of tense or modal modifications. However, their future projected or non-actual status enables the user to evaluate them as having the possibilities of being brought about by the reader at some future moment. Therefore, the present study argues that they are used to indicate a desired future course of action that the writer would like the reader to carry out. In this sense, these non-finite instances of *we*-IPCs are better to be seen as modalized. Although small in number, they are significant in that they facilitate to invite the reader to be on the train of the writer's thought.

With respect to the Thematic status, it is noteworthy that all *we*-IPCs appear in the Thematic position. The finding confirms the framing or prefacing effect of IPCs vis-à-vis the whole clause complex.

5.2.3 A Cross-Genre Analysis of *we*-IPCs

Similar to the analysis of *I*-IPCs, a comparative analysis will be conducted with respect to *we*-IPCs in ELBR and ELJE. Table 5.7 compares *we*-IPCs in the two genres by frequency of occurrence.

Table 5.7 Cross-Genre Comparison of *we*-IPCs by Frequency

Genre type	Number of Occurrences	Frequency/10,000 words	Frequency/100 Sentences
ELBR	134	6.5	2.1
ELJE	308	13.4	4.5

As can be seen in Table 5.7, the ELJE writer is found to have employed *we*-IPCs on 308 occasions. Compared with 134 tokens in the corpus of ELBR, the number suggests that the ELJE writer tends to use more *we*-IPCs than her ELBR counterpart. The contrasting frequencies of occurrence are also indicative of the editor's much stronger preference for *we*-IPCs. The preliminary finding does reveal much more about generic differences with a set of comparative investigations conducted with respect to Projector expressions, processes, and overall structural allocation.

To begin with, with respect to Projector realizations, the editorial writer shows her overwhelming preference for *we* than the review writer does, as is displayed in Figure 5.8.

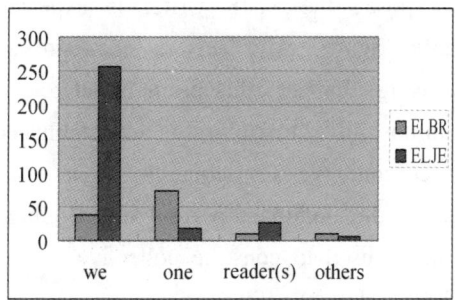

Figure 5.8 Cross-Genre Comparison of *we*-IPCs by Projector Realization

Figure 5.8 shows that the editorial writer uses *we*-IPCs initiated by *we* roughly six times than the review writer does. By contrast, the tokens of *one* in ELJE are less than one half of those in ELBR. The finding confirms the assumption that how the writer negotiates her personal status with the reader varies between genres. The sharp discrepancies may attribute to the following factors.

First, as was mentioned, 42% of all the ELJE texts are co-authored, while all ELBR texts are single authored. This may increase the editorial writer's choices of *we* while decreasing the review writer's choices of *we*. What is more important, while the reviewer tends to present her own persona as well as the reader's as individual participants in an organized academic conversation, the editor inclines to portray in the discourse a collective image representing the editorial board of the particular journal, the publisher, the anonymous reviewers, and the contributors to the issue under discussion. This is of course part of the conventions of the given genre.

Another influencing factor is linked to the expected social and communicative goals assigned to the particular genre. With promotion as the prime purpose, the ELJE writer is expected to forge an authoritative public figure, who acts as the spokesperson for the product in advertising. In fact, this promotional role is foregrounded by the fact that almost all editorial writers are established personages in the disciplinary community. Consequently, this generic identity of ELJE contributes to the dominant portion of *we*-initiated *we*-IPCs in ELJE, as *we* can be used to construe collective, authoritative voices (cf. Samson, 2004; Harvey, 1995).

In fact, the finding confirms Harvey's (1995) conclusion. Based on an observation of a sample of public reports, Harvey finds that the occurrences of *we* are revealing. In his data, most *we*s tend to emphasize collective authorship and responsibility. Additionally, Harvey's study shows that only a few of them correspond to the use of an inclusive *we* in the sense that it cooperates with other researchers or less informed readers to the argument. The present research reveals a similar result. That is, nearly all the *we*s are used to represent a writer-inclusive collective image.

The last contributing factor is in connection with the GSP of ELJE. As is already observed, different from review texts, editorial texts consist of a particular section which construes journal acknowledgement and announcement. In the GSP, it is represented by the element of JA&A. As Giannoni (2002) notes, the element has evolved to be highly formulaic, grammaticalized in that the convention for expressing gratitude is, among others, through the IPC of *we would like to* (n = 84).

With respect to process types, Figure 5.9 exposes a detailed presentation of *we*-IPCs in ELJE and ELBR.

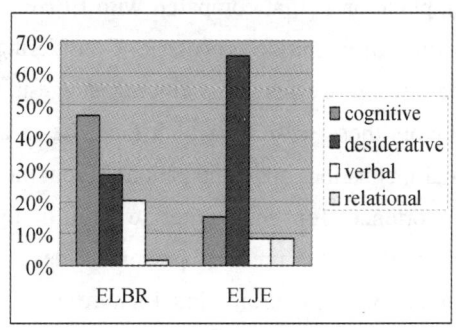

Figure 5.9 Cross-Genre Comparison of *we*-IPCs by Process Type

Figure 5.9 is significant in the sense of the following implications. First, the prominence of desiderative processes in ELJE suggests that the editorial writer tends to combine inclusive *we* with verbs that are indicative of desires and hopes. On closer examination, the study finds that *we would like to* (n = 72) and *we hope* (n = 44) are the most frequent tokens of all desiderative processes. The study also notes that these desiderative processes are mainly used for the purpose of volume promotion, as is illustrated in Example (140) below, in addition to gratitude conveying.

(140) *We hope that* this volume has contributed not only to enriching the field of critical discourse analysis, but also to opening up a new field that one could call 'critical metaphor analysis'. [E84]

The finding is indicative of one significant difference across the genres with respect to the use of desiderative processes. In ELJE, as is shown by Example (140), the majority of desiderative processes are employed by calling for the reader to focus on the inspiring and innovative points of the volume, whereas in ELBR, it is common for the writer to deploy such a process to express her wish for future improvement vis-à-vis the book under review.

A second implication is that compared with ELBR, ELJE shows a much smaller portion of cognitive processes. Considering the dominant portion of desiderative processes, this finding suggests that the ELJE writer strongly favors those *we*-IPCs which facilitate in an explicit way to express authorial inclinations and anticipations. From this perspective, it is of prime importance for the writer to fulfill the purpose of promotion, rather than to present personal ideas regarding the contributions. In addition, the promotional nature of the genre does not encourage the writer to present alternative or controversial views vis-à-vis these articles. As Bhatia (2004) states, the introducing of any negative comments will do no good to the promotion. In advertisement, the advertiser will never admit the weak point of the product. Similarly, in ELJE, the writer will avoid introducing opposing ideas, in case of the possibility of invoking the reader's negative views against the contributing articles.

A third implication lies in the different portions of relational processes across the genres. While in ELBR relational processes are too few to display any discursive significance, those in ELJE appear in emotive processes of "like" type (Halliday & Matthiessen, 2004:

225), with a percentage as high as 94%. Consider the following examples.

> (141) *We are fortunate, then, to* have Chouliaraki's analysis of televisual discourse, one that deals with the implications of the interactions between word and image. [E85]
>
> (142) *We are especially pleased to* have such a wide range of authors and particularly so that many of these authors are writing from outside the 'English-only' world of research. [E25]

As Examples (141) and (142) demonstrate, in such "like" type of relational processes, most attributes are evaluative in nature ((Halliday & Matthiessen, 2004: 224). Therefore, they are important grammatical categories in the enactment of appraisal. In the present case, findings disclose that with only one exception, all attributives are positive evaluation invoking, exemplified by *pleased*, *fortunate*, *delighted*, and *delightful*. They are often used to explicitly convey the writer's positive assessment of the articles in the issue, thus serving the anticipated promotional function. The only exception which arouses negative feelings is Example (143) below, in which the editor announces the retirement of her editorial staff members.

> (143) Finally (again) *we are sorry to* announce the retirement of Desmond Allison and Jo McDonough from the editorial board after 6 years of service. [E36]

It is obvious that in a similar vein to desiderative mental processes, these emotive relational processes impress the reader with the overt authoritative collective positive evaluation of the contributions. On the one hand, the successful membership of the disciplinary community privileges the writer's expertise over the reader's more peripheral participation in the genre. On the other hand, the collectiveness inherent in *we*-IPCs facilitates the writer to negotiate the right to speak both of and for the discipline. In this sense, with *we*-IPCs the editorial writer intervenes massively in the text to constitute themselves as spokespersons for the contributions and to maximize the likelihood of their being attractive to the reader.

Finally, a cross-genre analysis of *we*-IPC distribution vis-à-vis the GSP shows an unsurprising result. Figure 5.10 and Figure 5.11 illustrate respectively the allocation pattern of *we*-IPCs in different elements of the GSPs of ELBR and ELJE.

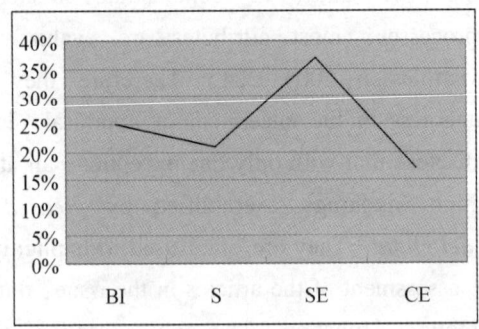

Figure 5.10 Generic Structural Distribution of *we*-IPCs in ELBR

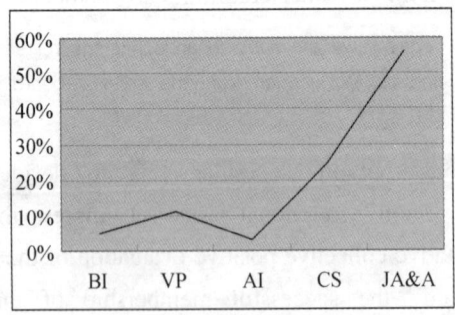

Figure 5.11 Generic Structural Distributions of *we*-IPCs in ELJE

It reveals that, as Figure 5.10 demonstrates, in ELBR, *we*-IPCs distribute evenly across the elements, with an expected much higher percentage in SE (37% of the total). The insignificance perhaps partly attributes to the relatively small number of *we*-IPCs in the genre. As far as ELJE is concerned, as Figure 5.11 shows, most *we*-IPCs are found in JA&A and CS (respectively 57% and 25% of the total). This finding is also within the expectation of the present study. As has been suggested, in JA&A, it is conventional to express acknowledgement with *we*-IPCs. Impelled by promotional purposes, the editorial writer confidently evaluates the contributions by weaving promotion into information delivering. This is most explicitly displayed in the element of CS, in which closing summaries are coated with positive evaluations by *us*, an established, authoritative, collective image.

5.2.4 *We*-IPCs as Intersubjectivity Boosters

It has been shown that *we*-IPCs are characterized by their genre-specific features in terms of lexicogrammatical realizations, the allocation of generality expressions, predominant processes, and tense choices. A cross-genre analysis demonstrates that this type of IPC behaves differently across ELBR and ELJE. However, it deserves particular attention that the principle underlying the differences is that *we*-IPCs are deployed by disciplinary community members to fulfill intended purposes, one of which is to augment intersubjectivity. Therefore, this subsection aims to explore the functions of *we*-IPCs from the vantage point of the writer's intersubjectivity awareness.

A quick survey of the literature shows that *we* functions in academic discourse in a variety of ways. Kuo (1999) identifies more than ten discourse functions of *we* in research articles, namely, explaining what was done; proposing a theory or approach; stating a goal or purpose; showing results or findings; justifying a proposition; hedging a proposition or claim; assuming shared knowledge, goals or beliefs; seeking agreement or cooperation; showing commitment or contribution to research; comparing approaches or viewpoints; and giving a reason or indicating necessity and expressing wish or expectation. His classification is mainly around the transmission of knowledge in discourse. Thus, Kuo's (1999) interpretation of *we* is primarily information-oriented.

A majority of scholars agree that *we* is "an interpersonal pronoun" (Freddi, 2005: 16). Freddi suggests that *we* may mean "it is well-known or a given fact" to include peers and that it can replace *one*. Freddi also notices that *we* may also serve hypothetical function (e. g. *if we*) and modal function (e. g. *we may*). In metadiscourse studies (cf. Hyland, 2005a), *we* is categorized under self-mention, contributing to the relationship established between the writer and the reader.

Inspired by these studies, based on the observation of the current database, several intersubjectivity-boosting functions of *we*-IPCs are identified. It should be noted that these functions do not exist in isolation. Instead, they have to be interpreted within their particular surrounding environment.

1. Perspective Aligning

One prime function of *we*-IPCs is to co-opt the reader into the unfolding argument by inviting the reader to take the writer's perspective, so that the reader agrees with the writer (Ädel, 2006: 76). These constructions often involve explicit calls asking the reader to identify with particular views. Consider the following examples.

(144) *We might therefore wonder whether* these basic typological differences

would have any impact on the development of final particles across language. Likewise, *we could ask if* final particles in Mandarin are implicated in turn construction and turn management in ways that differ from Japanese and Korean. [R17]

(145) *As one might expect*, the situations arising from the colonial status of Mozambique, and its associated linguistic development, have impacted upon the societal and governmental organization of the country and conceptions of citizenship within these structures. [R94]

In Example (144), the inclusive nature of *we* immediately suggests the presence of the author and the audience. Hence a feeling of togetherness is created and foregrounded. In this way the reader is invited to share the writer's upcoming views. A searching reading of the projected proposition reveals that the notion of sharedness is often invoked by the writer to smuggle contested ideas into their arguments. Meanwhile, the modal operators (i.e. *might*, *could*) enable the reader to follow the writer's viewpoint without the writer appearing too assertive. Thus, *we*-IPCs invite participant corroboration.

In Example (145), the *we*-IPC *as one might expect* enables the writer to construct the reader by presupposing that he holds such beliefs. The choice of the general *one* shows that the writer encourages the reader to assume that the proposition is unproblematic and that it enjoys broad consensus. In addition, by framing the ensuing text within the *we*-IPC, the writer suggests to the reader that she assumes he is well familiar with the disciplinary knowledge expressed in the ensuing text. In this way, the writer aligns both experts in the field and less informed readers. Finally, the *we*-IPC creates an authoritative voice by asking the reader to recognize something as familiar and well-accepted.

2. Position Setting

A majority of *we*-IPCs in the present corpora facilitate the writer to set intended positions for the reader. Positioning the audience involves predicting and responding to the audience's possible objections and/or alternative reactions (cf. Hyland, 2004a). By anticipating the reader's questions and objections, the writer can predict and head off criticism as she leads him through an argument. Thus, by assigning to the reader a role in creating the argument, the writer shows her acknowledgement of and respect to his potential views. In this way the writer highlights to the reader that his potential viewpoints made have indeed been predicted and considered. In fact, by using such *we*-IPCs, the writer assumes a level of complicity on the part of the reader. What is more significant, *we*-IPCs also set up a dialogue by weaving the reader's potential viewpoints into the text. Consider the following examples.

> (146) *Anglo- and- Germanophone readers might regret that* there is no mention of intonation (high-rise terminals), tag-questions, modality and particles as politeness strategies—but these aspects are well-covered for English in, for example, Holmes. [R20]
>
> (147) If *we accept that* there cannot be real synonymy and that there must be differentiating nuances of meaning or function of these connectives, the question that immediately arises concerns the correlates that determine their use and those subtle differences of meaning. [R12]

In Examples (146) and (147), both *we*-IPCs, though strikingly different in their forms, assign propositions to the reader. By stating overtly that an idea is projected onto the reader as in Example (146) or in-group members as in Example (147), the writer is publicly performing awareness of the reader and simultaneously inviting the reader to share in the construction of the argument in the text.

It should also be noted that both *we*-IPCs enhance reader

involvement by guiding his thinking through the argument in the text. In Example (146), in particular, the use of the low-value modal operator *might* and the fact projection, which suggests the fact that the reader is impinged on by the Phenomenon, thus leads the reader to accept more readily that his own potential opinion needs to be qualified. In Example (146), the *we*-IPC is adopted to set up some position in order to critically modify it, while its counterpart in Example (147) signals to the reader that the potential point of view deserves explicit confirmation. In this way the writer shows her familiarity with the research field and expresses peer solidarity by addressing her peer readership directly.

The data also identifies a special type of reader-positioning *we*-IPCs, namely, "directives" in Hyland's (2005b) words. As is acknowledged by Hyland (ibid), directives are perhaps the most overt rhetorical strategy of engagement because they directly instruct the reader to carry out an action or see things in a way determined by the writer. Therefore, the most imposing use of directives is positing the reader. Consider the following example.

(148) *Let's just hope* her message will also spread beyond academia. [R5]

As Example (148) indicates, directives such as *let's just hope* initiate reader participation by directing the reader to some idea or understanding. In the example, the reviewer aims to seek agreement and cooperation from the reader by using *Let's just hope* before proposing her proposition. Moreover, the imperative form suggests the illocutionary force of a polite request. Thus, it explicitly foregrounds the dialogic aspect of the discourse. As Hyland (2005b: 372) rightly observes, such directives typically lead the reader towards the writer's conclusion by emphasizing what he is expected to attend to in the argument. This is true in the case of Example (148), which is the ending sentence of the whole text.

3. Disciplinary Solidarity Fostering

This function is similar to Perspective Aligning in that the writer chooses to engage the reader by invoking a world of commonsense activity and suggesting a shared general knowledge with him. Nonetheless, *we*-IPCs in this category mainly facilitate the writer to augment disciplinary solidarity within the community rather than between the interactants as individuals. In this way, they help to underline shared membership of a disciplinary community. The writer usually presupposes a single or a set of mutual discipline-identifying understandings to claim authority as well as communality. In this sense, the *we*-IPC functions as a clear signal of membership by textually constructing both the writer and the reader as in-group participants with similar understanding and goals with respect to disciplinary knowledge, norms and conventions. Consider the following examples.

(149) *This means that* plenty of language proceeding must take place while struggling to get a text on the page, and, *as we know*, this language processing is considered to be essential in promoting language development (see Swain, 1985, 1995). [E1]

(150) *No one thinks that* brains carry out purely syntactic operations on items with determinate formal properties. *Most accept that* brains exploit the robust tracking that is associated with (non-symbolic) representations. [E3]

Both examples demonstrate how a sense of communal intimacy and an awareness of in-group solidarity are promoted through particular instances of *we*-IPC constructions. In Example (149), the *we*-IPC *as we know* explicitly marks a shared disciplinary membership with the reader. The writer puts forward a view while simultaneously indicating that it belongs to the disciplinary community. In fact, a collective voice emerges in the process of viewpoint stating. The *we*-IPC also enables more weight to be attached to the claim made. In addition, the writer cites established scholars to add strength to expressions of her opinion, and on the other hand, to show reference to the whole scientific community. It is also worth noting that the passive construction *is considered to* implies that the writer's claim is well-accepted within the disciplinary community. In this sense, *we*-IPCs are powerful resources which have evolved to serve the user's intended communicative purposes within particular social and cultural contexts.

Similarly, in Example (150), the writer resorts to two *we*-IPCs to strengthen her claim by linking it to a wider group. In this way, the disciplinary community is invoked. Apparently, the deliberate selection of the semantically contradictory IPC constructions construes the writer as a competent member of the academic community. Embedded in this construction, of course, is the announcement that the writer is acting as a spokesperson for her community. In accordance, the reader is anticipated to be a reasonable and thinking community member of the shared discipline. Thus, the *we*-IPC facilitates to foster disciplinary solidarity by shaping the author's view into appropriate disciplinary formulations.

4. Interpersonal Coherence

Similar to *I*-IPCs, *we*-IPCs in the present database are identified to signal relations vis-à-vis interpersonal conjunction. By anchoring these resources in their wider surroundings, the current study finds that *we*-IPCs are commonly deployed to facilitate or to clarify interpersonal coherence. Consider the following example.

(151)... the use of English in Central and Eastern Europe ... is then approached under the same linguistic fetish lens as French and German in British ads. However, even if *one agrees that* a meaningful distinction can be made between language use for communication and symbolic language use (as I don't), there is a crucial difference between these two texts... [R19]

In the example above, the *we*-IPC *one agrees* is used to create an interpersonal relation of concession, which is followed by a counter-claim. The premise of the *if*-clause is to be examined and the reader is presumed to be examining it at the same time, as if alongside the writer. With the *we*-IPC removed, the logical relation between the clauses would still hold. However, the concession operating on the interactive level would be wiped out. The *we*-IPC allows the writer to acknowledge the contentiousness of a particular proposition, the willingness to negotiate with those who hold a different view and the deference of the writer for those alternative views. Hence by showing her full awareness of alternative viewpoints through the *we*-IPC, the writer opens discursive space for negotiation. Meanwhile, the interpersonal coherence operates to render the text more understandable and interesting and to direct the reader towards the interpretative orientation the writer prefers him to develop regarding the projected discourse.

Example (152) below is an illustration of hypothetical-real type of interpersonal conjunction initiated by *we*-IPCs.

(152) *One might perhaps think that* focusing upon trilingualism is a bit random— why not look at quadrilinguals? *It should be remembered, however, that* situations in which the parents have different mother tongues, and in which children are raised in a milieu where a third language is dominant, are relatively common. [E87]

Here the conjunction is achieved through the co-opting of two

IPCs, which are marked by the italics. A comparative analysis of the two IPCs will contribute to clarifying the interpersonal coherence. In the hypothetical part, *might* and *perhaps* form a modality harmonic①. Together, they construct the modality of low value. In addition, the projection initiated by *think* is a hypotactic one, implying that the proposition in the projected clause is brought into existence by someone's consciousness. It does not exist in the real world. In the real part, the modality *should* is of higher modal value. Meanwhile, the projection is an embedded pre-projection. That is, the proposition exists as a matter of fact prior to the mental activity of remembering.

The coworking of IPC strategies thus enables the writer to claim a greater degree of authority and make her proposition harder to challenge. Seen in this way, IPC facilitates the writer to seek in-group agreement and cooperation. It is therefore shown that in pursuing her personal and disciplinary goals, the writer seeks to create a recognizable social world through deliberate choices of IPC which allows her to conduct interpersonal negotiations and to balance claims for the significance, originality and plausibility of her contribution against the convictions and expectations of the reader.

5.3 Summary

This chapter scrutinizes the discursive behavior of *I*-IPCs and *we*-

---

① Lyons (1977) employs the term "modality harmonic" to refer to the context where two or more forms express the same degree of modality such that there is a kind of concord running through the clause which results in the double realization of a single modality.

IPCs, with respect to their lexicogrammatical realizations relating to three metafunctions, and cross-genre investigations, followed by elaborations on their intersubjectivity-augmenting functions. It is concluded that discoursal features of both types of IPC are determined by the user's awareness of the interactive participants and the social and communicative functions the particular genre (in the present case, ELBR and ELJE) aims to accomplish. As has been argued, one primary function of ABR is to evaluate the academic product; hence the book reviewer is anticipated by the disciplinary community to provide balanced assessment, even negative evaluation if necessary. Consequently, the reviewer is found to often turn to either *I*-IPCs or *we*-IPCs when she feels that the interpersonal stake is high, in order to get the reader aligned, and to engage the reader in the current academic conversation.

However, it is different in the case of editorial writing. The prime purpose of journal editorials is to promote the academic product, therefore the writer resorts more to *we*-IPCs so as to establish collective authoritative image for the journal's editorial staff, reviewers and contributors. As Lerner & Kitzinger (2007: 549) point out, it is not that *I* and *we* do more than referring, but rather that it is possible to uncover what situated referring itself can accomplish as part and parcel of the organization of writing in interaction, that is, as part and parcel of situated social life.

Specifically, the *I*-IPC in ELBR shows its genre-specific features in terms of its lexicogrammatical realizations in the following aspects. To begin with, the cognitive mental processes are predominant. Second, with respect to tense and modalization, while the unmarked simple present and modalization is dominant, simple past is also observed to occupy notable portions of instances. Third, split projection is found common. Cross-genre investigations show that the *I*-IPC is of much lower frequency of occurrence in ELJE. It is also observed that it displays fewer variations vis-à-vis realizing resources.

As far as the *we*-IPC is concerned, the data shows that the reviewer has a strong preference for *one* as a general referent, which might be inclusive of either of the interactants or both of them. Within ELBR, similar to the *I*-IPC, the *we*-IPC also favors cognitive processes and simple present tense. In marked contrast to the *I*-IPC, rare instances of *we*-IPCs appear in past tense or split projection. Across the genres, it is found that the *we*-IPC is much more preferred by the editorial writer. An analysis of the distribution and allocation of the two types of IPC confirm the significance of IPC employment to facilitate the writer to achieve the anticipated social purposes in different elements of the particular GSP.

The next chapter will, in a similar manner, examine another two types of IPC constructions, namely, those IPC realizations without the interactant appearing as the Projector and those with a third party instead of the interactant functioning as the Projector.

Chapter 6

No-interactant and Non-interactant IPCs in ELBR

The previous chapter conducted respective analyses of *I*-IPCs and *we*-IPCs. The findings are revealing in that IPC shows noteworthy genre-specific features. This chapter continues the exploration into IPC constructions by investigating another two types of IPC which are identified in ELBR. Both are featured by the fact that the Projector is not construed by the interactant. The difference lies in whether there is no explicit Projector at all or the Projector is realized by a third party rather than the interactant. In the former case, no-interactant IPCs are involved whereas non-interactant IPCs in the second.

Similar to the analysis procedure in the preceding chapter, this chapter will explore no-interactant and non-interactant IPCs, with particular attention given to their realizing options, and allocations vis-à-vis the GSP elements of ELBR. In the same vein, cross-genre comparisons will be conducted, aiming to offer a better and clearer depiction of IPC constructions. Each section will end with a functional discussion of the targeted type of IPC with respect to intersubjectivity enhancement.

6.1 No-interactant IPCs

This type of IPC, as the name indicates, does not bring the Projector into visibility. That is, the selected structure of IPC does not represent the Projector. Structurally, no-interactant IPCs show no evidence of the participation of the interactant. Some scholars therefore treat no-interactant IPCs as impersonal projections (Halliday & Matthiessen, 2004: 475; Martin, 1992: 130). It is of necessity to, first of all, justify no-interactant IPCs since one primary parameter for identifying IPC is that it serves interpersonal functions and works on the interpersonal dimension. After the justification and classification, the section examines the discursive behavior of no-interactant IPCs in terms of their realizing instances and cross-genre variations. This section ends by elucidating intersubjectivity boosting functions of no-interactant IPCs.

6.1.1 Justification and Classification of No-interactant IPCs

It is well accepted that impersonal projection (Martin, 1992) or explicit objective modal assessment (Halliday & Matthiessen, 2004; Thompson, 2004) is a common device for the writer to express her subjective attitude or comment without appearing overtly in the text. That is, as Giuliana (2004: 196) interprets, by putting a certain proposition into a projection, the writer can use no-interactant IPCs to encode her personal views while simultaneously being objective. Hyland & Tse (2005) also state that no-interactant IPCs, in particular the anticipatory-*it* type, are powerful constructions for expressing evaluative meanings in academic discourse as they allow the writer to thematize the evaluation, making the attitudinal meaning the starting point of the message and the perspective from which the content of the ensuing clause is to be interpreted. Consider the following example.

> (153) *It is clear that* it covers an impressive amount of ground and it provides new data on a number of constructions. [R16]

On the surface, the construction *it is clear* in Example (153) is impersonal. However, it is understood quite well that the writer is the source of the comment. According to Hunston (2000) and Charles (2006b), such no-interactant IPCs are self-sourced "averrals without attribution". Thus, they operate on the interpersonal dimension by conveying the writer's viewpoint. As Halliday & Matthiessen (2004: 607) point out, objective expressions of IPC actually construe the writer's subjective judgment and evaluation.

However, it should be borne in mind that no-interactant IPCs can also be deployed to express possible views of the reader-in-the-text (cf. Thompson, 2001). The principle behind the concept of reader-in-the-text is that any text can in essence be seen as a record of a dialogue between the writer and the reader in which "the writer has to conduct her interaction by enacting the roles of both participants" (Widdowson, 1984: 59, cited in Thompson, 2001). Thompson & Ye (1991: N5) and Thompson (2001: 64) argue that no-interactant IPC constructions will normally be taken as signaling that the source could plausibly be the reader-in-the-text, as Example (154) below exhibits.

> (154) *It might be argued that* references to other works throughout the descriptive chapters are scarce. [R70]

As Example (154) shows, an individual reader may not accept the idea expressed in the projected clause as representing his own views, yet he must agree with the writer that some of his peers might well accept it.

Besides *it*-type no-interactant IPCs, the present study identifies some no-interactant IPCs appearing in existential processes as well, as Example (155) illustrates.

> (155)... there have long been 'folklinguistic' beliefs that certain ways of speaking English index gay male identity... [R75]

Such *there*-type IPCs are used, according to Morley (2000: 191), for presentational purposes to draw attention to the existence of the following element. The actual word *there* may be seen as a pronoun functioning as a dummy subject headword, which is followed by the verb and then the delayed identification of the meaning content of that headword by a further nominal phrase. In such constructions, the embedding projection may be used by the writer to express views of either or both interactants.

Similarly, the corpus reveals another type of no-interactant IPCs which resembles the *there*-type in that they function to turn the ensuing proposition into a clause through upranking, as Example (156) below shows. For the convenience of reference, this type of no-interactant IPCs is referred to by this study as *problem*-type no-interactant IPCs.

> (156) The problem is that only the main text is indexed, while the extensive and informative end-of-chapter notes are not. [N5]

Halliday & Matthiessen (2004: 199) regard such projections as facts (cf. Section 3.3). According to their observation, projections like Examples (155) and (156) are able to set up another clause, or a set of clauses as the content of thinking, or other projections. Martin *et al.* (1997: 190) also notice the *problem*-type of expressions. They state that such constructions function to set up a Value-Token structure, where the Token may be an embedded clause or even clause complex. Seen in this way, the *problem*-type no-interactant IPCs are similar to the *there*-type in that both may be used to create an interpersonal space in which the writer conveys the writer-reader's viewpoints while simultaneously not bothering to clarify whose viewpoints they are.

Interpersonally, a common property the three types of no-interactant IPCs share is that it is an inherent part of the construction that it needs a source, someone entertaining the belief which the real member then contradicts, qualifies, and confirms. This someone may be the writer, the reader, other people, or any combination of the three (Thompson, 2001).

However, it is worthy of note that the present research does find some projections which appear in the form of no-interactant IPCs but do not work on the interpersonal dimension. They are of course excluded. The cases are mainly of three categories, i.e. having a text-organizing function, referring to other parts of the text, or presenting propositional content with predominantly ideational functions, or expressing the author's rather than the writer-reader's views. Here are two examples.

(157) *It is suggested that* the languages in which condition (a) is grammaticalized represent a later stage of diachronic development with respect to those in which condition (a) is pragmatically derived from condition (b) (346-48). [R29]

(158) This finding points out how some processes can be more influential in the development of metaphoric expressions than others; *it also suggests that* corpus data can provide a reality check of categories (and theories) that are based on dictionary entries, as in Goossens's (1995) study, or purely on researchers' own intuitions. [R26]

In Example (157), it is not the interactant's argument that is presented, for it can not be glossed as *I suggest*. In the same vein, the projection in Example (158) refers back to *this finding* (of the author) rather than the writer's own finding. These examples are indicative of the fact that in defining no-interactant IPCs, it is fairly important to look more widely into the context in which they are used.

What is equally important, if not more, the genre identity of discourse is a determinant factor. The genres of ABR and the journal editorial are both parasitic to the author's academic product because the writer primarily evaluates or promotes the product rather than present her own products as in research articles. Consequently, impersonal projections such as *it is suggested* that normally express authorial views do not, in most cases in the two parasitic genres, express the writer's suggestions. Thus, most of these projections work on the ideational level, not co-opting with the interpersonal projection. One sound conclusion drawn is that IPC resources are genre-sensitive and context-specified.

To sum up, there are three types of no-interactant IPCs identified in the current corpus of ELBR, namely *it*-type no-interactant IPCs, *there*-type no-interactant IPCs and *problem*-type no-interactant IPCs. The subsequent section will tackle the three types of no-interactant IPCs from the perspectives of metafunction, cross-genre comparison and intersubjectivity augmentation.

6.1.2 Metafunctional Features of No-interactant IPCs

A preliminary investigation of the data shows that no-interactant IPCs overwhelmingly outnumber *I*-IPCs and *we*-IPCs, with a total number of 627 occurrences. That is, these constructions form the bulk of all IPC resources. This finding shows that the writer prefers no-interactant IPCs to *I*-IPCs and *we*-IPCs (cf. Sections 5.1.2 and

5.2.2). The data of ELBR also reveals that no-interactant IPCs exhibit the greatest variability with respect to process types. Table 6.1 represents the relative distribution of process types concerning no-interactant IPCs in the ELBR corpus.

Table 6.1 No-interactant IPCs in ELBR by Process Type

Process	Subtype	Number of Occurrences	Frequency
Relational	Attributive	395	63%
	Identifying	133	21.2%
Verbal		21	3.3%
Mental		45	7.2%
Existential		33	5.3%
Total		627	100%

As is shown in Table 6.1, relational processes are most favored in ELBR, making up 84.2% of all no-interactant IPCs. The majority of these relational processes relate to attributive relations (63% of the total) rather than identifying relations (21.2% of the total). Examples (159) and (160) below illustrate the two subtypes of relational processes respectively.

(159) Seen in this light, *it is not surprising that* the definition in (1) leads Dixon to conclude that what he calls adjectives... are universal. [R59]

(160) Although many of the chapters reiterate the demographic imperative for marketing oneself in two languages, *the more urgent community-based necessity is that* communities not squander their linguistic resources. [R5]

The findings are of at least four important implications. First, the ELBR writer is inclined to employ strikingly more IPC resources in which no Projectors are involved (i.e. impersonal projection). Compared with the number of occurrences of *I*-IPCs (213 instances) and *we*-IPCs (125 instances), the repeated fondness and very conspicuous preference for no-interactant IPCs substantiates Freddi's (2005) statement that in linguistics discourse impersonal attribution proves to be a general tendency.

In addition, the prominence of no-interactant IPCs is in line with the well-held viewpoint that academic discourse appears to be impersonal, objective and faceless. As Taylor (1989: 144) advises his readers, while academic writing should constitute the writer's judgments and beliefs, explicit expressions should be used sparingly. His words partly account for the high percentage of impersonal projections in the current corpus.

Third, with the absence of the Projector, no-interactant IPCs offer more flexibility and larger discourse space for the reader to interpret the source of the proposition. As Fairclough (1992) maintains, the use of no-interactant IPCs makes it unclear whose views are being presented, whether the writer is presenting her own views as being universal, or acting as a vehicle for the views of the group and the community.

Finally, within no-interactant IPCs, the overwhelming dominance of relational processes suggests that the use of relational processes is a prototypical mechanism for the ELBR writer to manage intersubjectivity. In fact, Hunston & Sinclair (2000) and Hewings & Hewings (2002) have noticed this function of anticipatory-*it*-type no-interactant IPCs. They argue that such constructions allow the writer to encode an evaluation which influences how the subsequent clause is to be interpreted. By identifying relational processes which highlight the Value-Token sequence within the sentence (as in Example (160) above), or by foregrounding the Value by putting it prior to the Token through extraposition (as in Example (159)), the writer explicitly signals to the reader her perspective to what to follow. In Hyland & Tse's (2005) words, such constructions "initialize" the writer's perspectives.

Within the relational processes, the attributive type is characterized by adjectival predicates (89.4% of the total), as Example (159) above shows. This is consistent with the findings of Rodman's (1991) study of anticipatory *it* in journal articles, where about 40% of predicates are adjectival. However, the finding is in contrast with Hyland & Tse's (2005) observation that there are only a handful of non-verbal forms (principally nouns) in their corpus of article abstracts. Hyland & Tse (2005) offer a sound explanation for the discrepancy. According to their study, the abstract writer does not use such structures to guide the reader through an argument, convey affect, introduce new topics, or summarize information. Instead the writer is largely seeking to comment positively on her main findings, indicating both a degree of certainty and a particular kind of activity.

In addition, the present finding is also in line with Diani's (2004) analysis of review articles in linguistics. The four adjectives (*clear*, *important*, *necessary* and *interesting*) of the highest frequencies (respectively 44 occurrences, 39 occurrences, 19 occurrences, and 10 occurrences) found in the present corpus are also among Diani's (2004: 203) top ten adjectives in terms of frequency. This shows that such patterns are favored by the writer within the discipline.

Much less obvious than the previously mentioned mechanisms are verbal, mental and existential processes, which return to 3.3%, 7.3% and 5.2% respectively of all no-interactant IPCs found in the corpus. Altogether, the three types of processes account for a mere 15.8%. The following examples represent the three processes respectively, with Examples (154) and (155) rementioned just for the purpose of convenience.

(154) *It might be argued that* references to other works throughout the

descriptive chapters are scarce. [R70]

(161) Since that volume *it seems that* studies of institutional interaction (or talk) now predominate in CA research. [R52]

(155)... *there have long been 'folklinguistic' beliefs that* certain ways of speaking English index gay male identity... [R75]

The lowest percentage of verbal processes in ELBR indicates that the writer is reluctant to use this type of processes in no-interactant IPCs. The finding sharply contradicts Freddi's (2005) conclusion which is based on a study of introductory chapters of 10 textbooks in linguistics. Freddi finds that in his corpus verbal processes are in numerous occurrences like *it can be argued* and *it has been suggested* with *that* as the most frequent collocate to the right of *argued* and *suggested*. One probable explanation for the discrepancies is that no-interactant IPCs are genre-sensitive. The argumentative nature of linguistics textbooks (Freddi, 2005) requires high percentage of verbal/argumentative processes, which highlight the writer's viewpoints. By contrast, ELBR texts tend to be more informative and evaluative. Thus, these verbal processes are not so favored as in textbooks.

Within ELBR, the variation can be accounted for from the vantage point of ambiguity avoidance. While no-interactant IPCs offer the writer more referencing flexibility, the absence of the Projector also causes potential ambiguity. That is, with no-interactant IPCs like *it is argued*, the writer has to clarify whose argument it is. A finer-grained analysis shows that ELBR texts are rich in verbal expressions like *it is argued*, with as many as 277 instances. However, most of these instances are used by the writer to refer to the author's argument. Thus, it shows that the use of such verbal processes is linked to generic norms and conventions.

The frequency of mental processes in no-interactant IPCs is also reduced to a great extent, compared with their conspicuous predominance in both *I*-IPCs and *we*-IPCs (cf. Sections 5.1.2 and 5.2.2 respectively). The mental process also differentiates itself from those in other IPC resources in terms of lexicogrammatical realizations. A close scrutiny reveals that out of the 45 no-interactant IPCs in mental processes, *it seems* (n = 29) and *it appears* (n = 8) are of important presence. The interesting finding is of two implications. First, these results show how conscientious the writer is when constructing her discourse. There is ever a need to balance presence and absence, generic and specific, intimate and distant, alone or grouped, and so forth (Rundblad, 2007). Second, there seems to be a grammatical conspiracy with respect to the distribution and allocation of lexicogrammatical realizations of IPC.

The low frequency of existential processes is well accounted for by Gómez-González (2001: 205-06). She argues that the relative scarcity of existential-*there* constructions in her corpus can be justified in processing terms. They bring about the delay of the notional Subject until the end of the construct. By doing so, the reader's short-term memory is put under strain and the process of comprehension becomes slower. Obviously, this is an undesired effect due to the fact that the ELBR writer is more concerned with intersubjectivity management.

In terms of tense and modalization, no-interactant IPCs in ELBR are exhibited in Table 6.2.

Table 6.2 No-interactant IPCs in ELBR by Tense and Modalization

Tense	Number of Occurrences	Frequency
Simple present	488	77.8%
Modalized	98	15.7%
Non-finite	32	5.1%
Others	9	1.4%
Total	627	100%

As is displayed in Table 6.2 above, no-interactant IPCs in simple present tense are profoundly preferred by the ELBR writer (77.8% of the total). The use of those modalized instances also deserves consideration, covering 15.7% of the total. Altogether the two types of resources possess 93.5% of all no-interactant IPCs. The finding is not surprising, considering the fact that simple present tense and modalization are typical of IPC. Of the two types, the writer's obvious preference for simple present tense aids in generating a strong sense of "here-and-now", which signals to the reader the immediacy of the writer-reader interaction and the ongoing nature of the interaction, as is shown in the following example.

(162) In the absence of such ethnographic data, *it is puzzling to* see comments about what the participants do in their everyday lives... [R32]

In Example (162), the no-interactant IPC *it is puzzling* facilitates the writer to create a sense of "now" in the discourse. The present tense construes the academic activity of ELBR writing as a conversation involving the writer and the reader.

In addition, it is hypothesized that the frequent use of present tense is partly related to the infrequent use of modalization. As far as no-interactant IPCs in simple present tense are concerned, the analysis reveals an exceptionally strong relation between anticipatory *it* and *is*, followed by an evaluative or attitudinal adjective, as is illustrated in Example (162) above.

However, it is not believed that this combination is specific to the genre of ELBR, considering the findings of other researches (e.g. Groom, 2005; Hewings & Hewings, 2002; Herriman, 2000). Used to convey the writer's viewpoints, the combination seems a general pattern across genres and disciplines. Seen in this way, the striking preference for such no-interactant IPC constructions is not unexpected.

A closer look at those modalized cases reveals that the ELBR writer is inclined to choose modalities of medium and low values such as *would* (n = 21), *may/might* (n = 12) and *should* (n = 7). Taken together, modalities of non-high values account for 70% of all modalized no-interactant IPCs. This is consistent with the findings in the previous chapter. Thus, it indicates that there is a tendency across the various types of IPC resources to use modalities of non-high values. With respect to no-interactant IPCs, this might be accounted for from the perspective of intersubjectivity management. Consider Example (163) below.

> (163) *It would be interesting to* view these messages from a Message Design Logic (O'Keefe, 1988) perspective or even over time looking at how these conversations embody Baxter and Montgomery's (1998) relational dialectics theory. [R39]

As Example (163) demonstrates, the modalized no-interactant IPC *it would be interesting* is deployed to introduce the reader's plausible views with respect to the author's proposition. In this way, the writer shows her full awareness of the reader by construing his voice into the discourse through modalization. The employment of these modalities suggests that on the one hand, plausible alternative views from the reader or elsewhere are fully considered, and on the other hand, that the reader is invited to engage in the discussion and judgment of these alternatives.

In terms of the Thematic position, no-interactant IPCs in the present corpus are found to be assigned to the initial status in a percentage as high as 98% of the total instances. The corpus reveals three types of thematized no-interactant IPCs, as are represented respectively by the following examples. Overall, there appears to be an obvious tendency to locate no-interactant IPCs towards the very initial slot of the clause complex as the one in Example (164) below, or on some occasions, the position right after the textual Theme as the one in Example (165) below. Taken together, the two types of thematized no-interactant IPCs occupy 97.7% of all no-interactant IPCs (67.2% and 30.5% respectively). Embedded textual Themes as the one in Example (166) below are rare (0.3% of the total).

> (164) *It must be noted, though, that* translations do not always capture fine-grained distinctions. [R70]
>
> (165)... but *it is clear that* she is building on stance as it has been employed in work by Biber and Finegan (1988, 1989) to make connection between linguistic markers and the attitudes and psychological attitudes of language users. [R17]
>
> (166) *It seems, however, that* for him thoughts take a definite shape when cast in the form of sentences, whether uttered or implicated. [R29]

The finding is in line with those in the previous chapter. The overall tendency to initialize IPC on the one hand reflects the unmarked working mechanism of IPC, i.e. the ideational projection comes to stand for interpersonal projection. As was stated in Section 3.3, ideational projection is featured by syntactic dominance. On the other hand, the strong preference for initializing no-interactant IPCs can be accounted for by the frame-setting property of IPC. Choosing to initialize no-interactant IPCs, the writer pre-sets frames and perspectives for the interpretation of the ensuing proposition. Thus, the writer signals to and invites the reader to understand the ensuing clause within the suggested frame. Considering these facts, it is natural for the overall predominance of thematized no-interactant IPCs.

The finding that embedded textual Themes are of extremely low frequency in ELBR contradicts Martin's (1995: 157) statement.

According to his observation, interpersonal Themes frequently embed within them textural Themes. This discrepancy between the present observation and Martin's conclusion, though interesting, can not be accounted for without consulting larger bulks of authentic data. On the one hand, it is not clear whether Martin's conclusion is based on data observation or intuition. On the other hand, there is the possibility that the present finding might not be generalized beyond the genre and discipline.

6.1.3 A Cross-Genre Analysis of No-interactant IPCs

When it turns to the comparative investigation of no-interactant IPCs across ELBR and ELJE, the present study finds that these resources are of quantitatively almost equal focus, as Table 6.3 represents.

Table 6.3 Cross-Genre Comparison of No-interactant IPCs by Frequency

Genre type	Number of Occurrences	Frequency/10,000 words	Frequency/100 Sentences
ELBR	627	30.4	9.7
ELJE	809	35.1	11.9

Roughly speaking, there appears no sharp discrepancy with respect to the percentage of no-interactant IPCs in either genre, with those in ELJE being of a slightly higher percentage. This finding implies that both the review writer and the editorial writer show much stronger preference for no-interactant IPCs over *I* -IPCs and *we* -IPCs (cf. Table 5.3 and Table 5.7). This tendency might be generalized to other academic text types both within and outside the discipline. However, it is beyond the scope of the present study. As far as the current study is concerned, the overwhelming predominance of no-interactant IPCs is, in the least resort, indicative of the fact that it is considered appropriate by this disciplinary community.

The discursive behaviors of no-interactant IPCs across the genres are also similar with respect to the distribution and allocation of process types involved, as Table 6.4 exhibits.

Table 6.4 Cross-Genre Comparison of No-interactant IPCs by Process

Process	Subtype	Frequency in ELBR	Frequency in ELJE
Relational	Attributive	63%	61%
	Identifying	21.2%	17.9%
Verbal		3.3%	6.9%
Mental		7.2%	10%
Existential		5.3%	4.2%
Total		100%	100%

As Table 6.4 indicates, there is no obvious cross-genre discrepancy in terms of process types and frequency of occurrences. Of particular note here is the choice of verbal processes, which achieve a rate of 6.9% of all no-interactant IPCs in ELJE and are found only to occupy 3.3% of those in ELBR. This variation has a close link to tense choices across the genres. Therefore, it will be explained on the pages which conduct a comparative study of tense. Overall, it might be concluded that within the discipline, as far as process is concerned, no-interactant IPCs do not show explicit genre-specific features. Considering the different communicative purposes of the two genres, this finding may be surprising. A best estimation is that the review writer and her counterpart use similar types and portions of processes to accomplish different goals. If it is the case, no-interactant IPCs must be different in other aspects.

In order to bring into vision in what ways these resources are used in the process of interaction between the writer and the reader across the genres, the present study turns to the lexicogrammatical realizations of the values in these relational processes, since they possess the exceedingly largest portion in both genres. In synthesizing the classification system for pattern/meaning association proposed by Francis *et al.* (1998), Groom (2005) and Hewings & Hewings (2002), the present study reexamines all no-interactant IPCs in both corpora.

The finding is revealing in at least two aspects. The first is related to frequency variation of desirability/expectation-signaling no-interactant IPCs across the genres. In ELBR, there is an important presence of such instances, making up 83 occasions of the total value realizations, compared with ELJE, which shows much fewer instances (24 items in total). In ELBR, items of the highest frequencies are *interesting* (n = 23), *helpful* (n = 12), and *surprising* (n = 9). By stark contrast, in ELJE, only a few instances are identified (there is even no one single instance of *helpful* identified). When looking more widely at the use of these items in the corpus, the study notices that these value-carrying items are mostly used by the reviewer to convey her indirect criticism on the book under review by offering constructive suggestions, as the following example indicates.

(167) At a minimum, *it would be helpful to* distinguish between workers and management. [R5]

As Example (167) shows, the no-interactant IPC *it would be helpful* suggests the reviewer's criticism on the book under review. The reviewer uses the desire-signaling adjective (i.e. *helpful*) to point out the demerits of the book, and simultaneously suggesting preferable improvements.

The second is related with frequency variation of items indicating importance/significance (e.g. *important*, *significant*, *essential* and *crucial*) across the genres. ELJE witnesses a noticeably higher frequency (154 items in total) than its counterpart does (81 items in total). The following example is provided for the purpose of illustration.

> (168) For this, *it is essential that* more papers, such as the ones presented here, are made available. [E37]

In Example (168), the editorial writer employs the importance-indicating no-interactant IPC *it is essential* to comment positively on the papers under discussion.

These two findings are not beyond expectation, considering the main aims of ELBR and ELJE. In the review text, the writer is supposed to give information on the academic product to the reader while evaluating it in an accepted and appropriate way. The prominence of desirability/expectation-signaling no-interactant IPCs is of multifunction. To begin with, the review writer as a qualified expert and judge can not only point out the demerits of the book but offer comments and suggestions for improvement. Thus, she attempts to convince the reader of her evaluation. In addition, these no-interactant IPCs facilitate to invite the reader (inclusive of the author) to engage in the academic activity by pondering whether these views are acceptable and how they can be put into practice.

When it turns to ELJE, which is characterized by its use of persuasive and promotional techniques, the primary aim is not so much as to inform the reader of an academic product but to exert influence on the reader's behavior by using emphatics/importance suggestions. As is shown in Example (168) above, the ELJE writer deploys such IPC devices for the purpose of advertising. The use of the no-interactant IPC foregrounds the significance of the papers under discussion.

As with other types of IPC, the present study conducts a comparison across the genres with respect to tense and modalization of no-interactant IPCs. The results are displayed in Figure 6.1.

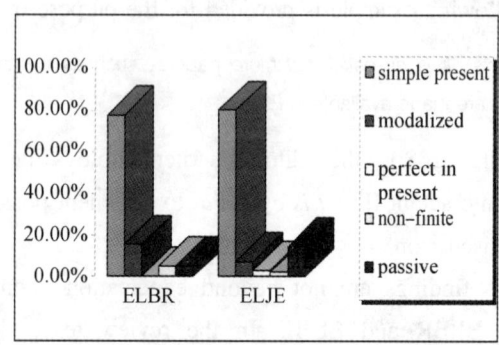

Figure 6.1 Cross-Genre Comparison of No-interactant IPCs by Tense, Modalization, and Passivity

Figure 6.1 is of the following important implications. First, simple present tense is seen to be prevailing in both genres. There is no obvious difference in percentage terms in the two genres. The finding confirms the SFL view that simple present tense is one of the two unmarked options that realize IPC.

Second, modalized no-interactant IPCs occur more frequently in ELBR (15.8% of the total) than in EBJE (7.4% of the total). The following examples represent modalized items in ELBR and ELJE respectively.

(169) *It might have been useful to* include references to some of the more reputable online sources of follow-up material along with the more traditional resources in this section. [R90]

(170) In this issue we have—fortuitously, *it must be acknowledged*—a focus on essay and other prompts for writing assessment. [E99]

As is shown above, the no-interactant IPC in Example (169) construes the writer's constructive suggestion whereas that in Example (170) draws the reader's attention to the feature and significance of the articles in the issue.

The discrepancy may attribute to two key factors. One is linked to the review writer's consideration of the reader. That is, modalization is used to entertain plausible alternative views deriving from the reader-in-the-text, which will be confirmed or contradicted in the ensuing text. The other is associated with the reviewer writer's negative comments with respect to the book under review. By deploying modalized no-interactant IPCs, the reviewer softens her unfavorable comments. By contrast, in ELJE, the writer is not expected to use such modalized no-interactant IPCs to introduce alternative views or to point to the demerits of the articles. The editorial writer, who is more interested in the promotion of the product, tends to steer away from using such no-interactant IPCs. One primary reason is that they generate controversial views and distancing in the text, which conflicts with her aim of creating a degree of interaction and closeness with the reader. Thus, in cases in which such no-interactant IPCs are employed, they are not used for the same purposes as in ELBR. Thus, the discrepancy shows that not only difference in frequency but also the meaning of similar expressions have to be interpreted and explained by referring to the type of text in which they are deployed.

Third, while neither genre shows notable presence of no-interactant IPCs in perfect in present, the frequency of the total in ELBR is extremely low (only 2 cases), compared with that in ELJE (25 cases). Example (171) below represents such items in ELJE.

> (171) *It has been argued that* this analysis explains the fact that the order of adjectives is the same in Welsh as in English. [E52]

As Example (171) shows, most of such no-interactant IPCs (79% of the total) are of verbal processes. This partly accounts for the fact that verbal processes in ELJE are more than twice those in ELBR (cf. Table 6.4). The strikingly low frequency of such no-interactant IPCs in both genres suggests that the writer is reluctant to deploy such strategies for academic interaction. One possible explanation may be that perfect in present is one marked option for IPC. Another interpretation may be relevant to the conventions and norms of the particular genre and discipline. However, this is only a hypothesis which requires more data-based investigation than the present study could cope with.

Finally, the frequency of passivized no-interactant IPCs turns out to be conspicuously different in the two genres, with 4.8% of all no-interactant IPCs in ELBR and 15% of the total in ELJE. Examples (172) and (173) below are typical passivized no-interactant IPCs in the two genres.

(172) *It is hoped that* the efforts of the authors included here will inspire readers to further pursue such endeavors. [E48]

(173) Although *it must be understood that* this limits what we can know, it is not a limitation that is not overcome in this book. [R39]

The relatively higher frequency of such constructions in EJLE attributes to those no-interactant IPCs in the tense of perfect in present, as Example (172) indicates. They account for 10.6% of the total. By contrast, as was mentioned, perfect in present is found scarce in ELBR. Another contributive factor is linked to the writer's purely rhetorical considerations. As Example (172) shows, the writer might use *we hope* instead of *it is hoped* to express almost the same meaning. The passive no-interactant IPC might be used for the purpose of repetition avoidance and achieving variation in expression. A third influential element is connected with the communicative purposes of the particular genre. In ELJE, the writer is expected to promote the academic product. Therefore, it is natural for her to resort to no-interactant IPCs such as *it must be understood* in Example (173) to explicitly highlight her intentions and thus invite the reader to follow her in understanding the importance of the academic product.

With respect to Theme-Rheme patterns, no-interactant IPC occurrences in the genres show more similarities than discrepancies. That is, both corpora see exceedingly high percentages of thematized no-interactant IPCs (98% of the total in ELBR and 96% of the total in ELJE). The finding confirms the significance of IPC in framing and filtering the ensuing clause. It is also consistent with the findings concerning other types of IPC resources (cf. Sections 5.1.3 and 5.2.3).

However, a further investigation of the distribution reveals one noticeable cross-genre discrepancy. Compared with ELBR, ELJE exhibits far more thematized no-interactant IPCs in which textual Themes are embedded (46% of the total, compared with 0.3% of the total in ELBR). A quick count of the occurrences shows that there is a noticeable tendency for the editorial writer to insert certain textual Theme within the no-interactant IPC construction. While in contrast with the finding based on ELBR texts observation, this finding is in line with Martin's (1995) statement. As was mentioned previously, the phenomenon needs to be examined in more cross-genre and cross-disciplinary texts. As far as ELJE is concerned, the preference for embedding other elements within no-interactant IPCs basically depends on the communicative prominence the editorial writer wishes to give to the no-interactant IPC. This may justify the frequent use of such no-interactant IPCs, as the promotional nature of these texts requires the writer to highlight the no-interactant IPC, in order to draw the reader's attention to it.

A final consideration should be given to the distribution of no-interactant IPCs with respect to the GSP elements of the two genres. Figure 6.2 and Figure 6.3 exhibit respectively generic structural distributions of no-interactant IPCs in ELBR and ELJE.

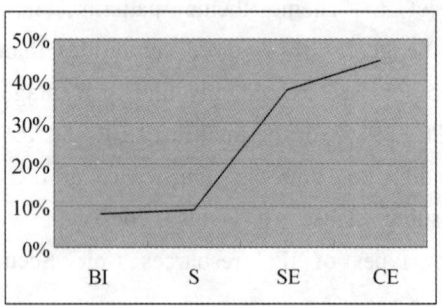

Figure 6.2   Generic Structural Distribution of No-interactant IPCs in ELBR

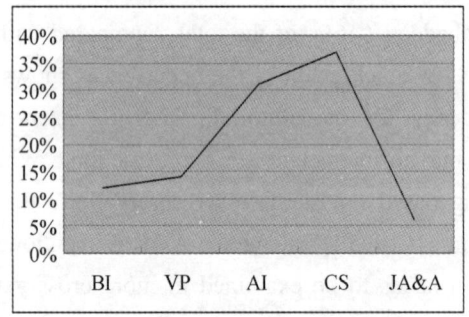

Figure 6.3   Generic Structural Distribution of No-interactant IPCs in ELJE

Concerning the GSP of ELBR, as Figure 6.2 displays, no-interactant IPCs are seen in all the elements. However, on closer inspection, the study finds that their distributive intensity varies across the elements. To be specific, these resources are profoundly predominant in the element of CE (45% of the total), with the element of SE ranking the second (38% of the total), whereas no-interactant IPCs identified in the elements of BI and S are of similar percentage (respectively 8% of the total and 9% of the total).

In ELJE, as is shown in Figure 6.3, no-interactant IPCs exhibit interesting distributive intensity. The elements of AI and CS see the majority of all instances (63% of the total) with that of CS seeing slightly more occurrences (36% of the total). The elements of VP and BI are similar in seeing almost the same percentage of no-interactant IPCs (respectively 19% of the total and 12% of the total) whereas the element of JA&A witnesses only a handful of no-interactant IPCs (6% of the total).

These findings are of some noteworthy implications. First, across the genres, no-interactant IPCs tend to be used more frequently in the final elements (i.e. the element of CE in ELBR and the element of CS in ELJE). This finding confirms the importance assigned to the element in each genre. In ELBR, the writer is expected to express her overall evaluation of the book in the element of CE. While she is reluctant to resort to *I*-IPCs or *we*-IPCs which explicitly suggest the authorial presence, she is more inclined to employ no-interactant IPCs which sound more objective and impersonal. Thus, it appears that the review writer manages the tension between catering to the community expectation (i.e. offering her personal judgment) while simultaneously forging alignment with her audience. In ELJE, however, the writer is anticipated to promote the articles. Consequently, she is conscious to use no-interactant IPCs to make the reader favorably impressed by her presentation of the articles. Therefore, in either case, the writer is seen to invest more in the deployment of IPC.

Second, the two genres are different with respect to the overall distribution of no-interactant IPCs. To be specific, in ELBR, the frequencies of no-interactant IPC occurrences vary across different elements to a much greater extent than their counterparts in ELJE. That is, except the element of JA&A, ELJE sees a roughly even distribution of the resources. This finding is consistent with the generic identities of each genre. In ELJE, promotion is mapping onto nearly every element of the GSP. In Bhatia's (2004) words, there is no tension between the functions of promoting and informing. Therefore, the writer has more freedom to use no-interactant IPCs for the purpose of reader alignment and ultimately product promotion. In ELBR, however, as has been mentioned, the writer has to manage to soften the conflict between the goals of the genre (i. e. interpreting and evaluating the particular book) and her private intentions (i. e. ensuring the acceptability of her assessment by the audience). As a result, on the dimension of GSP, there emerge different distribution patterns across the two genres. While ELJE sees a somewhat even distribution of no-interactant IPCs across the elements, ELBR shows an obviously higher no-interactant IPC intensity in certain elements in contrast with others, as is shown in Figure 6.2 above.

6.1.4 No-interactant IPCs as Intersubjectivity Boosters

As was stated in Section 6.2.1, no-interactant IPCs have received constant interest in the field of discourse analysis. A quick survey of the literature shows that no-interactant IPCs have been approached in terms of their discourse functions. It appears reasonable for the present study to offer a general picture of what has been concluded before conducting an analysis of the intersubjectivity-boosting function of no-interactant IPCs.

The literature reveals that previous studies mainly focus on anticipatory-*it*-type no-interactant IPCs. From the perspective of Theme-Rheme, Whittaker (1995) and Martin (1995) interpret them as interpersonal Themes. Gómez-González (2001) concurs with Whittaker in stating that such expressions facilitate the writer to objectify modality. In a similar vein, Rowley-Jolivet & Garter-Thomas (2005) conduct a cross-disciplinary analysis of information structure of no-interactant IPC constructions, and suggest that their use primarily confirms the end-weight principle. Thompson (2007) argues that Thematic boundaries of such constructions are dependent upon the particular context in which they are used. Out of a similar consideration, Fetzer (2008b) examines the connection between theme zone and its function in discourse. Fetzer argues that the concept of theme zone is of key importance for the construction of discourse coherence and should be assigned the status of a contextualization cue.

However, more researches are found to concentrate on how no-interactant IPCs are employed to express the writer's subjective attitude or judgment (e. g. Markkanen & Schröder, 1997; Hunston, 2000; Hewings & Hewings, 2002; Neff et al., 2004; Rezzano, 2004; van Hell et al., 2005; Charles, 2006b). Most of the studies come to the conclusion that subjectively no-interactant IPCs express the writer's detachment from the ensuing proposition and thus help to avoid responsibility, and that stylistically such devices facilitate to forge objectiveness of the discourse. Herriman (2000) offers a comprehensive discussion of the functions no-interactant IPCs usually perform:

 A. to make the attitudinal meaning into an explicit and negotiable proposition;
 B. to make it possible to elaborate the description of the attitudinal meaning in considerable detail if wished;
 C. to make it possible to conceal the source of the attitudinal meaning if wished;

D. to make the attitudinal meaning into the perspective from which the content of the extraposed clause is interpreted; and

E. to create end-weight in the clause complex.

It is easy to conclude that Herriman's classification in principle is subjectivity-oriented, as in line with other approaches. What is at the center is how no-interactant IPC patterns are used by the writer to express or to hide her own attitude or responsibility under the headings of attenuating and mitigating expressions.

From the perspective of intersubjectivity, on the basis of authentic data observation, the present study aims to further the exploration on no-interactant IPCs by bringing into vision their intersubjectivity enhancing function. A scrutinizing observation of the data reveals the following related aspects.

1. Dialogue Anticipating

A considerable portion of no-interactant IPCs identified in the current corpora are used by the writer to create dialogic space in which the reader is drawn into the exploration of knowledge by being invited to accept that the proposition prefaced by the no-interactant IPC is a plausible opinion to hold. In this way, by entertaining the possible views of the imagined reader, the writer aims to construct a sense of dialogic interaction. What is more important, the use of such no-interactant IPCs brings underlying interaction to the surface by giving clear signals to the reader that he is anticipated to join the writer in going through the unfolding process of reasoning, in deciding what to include, what line of reasoning to follow, and so on. This is usually done by framing the projected with a modalized no-interactant IPC. Consider the following examples.

(174) With regard to 'surely', *it could be argued that* more emphasis should have been laid on the strikingly different pragmatic effects that it can create

depending on the context... [R70]

(175) *One hypothesis would thus be that* the North East Caucasian phenomenon reflects a reanalysis of an erstwhile auxiliary verb, which would thus... [E59]

In Examples (174) and (175), the use of no-interactant IPCs suggests that the proposition is intended to be seen as coming from the reader-in-the-text or from elsewhere. In fact, as the unfolding text shows, it is also the viewpoint that the writer is arguing for. From the perspective of intersubjectivity, the selection of no-interactant IPCs may help to encourage the reader to react actively to the ongoing text. To be specific, in Example (174), the verb *argue*, which is typically used to introduce argument (Ädel, 2006: 85), can stimulate the reader's interest by encouraging him to speculate whether he himself would put forward the proposed proposition and whether he would agree or disagree on the opinion. In addition, qualified by the low-value modality *could*, which functions to soften the taking of position in argumentation, the framing no-interactant IPC suggests that the projected proposition is only one possible opinion, and that it needs to be justified. In this way, the ELBR writer anticipates the common reader to offer his own judgment and decision. In fact, the writer may expect the author to take the proposition as a possible suggestion rather than a direct criticism. Thus, while anticipating academic exchange from the common reader, the writer expects the author to join in the dialogue as well.

Similarly, in Example (175), the ELJE writer uses an intensive identifying process *one hypothesis would thus be that* to bring into vision one plausible speculation emerging somewhere from the readership. The reader is thus expected to ponder over the idea and to judge whether the hypothesis holds or not. Again, the reader is impelled in a gentle way to think actively and thus to remain involved in the hypothetical dialogue. In this way, alternatives are entertained or acknowledged and the dialogic space for those alternatives is thereby expanded. One possible motivation behind is that, as Simpson (1993: 181) argues, communication is necessarily a two-sided act, where meaning is not under exclusive control of any one side of the interaction. The writer therefore has to acknowledge plausible questions or doubts that the reader might raise after reading the preceding segment of text. In the case of Example (175), this is achieved through the use of modalized no-interactant IPCs.

2. Attention Drawing

A second function commonly associated with the use of no-interactant IPCs involves drawing the reader's attention to the ensuing proposition. As has been stressed, one syntactic feature of most no-interactant IPCs is that they are scopal. That is, they are structurally dominant and thus filter the projected proposition. This scopal or introductory function of no-interactant IPCs, as Myers (1989: 14) states, tells the reader what weight the statement is to have. In this way, the no-interactant IPC constitutes an explicit expression of the writer's desire to control the reader's inferences, to lead him towards an action that she considers to deserve particular attention, because of its significance, newsworthiness, prominence, etc.

Under scrutiny, the corpora suggest four subcategories of attention-drawing functions of no-interactant IPCs. Of the first category, no-interactant IPCs may be employed to draw the reader's attention to aspects of the discourse that might otherwise go unnoticed. In this sense, no-interactant IPC constructions serve as reminders to the reader. Consider the following examples.

(176) However, *one shortcoming* that I as a K-12 teacher educator found *is that* this book focuses primarily on college level writing research and instruction. [R64]

(177) *What is of particular interest is that* Aldridge shows explicitly the implications of extending her analysis of Tagalog to Standard Indonesian. [E47]

As the examples above illustrate, the Value-Token type of relational processes (with *shortcoming* and *particular interest* as the Values in the cases respectively) highlights the evaluation orientation the writer intends to remind the reader to take. In such cases, no-interactant IPCs are deployed to remind the reader to pay special attention to the framed proposition, either negative evaluation as in Example (176) or positive assessment as in Example (177).

Of the second category, no-interactant IPCs are observed to serve as emphatics, foregrounding something important to the disciplinary knowledge construction or the discourse community, or introducing certain new topics. Consider the following examples.

(178) *The point is that* these strategies remain mostly 'under the surface' and have to be explicitly uncovered for analysis (but not for effect). [E71]

(179) Whilst I started this review with a comment on the book's lack of thrills and spills, *it cannot be ignored that* this book does in fact contain a significant amount of useful and well-researched debate, much of which may be the source of some interesting debates. [R94]

In Example (178), the no-interactant IPC in the very initial position of the clause complex puts at the center of the stage what the writer intends the reader to focus his attention upon. In a similar vein, the no-interactant IPC in Example (179) emphasizes the contribution the book under review makes to the disciplinary community. It should also be noted that the intersubjectivity boosting function of the no-interactant IPC is intensified by the embedded negation. As Verhagen

(2005) argues, negation is an explicit expression of intersubjectivity.

In the third category, no-interactant IPCs are used to provoke displacement of attention (Namsaraev, 1997). In such cases, no-interactant IPCs are used as a strategy to arouse a displacement of the focus of the reader's attention to the prefacing no-interactant IPC rather than to the subsequent statement. Consider the following examples.

(180) Especially in the media chapter, *it becomes apparent that* in films (...) and TV series (...) "grammatical correctness" is not always necessary. [R5]

(181) However, *it is a pity that* no space could be found for an extract from Spain since Spain has become a major powerhouse in EAP in the new millennium. [R30]

In the instances above, the reader's possible negative reaction to the filtered statement is either "No, it is not apparent" to Example (180) or "No, it is not a pity" to Example (181). The structural dominance of the two no-interactant IPCs thus makes it possible for the language user to digress the reader's attention to the interpersonal dimension of the clause complex. In this way, the no-interactant IPC indicates to the reader how the statement is to be taken (e.g. as pre-projected facts in the two cases).

The final category is closely linked to *there*-type no-interactant IPCs. As was discussed in Section 6.1.2, this type of IPC primarily functions to convey a construction to present something and to bring it into the reader's awareness, as the following illustrations suggest.

(182) ... *there is a possibility that* the decision to continue with a pregnancy may be made on the basis of them. [E84]

(183) In choosing not to critique examples of research, *there is an implication that* "application" of a philosophical perspective (i.e. figuring out its meaning in practice) is straightforward. [R23]

As has been shown, the four categories of no-interactant IPCs operate to attract the reader's attention to either the coming statement or the IPC itself. The specific syntagmatic feature of no-interactant IPCs enacts the function. One particular point about the variability of attention-drawing no-interactant IPCs is that on many occasions the choice is simply out of rhetorical consideration, such as avoiding repetition or showing the writer's language competence (cf. Thompson, 2003).

3. Consensus Forging

A third type of function performed by no-interactant IPCs is related with the writer's endeavor to forge consensus between her and the reader. On closer observation, the study reveals that the current corpora are rich in such resources. As has been well discussed, in academic discourse, the experienced writer is always aware of the presence of the reader and their shared community membership of the particular discipline (cf. Hyland, 2005a). It stands to reason that the writer is obliged to negotiate common ground and to confirm solidarity within the community. One motivation behind the negotiation is that the reader may not share the writer's knowledge, expectations or norms (Fant, 2005). It should be mentioned that this function is widespread across nearly all types of IPC resources, as was shown in the previous chapter and will be shown in the next section.

As far as no-interactant IPCs are concerned, the writer-reader consensus is created and forged mainly through three types of strategies. First, the writer may resort to general attribution, stressing that the framed points are considered facts in the community and/or are self-explanatory. Consider the following examples.

(184)... *there is a growing consensus that* we should be concerned not only with the way language are (individually) and the way language is (in general) but also with why language is the way it is. [E51]

(185) For one thing, *there is well established evidence*, syntactic and prosodic, *that* the conjunctive element forms a constituent with the following conjunct; so most current analyses across different syntactic frameworks exhibit at least that degree of asymmetry: [XP [and YP]]. [E58]

As is demonstrated in the examples above, by using no-interactant IPCs, the writer refers either to widely-accepted knowledge (as in Example (184)) or taken-for-granted fact (as in Example (185)) that are no longer contested. The writer is seen to stress the fact that her argument is based on knowledge that everyone in the field is familiar with. The no-interactant IPCs work to generalize the source of statement and thus present it as a view which is uncontested or at least widely accepted. By employing *there*-type no-interactant IPCs which typically function to construe already-existing facts in the world, the writer represents herself as simply agreeing with the reader, as recounting a view of the dialogic partner and by people in general. In this way, the no-interactant IPCs facilitate to construct consensus between interactants in the discourse.

Second, certainty-expressing no-interactant IPCs are observed to enhance writer-reader consensus. According to Hyland (2000) and Koutsantoni (2004), expressions of certainty do not allow room for disagreement or negotiation by imposing positions on the reader and controlling his inferences. However, such expressions construed by no-interactant IPCs work towards the acceptance of views by acknowledging readers as knowledgeable in-group colleagues or peers who know well the ideas presented and are capable enough to follow the writer's reasoning and thus make the same inference. Consider the following examples.

(186) And although "semiotics" to some humanities scholars may have the ring of yesteryear's scholarly fashion, *there is no doubt that* semioticians have always shown a theoretical interest in multimodal texts, so that... [R72]

(187) But on the other side, *it is clear that* people do not reason consciously from the linguistic input to explicatures and implicatures. [E37]

As the examples above display, by claiming that a viewpoint is of *no doubt* or *clear* the writer, suggests that it should be taken in this way by both interactants, based on their ability to make the same inferences (Hyland, 1998). Therefore, such expressions are closely related with intersubjectivity management. That they operate to forge in-group consensus is due to the fact that they make it very difficult for the reader to disagree with or oppose the statement. In Hoey's (2000: 33-34) words, the reader who does not find the statement clear may suspect his own judgments rather than the writer's, and might think he himself is missing the obvious. Thus, in using certainty-expressing no-interactant IPCs, the writer achieves community consensus by "obliging" the reader to conceive propositions presented as given and to agree with her.

Third, a notable portion of no-interactant IPCs are found to work on the intersubjectivity plane of discourse, which is characterized by negation or double negation. Consider Example (188) below.

(188) *There would be nothing odd in* considering certain implicatures of an utterance when discussing its truth or falsity, if the truth/falsity assessment were (as in Austin, 1962: 142-45) a matter of global correctness of the speech act with respect to the relevant portion of the world. And *it might not be impossible to* explain why certain alleged implicatures contribute to determining the truth/falsity of complex sentences, in terms of the speech acts to be assessed. [R29]

As the two no-interactant IPCs in Example (188) indicate, this type of IPC works on at least two dimensions with respect to intersubjectivity. On one dimension, the denial *There would be nothing odd...* is dialogic in the sense that it provokes and presents itself as responding to the claim that *There is something odd...* Thus, a prior and alternative position is explicitly engaged with dialogistically. It is the same with the case of *it might not be impossible...* On the other dimension, these no-interactant IPCs which convey disagreement① can be seen as the writer's endeavor to make the reader see her point of view, to invite the reader to jointly criticize previous research or alternative views. In this way, the writer makes it clear that the interactants agree that more research is needed in order to rectify the existing limitations and oversights, which is necessary for the benefit of the whole of the community and the progress of the discipline.

As has been demonstrated, there emerge in the corpora three types of no-interactant IPCs that are often deployed by both the ELBR writer and the ELJE writer for the purpose of augmenting consensus. The variability should be seen, on the one hand, to depend on the audience, the communicative purposes and other aspects of the social context, and on the other, to reflect the ways individuals use language to orient to and to interpret routine communicative situations (Hyland, 2005a: 87-89).

4. Interpersonal Coherence

Similar to the cases of *I*-IPCs and *we*-IPCs (cf. Sections 5.1.4 and 5.2.4), various relations vis-à-vis interpersonal conjunction can be established by no-interactant IPCs. As Thompson (2001: 64;

---

① Traditionally, disagreement is interpreted as disaffiliative and as largely destructive of social solidarity (cf. Heritage, 1984: 269). However, in academic discourse, as the present corpora show, disagreement can be deployed to enhance intersubjectivity.

2005) points out, the writer may choose to construct argumentation either logically or interpersonally. As has been argued by the present study, IPC operates primarily on the interpersonal plane of discourse due to the fact IPC always involves the interactant of a particular communicative event. Under scrutiny, the corpora reveal that three types of interpersonal coherence are commonly carried out by no-interactant IPCs.

The first type is hypothetical-real. Here the hypothetical part construes the objection simultaneously as both a possible opinion and a mistaken one; and the ensuing part expresses the real. On the interpersonal dimension, the reader is prepared more fully for the switch of positions and recapitulates the main issue. In this way, the segment of text is dialogically overtoned because it conveys a sense of the importance of interacting with the reader in a conventionally accepted way (Thompson, 2001). Consider the following examples.

> (189) Although *it might appear natural to* think of head movement as belonging to the narrow syntax, this assumption has been questioned in recent years. [E98]
>
> (190) There are perhaps two further "missing inputs" that might have been included, although *it might be hard to* fit them within the page budget. [R30]

In Example (189), the no-interactant IPC *it might appear natural* makes it possible to bring into surface the voice of the reader who, having read the analysis up to that point, might plausibly be assumed to have formed a hypothesis about the content. The hypothesis is of course to be contradicted. The hypothetical-real works to display the thinking process in which participants in the academic dialogue co-work to decide whether the problem raised by the reader-in-the-text is a real one and then move towards providing the real. Example (190) displays the real-hypothetical type of interpersonal conjunction. In this relation, the no-interactant IPC works in a similar vein to that of hypothetical-real, except that in real-hypothetical the hypothesis is not construed as the view to be contradicted, rather as an afterthought.

Another type is concession-assertion. It is interpersonal and dialogic in that it acknowledges an alternative while simultaneously acting to challenge or confirm it. Again, the proposition is projected as coming from the reader-in-the-text and thus needs to be accepted or conceded before a counter-assertion is made, for the purpose of fostering interpersonality. Consider Example (191) below.

> (191) *We may not want or need to* describe such knowledge in the explicit terms of contemporary cognitive science, or as a property of people's 'minds', but *it is hard to* deny that knowledge is *also* a cognitive notion—besides a social one, as is obviously the case for sociocultural knowledge as shared by an epistemic community. [E90]

In the instance above, two IPC constructions (a *we*-IPC and a no-interactant IPC) are deployed to construe the interpersonal coherence of concession. By the *we*-IPC, the writer expands the discourse space by entertaining alternative opinions of members of the community. The modality of low value (i.e. *may*) suggests this is only one of a number of possible reactions coming from the audience. This alternative, however, is proposed just for it to be conceded. In the ensuing clause complex, the prefacing no-interactant IPC with its simple present tense and emphasizing lexical items, highlights the force of counter-assertion. Seen in this way, the employment of IPC enacts a discourse space on the interpersonal plane, where the negotiation and interaction between interactants are brought into vision.

The corpora also reveal a basis-desirability type of interpersonal conjunction, which is typical of ELBR texts but rare in ELJE essays. In this type of relation, a plausible desirability (usually mildly directing to the shortcomings of the academic product) is put forward as one alternative the reasonable reader would hold. As Example (192) below shows, the desirability is typically in modalized past in present. What is of note is that the desirability is reasonable because it derives from certain facts explicitly stated in the book. The facts serve as the basis of the desirability.

> (192) All the newspapers are treated as a single data source and, although *one could hypothesize for example*, *that* the tabloids would be more favourable to Diana than the broadsheets, no classification arises from an analysis based on common linguistic or ideological features. *It would have been interesting to* know whether the treatment of what Diana said defines loyalties or affinities other than the traditional ones, such as those along party lines. [R54]

In Example (192), the first sentence serves as the basis for the desirability that is marked by the no-interactant IPC *it would have been interesting to...* In the basis part, the writer familiarizes the reader with the fact that *no classification arises...* On reading this segment of text, the reader gets prepared for the subsequent suggestions. He is expected to think about the demerit. In the expectation part, the no-interactant IPC makes it natural to bring to the center of the stage the desired improvement. Thus, the reader is invited once again to engage actively in the reasoning and thinking process the writer goes through as the text unfolds. It should also be mentioned that in the basis part, the no-interactant IPC *one could hypothesize* creates a concession-assertion type of interpersonal conjunction. It can be argued that the IPC resources co-work to form an IPC syndrome for the purpose of intersubjectivity management.

To sum up, the study has concentrated on the corpus-based analysis of no-interactant IPCs in terms of their discursive behavior.

The analysis confirms the statement that the behavior of no-interactant IPCs is genre-specific and context-sensitive.

6.2 Non-interactant IPCs

This section examines a fourth type of IPC, in which the Projector construes a third party rather than the interactant. However, it is different from experiential projections because it does simultaneously invoke the interactant's evaluation of or reaction to the framed proposition. After justifying this type of IPC, the study will describe its discursive features, in a similar vein to the previous section.

6.2.1 Justification of Non-interactant IPCs

When using non-interactant IPCs, the writer introduces a proposition by signaling that it comes from another source. However, it is the writer's view that is represented through another voice, i.e. the writer engages herself in a transparent pretense. The typical instance of non-interactant IPCs is *as xxx admits/points out* as in the following example.

(193) In particular, *as Carston admits*, the semantics of the apparent counterparts in natural language of logical operators need no longer be identical to the semantics of those operators. [R29]

As the example above demonstrates, non-interactant IPCs concern attribution, or evidentiality, i.e. the source of information. From the intersubjective vantage point, attribution defines the reliability of the proposition the writer presents and its potential impact on the reader (Hyland, 2005b: 178). However, non-interactant IPCs are a special type of attribution, i.e. delegated averral①, or evidential DIST (cf. ① on p. 137) clause in Vandelanotte's (2004) interpretation. It should be noted that this type of interpersonal projection (cf. Thompson, 2005) is different from experiential projection as is shown in Example (194) below.

> (194) Grudgingly, *Manning admitted that* the others' guess had not been too bad a one. (Halliday & Matthiessen, 2004: 607)

While Example (193) invokes the writer's point of view vis-à-vis the projected proposition, Example (194) does not enact the interactant's admission because Manning's admission is construed as part of the experiential representation (Halliday & Matthiessen, 2004: 607). That is, Example (194) does not operate on the interpersonal dimension. Nuyts (2001) concurs with Thompson (2005) in interpreting Example (194) as descriptive while Example (193) performative. Structurally speaking, non-interactant IPCs are subordinate and detached as Example (193) shows whereas the projected clause is structurally indistinguishable from a clause that is averred by the writer (Thompson, 2005). It is in this sense that such projections are included in the category of IPC.

It should be borne in mind that there is genre variation in terms of non-interactant IPC realizations (Halliday & Matthiessen, 2004: 605). Both Vandelanotte (2004) and Thompson (2005) notice that news reports favor non-interactant IPC formulations illustrated in Example (195) below.

---

① "Delegated averral", according to Thompson (2005: 782), is used by Thetela (1997). However, a check of the original work shows that Thetela (1997) does not use the term.

(195) Competitive sport should be available to children of all ages, *Tony Blair said yesterday*. (Thompson, 2005: 784)

According to Vandelanotte (2004) and Thompson (2005), mentioning the source of the information is of subsidiary importance, but it is part of the convention of a news report. In this view, such evidential clauses serve merely to indicate that the information is not mysteriously part of the general knowledge of the journalist, but rather originates in someone else's discourse. Similarly, Rezzano (2004) and Neff *et al.* (2004) identify in research articles a special type of authorial attribution as is shown in Example (196) below.

(196) *This study reveals that* the majority of children under 6 years of age have a naïve conception of speed. (Rezzano, 2004: 111)

They argue that instances like Example (196) signal authorial voice since the author transfers the attribution of the agency to "abstract rhetors" (Neff *et al.*, 2004: 146). Instead of presenting themselves as the Projector, the authors choose their products or research to stand for their authorial voices. In this way, the scientific facts are allowed to speak for themselves. However, this type of projection is found rare in ELBR due to the parasitic nature of the genre. As was discussed in the preceding chapter, the reviewer is usually expected to interpret and comment on others' academic products rather than to present her own work. Therefore, it is not the norm for the reviewer to employ "abstract rhetors" to stand for her own research.

It stands to reason that these non-interactant IPCs, similar to those in the present study, turn out not to be a straightforward speaker's claim. In essence, they are used as evidential head to filter a given proposition, facilitating the language user to regulate the interaction by providing evidential qualification (Nuyts, 2001: 386). The choice of non-interactant IPCs may then be seen as a deliberate decision on the part of the writer. By weaving her voice into that of the author or an expert, the writer, as Samson (2004: 200) suggests, projects herself in the texts. In this manner, the writer shows her authorial presence which plays an important role in securing the correct interpretation of the text. Meanwhile, it can be seen as the writer's endeavor to establish her academic prestige, in the attempt to construct a successful relationship with her interlocutors by taking into consideration their expectations.

6. 2. 2 Metafunctional Features of Non-interactant IPCs

Compared with no-interactant IPCs, non-interactant IPCs are much smaller in number. The current corpus of ELBR witnesses only 125 non-interactant IPCs, displaying the lowest scores within all IPC resources. The fact indicates that the type of IPC is not frequently deployed by the reviewer. However, these IPC devices do deserve a scrutinizing investigation because of their special syntactic and semantic characteristics and their particular contribution to ELBR as a genre. In a similar vein to the analysis of other types of IPC, the non-interactant IPC will be examined.

Let us begin by examining the Projector types in non-interactant IPCs. A data analysis shows that there are mainly two types of Projectors: authors and experts. Table 6. 5 summarizes and categorizes the types of Projectors.

Table 6.5 Non-interactant IPCs in ELBR by Projector Type

Projector type	Number of occurrences	Frequency
author	103	82.4%
expert	10	8%
others	12	9.6%
Total	125	100%

As Table 6.5 demonstrates, there are 103 instances (82.4% of the total) of non-interactant IPCs construing the author as the Projector, in contrast to 10 non-interactant IPCs (8% of the total) with an expert (e.g. experts or established figures well recognized in the community) as the Projector. The corpus also reveals that 10% of all tokens choose the academic product or part of the product (e.g. the articles, the book, the title) as the Projector. The three types are respectively illustrated by the examples below, namely, the author type as in Example (197), the expert type as in Example (198), and the product type as in Example (199).

(197) *As Wu notes in her conclusion*, she has brought these three areas together in a work which "provides a window into how Mandarin speakers construct their epistemic and affective stances" (p. 239). [R17]

(198) But *as Knot et al. (2001: 197) have noted*, "at the discourse level, the dividing line between cognitive linguistic approaches and traditional approaches seems less clear-cut than at the sentence level"... [R12]

(199) Moreover, *as the book tries to demonstrate*, a strict classification of linguistic phenomena in terms of formal categories is not adequate as the analyses are based on semantic, syntactic and pragmatic factors which are not amenable to representation in rigid categories or constructions. [R46]

As the examples above demonstrate, in ELBR, non-interactant

IPCs enable the writer to select an explicit sign of how she wishes to present the cited information (i. e. by resorting to the author type, the expert type or the product type).

The predominance of author-type non-interactant IPCs (82.4% of the total) indicates the writer's emphasis on the fusion between her voice and that of the author (de Oliveira & Pagano, 2006). In using such non-interactant IPCs, the review writer takes possession of the original discourse and presents it in such a way as if it were her own. This obvious prominence indicates that in ELBR it seems the norm that in using non-interactant IPCs the writer presents the cited author and places him in subject position.

A consideration on the process preference in these non-interactant IPCs also needs to be made. Verbal processes stand out as the most frequently preferred process (93.4% of the total). What is notable of these verbal processes is that overwhelmingly predominant are "positive" and "factive" verbs (Thompson & Ye, 1991) (96% of the total verbal processes). According to Thompson & Ye's (1991) framework, in using positive projecting verbs (e. g. *point out* and *note*) and factive projecting verbs (e. g. *acknowledge*, *notice* and *show*), the writer portrays the author as presenting the information/ opinion as true/correct. Consider the following examples.

(200) *As the author herself points out several times in the book*, learner autonomy can be achieved only when learners are fully trained in terms of what to look for in concordances and how to interpret the patterns found in them. [R60]

(201) Indeed, *as the author acknowledges*, discourse strategies are just one out of many parameters of gender enactment in contemporary workplaces. [R69]

As is illustrated by the examples above, these non-interactant IPCs facilitate the writer to foreground the ensuing statement as accepted fact (as in Example (200)) or established theories (as in Example (201) above). In this way, the writer on the one hand weaves her own voice into that of the author so that writer-author alignment is achieved. On the other hand, the writer fosters her in-group status by stating that she is well aware of the disciplinary knowledge and of the book under review. This also implies that when resorting to non-interactant IPCs, the review writer is inclined to influence the reader's response to the claim filtered by the evidential head in a positive way. In most cases, such non-interactant IPC tokens signal to the reader what should be considered significant.

A quick count of the verbs indicates that the ELBR writer prefers a limited number of lexical items (15 verbs in total). The analysis reveals that most of these verbs occur more than once. In particular, *point out* occurs 29 times, standing out from the other lexical items. It is also observed that *note* (n = 14) and *show* (n = 8) have relatively higher frequencies than the rest. The following example represents those non-interactant IPCs in which *point out* occurs.

(202) One of the main findings presented in chapter three, which, as the author points out, corroborates and extends to other kinds of reference the work of Fox (1987) on person reference ... [R78]

The high frequency of *point out* may reflect a common purpose of the review genre, in light of Hemais's (2001) explanation for the functions of such verbs in the discourse. According to her, such positive verbs are signs of the writer's sense of need to make the filtered claim strongly. The observation confirms the ELBR writer's preference for positive and factive projecting verbal processes in constructing non-interactant IPCs.

Therefore, it stands to reason that non-interactant IPCs are often deployed deliberately and consciously by the reviewer to provide the reader with sufficient cues to assist desired comprehension. It can be argued that in such cases the writer tends to draw on her knowledge of the discipline and its preferred discoursal patterns to create text, and more importantly, to facilitate knowledge transfer by speaking as an expert in the particular way, i. e. by weaving her voice into that of the author.

Considerations should also be given to the choice of tense in these processes. In ELBR, non-interactant IPCs in simple present tense account for a percentage as high as 97% of the total. A closer observation shows that all author-type non-interactant IPCs are in simple present tense whereas the instances in past in present, though small in number (7 items in total), are all of the expert type.

The finding is in line with the conspicuous prominence of the positive and factive verbal processes in the corpus. As has been noted, these verbal processes tend to construe the projected propositions as true information and/or correct opinion. In a very similar vein, through the frequent selection of the present tense for the projecting verbs, the ELBR writer seems to remove the represented discourse from a time perspective, conceding it the status of facts and indisputable truths (de Oliveira & Pagano, 2006). In this way, the writer seeks to control how the reader responds to a particular claim. The co-opting of verbal processes and present tense facilitates the ELBR writer to highlight her individual claims, while simultaneously fitting them into the framework of disciplinary knowledge and practice.

In terms of the Thematic position, non-interactant IPCs appear to be more complex than the other types of IPC. Generally speaking, there are two points worthy of notice. To begin with, typically, structural detachment is established between the non-interactant IPC and the projected discourse, as is exhibited in Examples (203), (204) and (205) below.

(203)... modularity can, *as they say*, 'be the endpoint of domain-general mechanisms operating on material drawn from different input domains' (p. 80). [R41]

(204) *As the author admits himself*, this arrangement is 'a bit of a distortion, since children don't first learn sound, then words, then sentences' (p.5). [R44]

(205) However, *as Gavioli shows*, this problem can be addressed, at least to some extent, ... [R60]

As is shown, in Example (203), the non-interactant IPC is assigned to the Rhematic position. In Example (204), the non-interactant IPC is assigned to the very initial slot of the Theme whereas the non-interactant IPC in Example (205) is assigned to the Thematic but non-initial position. It should be noted that, despite the position variation, the detachment of non-interactant IPCs is in essence the writer's rearrangement of the grammar of ideational projection for the purpose of minimizing discursive distance between herself and the reader (Thompson, 2004: 162; Martin *et al.*, 1997).

Second, the Thematic properties of non-interactant IPCs in ELBR show their differences with respect to frequency. Table 6.6 represents the differences.

Table 6.6 Non-interactant IPCs in ELBR by Theme-Rheme Distribution

Type	Rhematic	Thematic and Initial	Thematic and Non-initial
Frequency	48%	29%	23%

As Table 6.6 exhibits, the ELBR writer shows a relatively strong preference for Rhematic non-interactant IPCs, as is represented in Example (203) above. With respect to Thematic and initial position and Thematic and non-initial position, non-interactant IPCs are found not to exhibit sharp discrepancies.

The observation is interest-provoking in that the ELBR writer seems to be impelled by the tension between putting emphasis on the cited author and on what she actually claims. Within the micro IPC construction, the author receives emphasis by being assigned to the subject status. Within the macro sentence arrangement, the proposition tends to be stressed. In this way, the writer attempts to reach a balance. A probable motivation behind is the tension between the communicative purposes of ELBR as a genre, i. e. informing and evaluating. Seen from the alternative perspective, the peculiar feature of non-interactant IPCs makes it possible for the writer to construct her text in a multifunctional way.

6. 2. 3 A Cross-Genre Analysis of Non-interactant IPCs

A preliminary examination of the data reveals that non-interactant IPCs in ELBR and ELJE are of exactly the same number of occurrences (125 instances in each corpus). The low frequency of non-interactant IPCs in both genres indicates that both the review writer and the editorial writer in the discipline are cautious about using non-interactant IPCs. One possible explanation for the finding is that talking to the disciplinary community members should be accomplished in various ways, drawing on different criteria of appropriacy, and motivated by different purposes. Another possibility is that, compared with other types of IPC resources, the non-interactant IPC is more constrained by its syntactic structure.

On scrutinizing observation, the study finds that non-interactant IPCs do behave differently across ELBR and ELJE, despite the fact that both genres see the exactly same number. The difference mainly reflects in three aspects, namely, Projector types, process preference, and the Thematic position. To begin with, as Table 6.7 displays, a notable discrepancy is observed between the two genres with respect to the portion and distribution of Projector realizations.

Table 6.7   Cross-Genre Comparison of Non-interactant IPCs by Projector Type

Genre type	Author		Expert		Others	
	Number	Frequency	Number	Frequency	Number	Frequency
ELBR	103	82.4%	10	8%	12	9.6%
ELJE	85	68%	31	24.8%	9	7.2%

As can be seen in Table 6.7, compared with ELBR, ELJE shows a lower frequency of author-type Projectors and a much higher frequency of expert-type ones. To be specific, while author-type Projectors in ELJE are 14.4% fewer than those in ELBR, expert-type ones in ELJE are triple as many as those in ELBR. The findings indicate a tendency of the ELJE writer to invest much more than her ELBR counterpart in incorporating expert voices into her discourse. A second indication is that in both genres author-type Projectors are predominant (82.4% of the total in ELBR and 68% of the total in ELJE).

The similarity and discrepancy can be accounted for from the following aspects. First, in both genres, due to their parasitic nature, the review and the editorial have to be developed by basing on the author's product. For the review writer, it is the author of the book under review that she sheds assessment on. For the editorial writer, it is the contributions to that particular volume that she aims to promote. Therefore, it stands to reason that in both ELBR and ELJE, the author visibility is of a high degree.

Second, the striking percentage increase of expert-type Projectors in ELJE may attribute to the fact that the editorial writer is anticipated to fulfill the promotional purposes assigned to the genre. By higher investment in citing established figures, the editorial writer displays her strong desire to control the thoughts, inferences, and actions of the reader, and simultaneously demands his agreement and sharing of her view. The delegated averral underscores what the writer anticipates the reader to believe and thus guides the reader towards also evaluating them positively. In this way, by emphasizing certainty in the author's claims and by presenting them as shared by the personage and the writer herself, the writer endeavors to channel the reader towards accepting the author's claims because they are shared by the well-known figures in the disciplinary community, i. e. both the editorial writer and the quoted expert.

Seen in this way, it can be concluded that expert-type non-interactant IPCs impose evaluations on the reader and facilitate the writer to demonstrate her power in the discourse. They achieve the effect by creating a sense of solidarity between the writer, the cited expert as well as the common reader. By contrast, the ELBR writer is expected to convey and justify her balanced comment on the academic product. She is thus not impelled by promotional purposes as strongly as the ELJE writer is, since her task is to evaluate but promote. Therefore, she appears to be less enthusiastic about using expert-type non-interactant IPCs. Rather, she is inclined to deliver a positive comment only when necessary, thus to forge a fair judge image for herself.

In terms of processes employed, both corpora witness an overwhelming predominance of verbal processes (93.4% of the total in ELBR and 91% of the total in ELJE). Nevertheless, a careful scrutiny shows a couple of interesting discrepancies across the genres. First, the corpus of ELJE does not contain any instance of non-interactant IPC in mental processes whereas that of ELBR does, though low in percentage (6.7% of the total). Second, in terms of verbal processes, the ELJE writer is found to avoid *admit*-type factive verbs (e. g. *admit, acknowledge, concede*) which indicate "accept and agree unwillingly that something is true or that someone else is right" (Thompson, 2001). By contrast, her ELBR counterpart employs these verbs on 17 occasions (13.4% of the total verbal processes). Consider the following examples.

(206) The damaged text: tasi: run... ki: lifa cannot mean, *as Chruszczewski thinks*, 'may these runes live long', since lifa is either the infinitive or 3rd person plural present indicative. [R76]

(207) Their approach is quantitative and their ultimate aim is to reveal children's unfolding sense of self. However, *as they admit*, "it is possible that our way of operationalizing self complexity and multiple selves was too crude". [R47]

The two examples above extracted from the corpus of ELBR exhibit how the reviewer employs non-interactant IPCs to build her argument for the author's opinion as in Example (206) or to display her alternative views as in Example (207). In the examples, the writer resorts to tentative or unfavorable expressions and consequently by employing *think* and *admit* respectively.

Considering the low frequency of non-interactant IPCs, these differences are noteworthy. A possible explanation for the ELJE writer's avoidance of mental processes and *admit*-type verbal processes could be linked to the preferred way in which the writer of different discourse roles views and constructs her argumentation. In ELJE, due to its promotional nature, the opinion of the author is definitely highlighted and favorably argued. The writer is expected, if possible, to avoid tentativeness (as mental verbs like *think* and *assume* connote) and unfavorable overtone (as *admit*-type verbs carry). The main reason is that any negative elements would have created conflicts for the advertising or promotional aspects of the genre (Bhatia, 2004: 135).

Thus, the absence of the two types of verbs is in fact the ELJE writer's deliberate choice. The finding confirms the idea that the resources the writer selects necessarily connect to particular audiences and social purposes, and that to achieve these purposes with these audiences at least partly depends on analyzing the reader and engaging with him in appropriate ways. Seen in this way, various categories of IPC enable the writer to address an audience with tactic and to exhibit a professional interpersonal competence which influences the effectiveness of the argument (Hyland, 1998b).

The data observation also shows that in terms of the Thematic position, non-interactant IPCs behave differently across the two genres. As was noted previously, the ELBR writer is inclined to use these devices in Rhematic or Thematic-but-noninitial positions. By contrast, the ELJE writer is found to use non-interactant IPCs in the very initial position of the sentence. Figure 6.4 exhibits the noticeable differences.

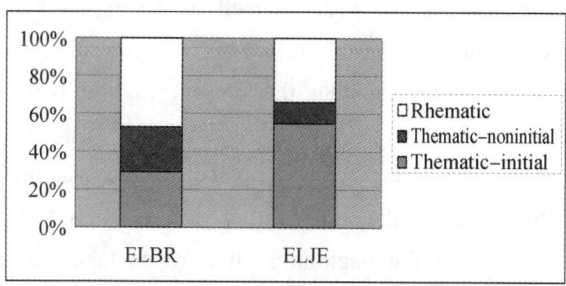

Figure 6.4   **Cross-Genre Comparison of Non-interactant IPCs by Theme-Rheme Distribution**

As is shown in Figure 6.4, the ELBR writer favors inserting non-interactant IPCs within the sentence whereas her ELJE counterpart tends to assign them to the initial status. The figure thus suggests that in employing non-interactant ICPs, the editorial writer chooses to construe it as the starting point of the information, which serves as the evidential head to frame and filter all the rest of the information within the text fragment. In ELBR, the prominence of non-initial non-interactant IPCs implies that the ELBR writer does not often give priority to these devices that signal "proposed claims" (Hunston, 1993).

A probable explanation for the discrepancy is associated with genre identity. As has been argued, the prime purpose of reviewing is to evaluate the academic product and to transfer knowledge within the disciplinary community. While attending to the dimension of writer-reader interaction and alignment, the writer also keeps well in mind information and knowledge transfer, and text organization. As a result, she may choose to deploy non-interactant IPCs with more casualness by inserting them in the middle of the sentence where she considers necessary and appropriate. In ELJE, by contrast, the promotional nature of the genre impels the writer to stress to the reader the credibility and importance of the author's proposition by foregrounding the like-mindedness of the writer herself as an expert and the cited expert or the author.

What is noteworthy is that the present finding partly confirms Myers's (1989: N3) viewpoint about attribution. Myers states that the effect of attribution varies with its place in the statement. When inserted in the middle of the statement, it is more likely to be a hedge, but when it comes at the beginning, it may be taken as a point of information, and not weaken the statement. In a similar vein, the present study argues that as a special kind of attribution, when initially positioned, delegated averral functions to put special emphasis upon the writer-author or writer-expert alignment so that the reader actually notices the saliency. The finding also matches the statement by Bhatia (1997) who argues that introductory texts (in the present case, journal editorials) often have a very distinct and recognizable promotional flavor, which often reminds one of "celebrity endorsements" in advertisements.

A final cross-genre comparison concerning non-interactant IPCs is linked with their distribution vis-à-vis the GSP elements of either genre. Figures 6.5 and 6.5 represent their allocation in the GSP elements of ELBR and ELJE respectively.

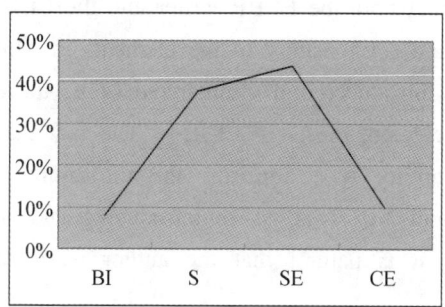

Figure 6.5 **Generic Structural Distribution of Non-interactant IPCs in ELBR**

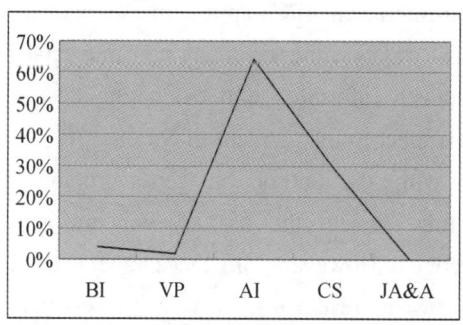

Figure 6.6 **Generic Structural Distribution of Non-interactant IPCs in ELJE**

In ELBR, as is shown in Figure 6.5, non-interactant IPCs are found to cluster in the elements of S and SE, amounting to 82% of all tokens (39% of the total and 43% of the total respectively). The rest are seen to disperse in the elements of BI and CE (8% of the total and 10% of the total respectively). As far as ELJE is concerned, the majority of non-interactant IPCs appear in the elements of AI (64% of the total), with the element of CS ranking the second (29% of the total). Much lower frequency of occurrences is found in the elements of BI and VP (5% of the total and 2% of the total respectively), while no non-interactant IPC tokens are identified in the element of JA&A.

It appears that both the ELBR writer and the ELJE writer tend to use non-interactant IPCs mainly in the elements in which the author's propositions are introduced and summarized (i.e. the element of S in ELBR and the element of AI in ELJE). The fact that most of these tokens are of author type confirms the informing function of the elements of S and AI. That is, in introducing and summarizing the author's views, it is natural that the author is of relatively higher visibility.

Two more noticeable points deserve elaboration as well. First, in ELBR, few non-interactant IPCs appear in the element of CE while in ELJE the element of CS witnesses many non-interactant IPCs. It seems that tension between informing and evaluating best accounts for the findings. With respect to the element of S in ELBR, the writer exhibits her agreement with the author on certain point when she feels necessary. In this element the primary concern is to interpret and transfer knowledge. However, in the element of CE, the prime function is to show the reader a final overall assessment of the author's work. It is conceivable that the writer keeps distance from the author by appearing to be just and fair. In ELJE, such tension does not exist at all (cf. Bhatia, 2004). In the element of CS, as in the element of AI, the writer's purpose is to promote the contributions under the disguise of information presenting and summarizing. Therefore, it is understandable for the editorial writer to allude to non-interactant IPCs to give the reader a final impression on the credibility and significance of the author's contribution.

Second, within ELJE, no non-interactant IPCs are found in JA&A. A reasonable explanation for the absence is connected to the genre convention. It seems, as the previous chapter shows, the element of JA&A favors *we*-IPCs most. Seen in this way, the allocation of IPC helps us to understand disciplinary communities and the different ways that they construct knowledge.

6. 2. 4 Non-interactant IPCs as Intersubjectivity Boosters

Non-interactant IPCs are not of relative high percentage in terms of occurrence frequency, as the corpora witness. However, both the review writer and the editorial writer do use them for a variety of purposes where necessary, such as avoiding presuming reference. The present study identifies primarily four discourse functions non-interactant IPCs perform with respect to intersubjectivity enhancement.

1. Rapport Managing

One noteworthy function of non-interactant IPCs revealed in the current corpora is to facilitate the writer to negotiate affiliation and establish rapport with the reader, in particular, the author of the book under review (in ELBR). By giving a particular author high author visibility through evidential non-interactant IPCs, the writer deliberately and strategically achieves establishing rapport with the reader, constructing some informality and/or familiarity.

The writer's choice may be due to at least two considerations. The first is to avoid appearing categorical or biased in her line of argumentation. The second is to resolve inherent tensions of the genre. These inherent tensions exist, for example, around the status of the reviewer as a relative expert in the field. From the point of view of the author, there is a tension to be resolved in terms of the extent to which he feels accommodated in the review, as part of the relevant discourse community. There is also the fact that the writer has to balance judgment and assessment of the author's contribution. Consequently, the writer may resort to non-interactant IPCs for resolving these tensions. Consider the following examples.

(208) *As the author argues and clearly demonstrates*, understanding what a particular compliment is being used to accomplish requires its analysis within its local sequential context. [R78]

(209) Indeed, *as the author acknowledges*, discourse strategies are just one out of many parameters of gender enactment in contemporary workplaces. [R69]

As the examples above show, the writer attempts to resolve inherent tensions by encouraging a rapport of positive anticipation through deliberate selection of non-interactant IPCs. In such cases, the writer constructs a stance which she assigns to the author, but which simultaneously expresses her own position. In this way, the reviewer shows her alignment with the author where necessary by demonstrating sameness. In addition, these positive praising strategies help to create closeness, intimacy, and rapport between the writer and the targeted audience. Structurally speaking, by giving the author the subject status in the Theme instead of non-integral within parentheses, the writer assigns high visibility to the author, and thus caters to the heteroglossic nature of academic genre (Bakhtin, 1986). On the other hand, the common reader is strongly encouraged to align with the speaker's explicit positive evaluation. Consequently, a positive solidarity of a shared sense of knowledge is created between the reviewer, the author and the common reader. In this sense, it stands to reason that these non-interactant IPCs function not only to make interpersonal connections with the audience, but sometimes overtly and sometimes subtly and implicitly to align the audience with the writer's position.

2. Acceptance Soliciting

A second function commonly found attached to non-interactant IPCs is to solicit the reader's acceptance of the writer's claims, and thus to reach consensus. Typically, the language user achieves this by referencing respected and authoritative people in the discipline. In this way, academic justification is provided so as to persuade the reader of the goodness of the writer's claims. In fact, in employing such IPC devices, the writer projects a heavier sense of assertion to reiterate her position, and to direct the reader to her position. By claiming that her view is in line with the already accepted research findings, the writer on the one hand shows her expertise and thus expresses confidence in the validity of her finding by evaluating it as consistent. On the other hand, the room for negotiation of claims is deliberately limited by imposing attitudes, interpretations, and assessments of truth-value, and by predisposing the reader towards certain references. Consider the following examples.

(210) More importantly, *as post-process movement theorists argue*, it is essential for an individual teacher to consider the social and political contexts where writing takes place. [R64]

(211) Most obviously, *as writers like Schütze (1996) have argued*, there are questions about the reliability of some of the data that is used in current

research. [E56]

In both examples above, the writers make endeavor to solicit their readers' acceptance of their claims by alluding to shared knowledge and understandings within the community. In this manner, the non-interactant IPCs *as post-process movement theorists argue* in Example (210) and *as writers like Schütze (1996) have argued* in Example (211) contribute to defining the writer's epistemic and attitudinal stance towards particular propositions and engaging the reader in the construction of claims. In Example (210), the reviewer crafts agreement and acceptance by appealing to well-established theories. In Example (211), the editorial writer demonstrates connections between her claim and confirmed information. The instances indicate that the deployment of non-interactant IPCs often involves conforming to the shared norms, expectations or knowledge of the disciplinary world. This is normally done by indicating endorsement of sources which are highly respected in the field and carry the status of objective facts. At the same time, the writer emphasizes her own status as a member of the scientific community by showing full awareness of these sources and by showing her relevance to the contributions in the particular volume (as in Example (211) above) or the academic product under discussion (as in Example (210) above).

3. Feedback on Ongoing Interaction

Another fairly important function of non-interactant IPCs is to intertexually respond to the original work. The writer has to elaborate certain context for the reader through citation since the reader cannot be assumed to possess the same interpretative knowledge. In fact, this may be more obvious in ELBR and ELJE than other academic genres since both are parasitic to the original work. That is, whether in reviewing or editorial writing, the academic "conversation" is centering on others' research products. The writer's expressing ideas or delivering assessment can not do without her referring constantly to the work under review or recommendation. The writer may render views which have been thought through well before by herself and/or by others, and which have been gradually built up or prepared for the reader in the course of the text. She may paraphrase the original wording of a source, reformulate the original information, or just reinforce the message. These can be achieved, of course, through citation in the typical way.

However, in using non-interactant IPCs to refer to attributed contribution, the function is multi-layered. Besides responding to previous statements, from the intersubjective perspective, the writer employs these delegated averrals to signal her awareness of the reader's attendance. By resorting to such IPC resources, the writer reminds the reader of the forum both the writer and the reader engage in. In the forum, the writer exchanges her viewpoints with the imagined reader constantly. As Hyland (2005a: 117) argues, this suggests an appropriate disciplinary orientation. In addition, these non-interactant IPCs foreground the aspects of the original work which are of particular interest to the writer and thus indirectly suggest that much attention be paid. Meanwhile, by explicitly weaving her view into the author's, the writer reminds the reader, where she feels necessary, of the ongoing academic interaction. The following examples are chosen to illustrate how feedback on interaction is done tactically through non-interactant IPCs.

(212) *As the author herself points out several times in the book*, learner autonomy can be achieved only when learners are fully trained in terms of what to look for in concordances and how to interpret the patterns found

in them. [R60]

(213) However, *as the papers in this special issue show*, prosody can also contribute to the identification of utterance meaning. [E73]

(214) And, unless some of the words used are empty, the soldier's view (*as expressed here by Collins*) extends beyond some simple, cold and calculating realpolitik. [E85]

As the examples above show, non-interactant IPCs serving feedback are of relatively flexible syntactic position. They may appear in the very initial position of the sentence as in Example (212), after a textual conjunction as in Example (213), or even in parentheses as in Example (214). In these cases, as Theleta (1997) writes, the writer interacts with the community by reporting or interpreting the results of the author's investigation.

Simultaneously, the writer engages the reader in the dialogue for the negotiation of the perspective she is in line with. For instance, in Example (212), the reviewer strongly advocates the viewpoint presented in the projected clause by highlighting her notice of the author's repeating the point and her agreement with the author on the point. Similarly, Example (213) demonstrates the importance assigned to the contributors and thus appeals to audience approval and a positive judgment or appreciation of the authors' contributions. Equally important, the non-interactant IPC serves as a summarizing feedback of the contributions to the current volume and impresses the reader with the particular significance of the research articles recommended. In Example (214), the non-interactant IPC in parentheses adds an informal overtone to the text while simultaneously showing the close interconnection of the writer's position with that of the particular author.

4. Interpersonal Coherence

The current corpora witness several types of interpersonal

coherence constructed by non-interactant IPCs. It must be noted that different types of IPC may facilitate the same or similar interpersonal conjunction. It is rare the case that a certain type of interpersonal coherence is constructed only through one category of IPC. The cases examined are merely representative of how IPC operates to regulate participation, control joint attention, disciplinary norms, and consequently augment intersubjectivity.

So far as non-interactant IPCs are concerned, the present study identifies three relations construed with respect to the interpersonal dimension of language use, namely, basis-assessment, assessment-basis and assertion-denial. They will be illustrated in the subsequent instances respectively.

(215) As Foucault (1984) has said, criticism 'consists of analyzing and reflecting upon limits' (p. 45); and in this spirit, Blommaert provides a useful analysis and reflection upon the limits of the field to date. [R55]

(216) In fact, even if the link is not made explicit in the literature, subjectivity is the underside of consciousness, because, as Searle (1997: 120) writes, "consciousness has a first-person or subjective ontology." [R12]

(217) This is a tall order for families, and yet across the world's societies, rarely do family members reflect upon and strategize about how to raise a moral, sentient, and knowledgeable child beyond selection of and reliance upon children's schools, religious organizations, and other institutions outside the family. Yet, as the articles collected in this volume indicate, morality is embedded in and is an outcome of everyday family practices. [E83]

Example (215) demonstrates how interpersonal basis-assessment is enacted with the use of non-interactant IPCs. Of the two segments of text separated by the semicolon, the former establishes the basis for the assessment conducted in the latter. To establish the basis, the writer resorts to the non-interactant IPC by quoting Foucault, one of the most famous thinkers. The IPC investment shows the writer's desire to persuade and to give positive credit to the author under review. Therefore, it stands to reason that the writer writes to persuade and intentionally shape her choice of what to cite (White, 2004: 108). By overtly showing her being in line with Foucault, the writer foreshadows the significance of Blommaert's research and her positive assessment vis-à-vis the author's contribution. In this way, the interpersonal conjunction is signaled and enhanced.

In Example (216), the writer's claim is immediately followed and supported by the delegated averral *as Searle (1997: 120) writes*, which functions to provide the basis for the preceding statement. As in many other IPC cases, it is still acceptable and reasonable if the IPC was removed: *Searle (1997: 120) writes*. However, the interpersonal implication would be wiped out. In fact, as has been constantly argued in the study, it is the writer's deliberate investment of IPC that helps to strengthen the interpersonal relations she intends to achieve.

Example (217) demonstrates how IPC is deployed by the language user to control dialogic space through affirming contrastive ideas before disclaiming them. Again the choice of non-interactant IPCs creates an interpersonal space in which the writer negotiates with the reader with respect to the perspective she invites him to take in judging the contrastive view. By aligning herself with the contributors via non-interactant IPCs, the writer stresses the significant contribution of the current volume to the discipline. Obviously, the articles taken as a whole are invariably a response to previous statements and are themselves available for further statements by others. Thus, knowledge is constructed with peers in academic dialogue in which perennial problems are recycled through personal engagement.

Seen in this way, non-interactant IPCs, together with other types of IPC, are strategic investment of the language user for the purpose of interpersonal negotiation.

6.3 Summary

This chapter conducts a detailed analysis of two types of IPCs, i.e. no-interactant IPCs and non-interactant IPCs. The analysis procedure undertaken in the previous chapter is applied in this one. The corpus-based investigation reveals that the discursive behaviors of both types of IPC are genre-sensitive and oriented by the supposed purposes of particular text types.

It is found that the use of no-interactant IPCs displays the greatest intra-genre variability of all IPC devices examined, suggesting that this may be an area where experienced users of the genre may be permitted a relatively higher degree of freedom to manipulate discoursal conventions.

In both genres, no-interactant IPCs strikingly outnumber other types of IPC. This finding indicates that both ELBR and ELJE writers are strongly inclined to resort to no-interactant IPCs to make their appeals more visible to their intended audiences. This finding confirms the statement held by Kress (1994) and Hyland & Tse (2005) and many others that academic writing is, or appears to be impersonal. The finding also suggests that, as was hinted at in the previous chapter, the choices of IPC are a deliberate and conscious decision on the part of the proficient writer. While the various types of IPC allow the writer to vary her expression of intended purposes and to select the most appropriate ways to conduct interaction with the audience, they should be taken as important devices with which the writer manages to mix private intentions with the socially defined purpose of securing ratification of her arguments (Bhatia, 2004).

The cross-genre comparative study shows that no-interactant IPCs are more frequently employed in ELJE. The finding substantiates the suggestion that academic discourse needs to be regarded as reflecting different social practices of disciplinary communities in constructing knowledge (Hyland, 2000; Simons, 2006). The results emphasize the point that social relationships within discourse communities constrain, though do not determine, the writer's linguistic choices.

Finally, in ELBR, the high intensity of IPC around the GSP elements which serve the function of evaluation confirms the argument that IPC is used to augment intersubjectivity when the interpersonal stake is high. In reviewing, when the writer delivers comments, either positive or negative, she consciously chooses IPC to align the reader, to rationalize her views and positions. In ELJE, the writer does not need to attend to such tensions. Instead, the generic anticipation allows her to infuse her positive evaluation into the introduction of new knowledge. Consequently, the resources are seen to spread all over the GSP elements, with a lightly higher percentage of occurrences in the closing summary part, out of the consideration of impressing the reader a final positive impression of the academic product advocated and promoted.

Chapter 7

Conclusion

This chapter is intended as a summing-up of the previous chapters which have examined the phenomenon of IPC as an intersubjectivity boosting device from a variety of perspectives. Within the theoretical framework of SFL, inspired by previous studies, the present research proposes a model for the functional analysis of IPC vis-à-vis its discursive behavior within ELBR. As the conclusion of the research, the chapter will review the prime aspects the current study has covered, summarize the major findings, discuss the significance of the current research, and finally suggest some feasible and interesting research projects related to the present study, which will turn out to be promising and fruitful if future studies are conducted.

7.1 Overview of the Current Study

IPC in this study refers to those linguistic devices which work on the interpersonal plane by usually co-opting ideational projection to do interpersonal work. A survey of the literature shows that the phenomenon has been approached from traditional perspectives which focus on its syntactic features, semantic connotations, and phraseological co-occurrences. The functional school is more interested in bringing out how IPC operates to convey the language user's subjective attitude and/or commitment. However, not sufficient attention has been given to the mechanism with which IPC works to facilitate the language user to highlight her full awareness of other participants involved in the same communicative event, to augment interactant-interactant alignment, and to simultaneously regulate and construct social norms. In this sense, IPC functions to enhance intersubjectivity. The present study endeavors to bring into clearer vision how IPC behaves on the plane of intersubjectivity. In this sense, the study contributes to the investigation on IPC by extending the research from the plane of subjectivity to that of intersubjectivity. It is argued that the specific metafunctional features of IPC empower IPC to fulfill the intersubjectivity-boosting function.

However, it stands to reason that the discursive behavior of IPC will, seen from above, be determined by contextual variables with respect to particular communicative events. Seen from below, its lexicogrammatical realizations must vary according to contextual variables. Thus, the study adopts SFL notions of metafunction and genre. In addition, the concept of projection is elaborated in order to examine how IPC operates by co-opting ideational projection. The theoretical framework is also inclusive of the interpretation of intersubjectivity. Guided by these theoretical considerations, the study proposes an analytical framework to approach IPC. The particular genre of ELBR is chosen for the purpose of observing the behavior of IPC.

The study then provides a detailed analysis of ELBR with particular attention given to its generic identities and its GSP. For the purpose of comparison, the corpus of ELJE is developed and analyzed in the same vein. The bulk of the project focuses on the quantitative analysis and qualitative interpretation of IPC resources identified in the corpora.

7.2 Main Findings of the Current Study

The prime findings of the current project will be elaborated with respect to the objectives proposed in the introductory chapter.

First, the literature survey reveals that, although the phenomenon of IPC has been approached under various terms by different schools, there are four points worthy of particular notice. One is that IPC has not been considered from the perspective of projection until very recently (Halliday & Matthiessen, 2004). Another is that few studies have focused upon the intersubjectivity-boosting function typical of such devices. The third is that little attention is given to the discursive behavior of IPC with respect to particular genres, especially different genres within the same discipline. Fourth, ELBR has escaped deserved attention with respect to its close connection with IPC.

Second, this study identifies four categories of IPC by examining whether and how the Projector in IPC construes the interactant. The primary concern for the classification is linked with the aim of the study, i.e. exploring IPC as an intersubjectivity booster.

I-IPCs construe the writer as the interactant in the most explicit way.

We-IPCs indicate the presence of either the writer or the reader or people in general, or any combination of them.

No-interactant IPCs refer to constructions in which no Projector is present. Thus, no interactant is directly construed in this type of IPC. Thus, the visibility has to be inferred.

Non-interactant IPCs do not display the presence of any interactant. Instead, they construe the presence of non-interactants. However, by genre-specific ways (for instance, *as xxx states*, in the present case), this type of IPC suggests the presence of the interactant, the writer in particular, by infusing her voice into that of a third party.

It is observed that the four types of IPC form a continuum in that the visibility of the interactant varies from the most obvious to the least observable.

Third, this study observes that the discursive behavior of IPC is of close connection with specific genres. It is found that within the genre of ELBR, the writer is expected to inform the reader of the content of the book under review while simultaneously evaluating it in an objective and convincing way. Thus, the close connection between IPC and the genre is found to be linked to the fact that the writer will resort frequently to IPC for interactant alignment and joint attention regulation, since in the genre the interpersonal stake is higher than that in others (cf. Hyland, 2000).

Fourth, the study also notices that ELJE, another genre within the same discipline, functions differently from ELBR. This genre is promotional, or being positively evaluative, in nature. The study observes that in the genre the writer uses IPC to reinforce the reader's acceptance of the academic product advertised. Thus, the present research brings into vision that the different behavior of IPC is primarily due to the different purposes assigned to different text types.

Fifth, it is found that IPC resources vary to a great extent in terms of frequency, lexicogrammatical realizations with process types, tense and modalization, and the GSP elements in particular, and genre variation. It is also found that each type of IPC devices performs a multiple functions in terms of intersubjectivity enhancement.

Within ELBR, in terms of frequency, no-interactant IPCs possess an exceedingly high percentage of all IPC resources identified. With a noticeable distance, *we*-IPCs follow in ranking the second. This finding confirms Swales's classification of academic discourse, which includes ELBR as one primary academic discourse. The reason is that in general academic discourse follows the convention of appearing to be objective and impersonal. Thus, the writer is more inclined to deploy no-interactant IPCs.

In terms of process types, different types of IPC display their favorable ones to various degrees. *I*-IPCs favor mental processes, *we*-IPCs and non-interactant IPCs verbal, whereas no-interactant IPCs relational. These variations on the one hand may be constrained by accepted linguistic expressions and the particular grammar. On the other hand, they show the writer's overall management of these linguistic strategies.

In terms of tense and modalization, the findings appear to be more complex. However, the general tendency is that simple present tense is predominant in all types of IPC. This finding confirms Halliday & Matthiessen's (2004) statement that simple present is the unmarked tense for IPC in English.

In terms of the Thematic position of IPC, the corpora reveal a clear distributive pattern. That is, whatever type, IPC tends to be assigned to the Thematic status of the clause complex. This confirms the significance of IPC vis-à-vis its scopal and frame-setting function.

In terms of allocation with respect to GSP elements, the majority of IPC resources are found to cluster around the elements of CE and SE, due to the evaluative function of these elements. The finding reinforces the assumption held by the current study that the writer will invest heavily on occasions where interpersonal tension is high.

Across the genres, IPC resources are found to behave differently as well. Generally speaking, the differences attribute to different purposes the genres are expected to fulfill. In ELBR, for instance, IPC is used primarily to enhance intersubjectivity at the moment when the writer predicts interpersonal conflicts. By contrast, in ELJE, IPC is employed mainly to invoke and sustain the reader's interest in the articles and hence to impress the reader in a favorable way for the ultimate purpose of promotion.

7.3 Significance of the Current Study

With reference to the objectives proposed in the initial chapter, the present study has made the subsequent achievements.

First, it provides a comprehensive and constructive survey of how IPC has been dealt with in traditional schools and recent approaches. The survey brings into vision what features of IPC have been identified and focused upon. Of particular note is that some misconceptions are clarified and limitations of these studies are pointed out.

Second, the current study constructs a preliminary framework for the identification and classification of IPC resources in the language of English. The framework makes it possible to analyze IPC in a systematic and comprehensive way.

Third, the study offers a detailed investigation into ELBR and examines the interconnection between IPC and the concept of genre. In addition, the genre of ELJE is also introduced and analyzed for the purpose of comparison. The analysis of IPC across the genres of ELBR and ELJE contributes to the study of genre from the intra-disciplinary perspective. Furthermore, the cross-genre analysis of IPC provides a feasible way to approach other linguistic phenomena.

Fourth, within the framework established, the current study offers a corpus-assisted depiction of four types of IPC identified in the present corpora. In this sense, the study provides a possible and plausible perspective in which phenomena like IPC can be approached.

Finally, the study exhibits how IPC behaves on the plane of discourse across different genres within the same discipline. The distribution and allocation of the lexicogrammatical realizations of IPC show how the strategy is employed in ELBR and ELJE to facilitate the writer's different social and communicative purposes. In this way, the study helps to bring into vision the dialogicality of different text types within the particular discipline. Thus, the study offers a complementary contribution to the current prevailing cross-disciplinary studies.

7.4 Limitations and Remaining Issues for Further Research

The study conducts a theoretical as well as practical inspection on the discursive behavior of IPC. As has been stated, the analysis has resulted in some significant findings. However, it has to be acknowledged that it is far from safe to say that the present study is immune to limitations. In fact, there emerge at least two limitations. First, although the present study has made endeavors to construct the corpora as typical and authentic as possible, the findings are anticipated to be seen as tendencies rather than statements. Some features might prove to be conspicuous or significant provided that the current corpora are expanded to a considerable extent. It would also be possible that there appear some contradictory observations due to the variation of contextual factors in the design and construction of corpus.

Second, the study does not tackle other linguistic devices that can also enhance intersubjectivity, despite the fact that it does mention en route the interrelationships between the use of IPC and other strategies, such as modality in lexical realizations. It should be mentioned that IPC is by no means the only possible way that human language has evolved to perform the function. In fact, it could be quite plausibly argued that IPC and other boosting devices cooperate frequently to facilitate the language user to accomplish the intended intersubjectivity management.

Therefore, it is predictable that remaining issues for future research lie in the following several aspects.

First, with the help of expanded corpora, in particular, those covering authentic data across genres as well as disciplines, further exploration into the general discursive behavior of IPC as a linguistic device will be of academic value. This will definitely deepen the understanding of the interesting phenomenon and ultimately of human language.

Second, the investigation of IPC may be expanded by studying how these resources co-occur with other linguistic devices in particular text types or in language in general. This might be achieved by observing genre-or-discipline-oriented corpora or database of considerable size (e.g. Bank of English). This is a promising area and will prove fruitful.

Third, it is hypothesized that the use of IPC is common in all human languages. Therefore, a comparative study can be conducted, for instance, between Chinese and English. Languages may vary in the aspects of syntagmatic arrangement, lexical preference and prosodic patterns. It will be interesting to find out how different languages have evolved to boost intersubjectivity via different IPC resources. Meanwhile, in cross-linguistic studies, it will be also of interest whether and how culture and social conventions play a role in the employment of IPC.

Fourth, although the primary motivation for the study is not pedagogical, its findings do have some implications on teaching English for Specific Purposes. Understanding how language constitutes and is constituted by interaction within a discipline is of noticeable importance for non-native speakers. To enter the particular disciplinary community, they are expected to participate in professional dialogues, to be in control of appropriate forms of argument and interaction in different genres. Thus, it is of necessity to create and foster non-native speakers' awareness of and sensitivity to the use of IPC.

Finally, the study of IPC can be interdisciplinary (cf. Christie & Martin, 2007) in that some scholars from other fields may contribute to the understanding of the mechanism with which IPC works by offering fresh perspectives. As has been displayed in the current study, the deployment of IPC in most cases involves clause complexing. Academics engaging in cognitive science, for instance, may provide sound explanations for how the brain processes when IPC is being deployed.

Bibliography

Aarsand, P. A. and K. Aronsson. Response cries and other gaming moves: Building intersubjectivity in gaming [J]. *Journal of Pragmatics*, 41: 1557-75, 2009.

Adams, M. In the profession: Re-viewing the academic book review [J]. *Journal of English Linguistics*, 35: 202-05, 2007.

Ädel, A. *Metadiscourse in L1 and L2 English* [M]. Amsterdam: Benjamins, 2006.

Aijmer, K. *I think* — an English modal particle [A]. In T. Swan *et al.* (eds.). 1-47, 1997.

Aijmer, K. and A. Stenstrom (eds.). *Discourse Patterns in Spoken and Written Corpora* [C]. Amsterdam: Benjamins, 2004.

Aktas, R. and V. Cortes. Shell nouns as cohesive devices in published and ESL student writing [J]. *Journal of English for Academic Purposes*, 7: 3-14, 2008.

Andersen, G. and T. Fretheim. Introduction [A]. In G. Andersen *et al.* (eds.). 1-16, 2000.

Andersen, G. and T. Fretheim (eds.). *Pragmatic Markers and Propositional Attitude* [C]. Amsterdam: Benjamins, 2000.

Ansary, H. and E. Babaii. A generic integrity of newspaper editorials: A systemic functional perspective [J]. *RELC Journal*, 36: 271-95, 2005.

Baker, M., G. Francis and E. Tgnini-Bognelli (eds.). *Text and Technology*: *In Honor of John Sinclair* [C]. Amsterdam: Benjamins, 1993.

Bakhtin, M. M. *The Dialogic Imagination*: *Four Essays by M. M. Bakhtin* [C]. M. Holquist (ed.). C. Emerson and M. Holquist (trans.). Austin:

University of Texas Press, 1981.

Bakhtin, M. M. The problem of speech genres [A]. In M. M. Bakhtin. *Speech Genres and Other Late Essays* [C]. C. Emerson and M. Holquist. (eds.). B. McCee. (trans.). 60-102. Austin: University of Texas Press, 1986.

Barnes, R. and D. Moss. Communicating a feeling: The social organization of "private thought" [J]. *Discourse Studies*, 9: 123-48, 2007.

Barron, C., N. Bruce and D. Nunan (eds.). *Knowledge and Discourse: Towards an Ecology of Language* [M]. Harlow: Pearson, 2002.

Baseman, K. How students argue scientific claims [J]. *Applied Linguistics*, 24: 28-55, 2003.

Bawarshi, A. The genre-function [J]. *College English*, 62: 335-61, 2000.

Bazerman, C. *Shaping Written Knowledge* [M]. Madison: University of Wisconsin Press, 1989.

Bednarek, M. Epistemological positioning and evidentiality in English news discourse: A text-driven approach [J]. *Text & Talk*, 26: 635-60, 2006.

Belcher, D. Writing critically across the curriculum [A]. In D. Belcher et al. (eds.). 135-54, 1995.

Belcher, D. Seeking acceptance in an English-only research world [J]. *Journal of Second Language Writing*, 16: 1-22, 2007.

Belcher, D. and G. Braine (eds.). *Academic Writing in a Second Language* [C]. Norwood, NJ: Ablex, 1995.

Benfield, A. Where epistemology, style, and grammar meet literary history: The development of represented speech and thought [A]. In J. A. Lucy (ed.). 339-64, 1993.

Benson, J. D. and W. S. Greaves (eds.). *Systemic Perspectives on Discourse. Vol. 1: Selected Theoretical Papers from the 9th International Systemic Workshop* [C]. Norwood, NJ: Ablex, 1985.

Berkenfield, C. Pragmatic motivations for the development of evidential and modal meaning in the construction of "be supposed to X" [J]. *Journal of Historical Pragmatics*, 7: 39-71, 2006.

Berry, M., C. Butler, R. Fawcett and G. Huang (eds.). *Meaning and Form: Systemic Functional Interpretations* [C]. Norwood, NJ: Ablex, 1996.

Bex, T. *Variety in Written English: Texts in Society: Societies in Text* [M]. London: Routledge, 1996.

Bhatia, V. K. *Analyzing Genre: Language Use in Professional Settings* [M]. London: Longman, 1993.

Bhatia, V. K. Genre-mixing in academic introductions [J]. *English for Specific Purposes*, 16: 181-95, 1997.

Bhatia, V. K. A genre view of academic discourse [A]. In J. Flowerdew (ed.). 21-39, 2002.

Bhatia, V. K. *World of Written Discourse: A Genre-based View* [M]. London: Continuum, 2004.

Biber, D. *Variation across Speech and Writing* [M]. Cambridge: Cambridge University Press, 1988.

Biber, D., S. Conrad and R. Reppen. *Corpus Linguistics: Investigating Language Structure and Use* [M]. Cambridge: Cambridge University Press, 1998.

Biber, D., S. Johansson, G. Leech, S. Conrad and E. Finegan. *Longman Grammar of Spoken and Written English* [Z]. London: Longman, 1999.

Birth, D. and M. O'Toole (eds.). *Functions of Style* [C]. London: Pinter, 1988.

Bloor, M. and T. Bloor. How economists modify propositions [A]. In W. Henderson *et al.* (eds.). 153-69, 1993.

Bloor, T. and M. Bloor. *The Functional Analysis of English: A Hallidayan Approach* (2nd Ed.) [M]. London: Arnold, 2004.

Bolívar, A. The negotiation of evaluation in written text [A]. In M. Scott *et al.* (eds.). 129-58, 2000.

Bredel, U. Polyphonic constructions in everyday speech [A]. In T. Ensink *et al.* (eds.). 147-70, 2003.

Brown, G. and G. Yule. *Discourse Analysis* [M]. Cambridge: Cambridge University Press, 1987.

Brown, P. and S. Levinson. *Politeness: Some Universals in Language Usage* [M]. Cambridge: Cambridge University Press, 1987.

Busch-Lauer, Ines-A. Perspective in medical correspondence: English and German letters-to-the-editor [A]. In T. Ensink et al. (eds.). 191-14, 2003.

Butler, C. S. *Systemic Linguistics: Theory and Applications* [M]. London: Batsford, 1985.

Butler, C. S. On the concept of an interpersonal metafunction in English [A]. In M. Berry et al. (eds.). 151-82, 1996.

Butler, C. S. *Structure and Function: A Guide to Three Major Structural-Functional Theories. Part 1: Approaches to the simplex clause* [M]. Amsterdam: Benjamins, 2003a.

Butler, C. S. *Structure and Function: A Guide to Three Major Structural-Functional Theories. Part 2: From clause to discourse and beyond* [M]. Amsterdam: Benjamins, 2003b.

Bybee, J. and M. Noonan (eds.). *Complex Sentences in Grammar and Discourse: Essays in Honor of Sandra A. Thompson* [C]. Amsterdam: Benjamins, 2002.

Caffarel, A., J. R. Martin, and C. Matthiessen. *Language Typology: A Functional Perspective* [C]. Amsterdam: Benjamins, 2004.

Caldas-Coulthard, C. and M. Coulthard (eds.). *Texts and Practices: Readings in Critical Discourse Analysis* [C]. London: Routledge, 1996.

Calsamiglia, H. and C. L. Ferrero. Role and position of scientific voices: Reported speech in the media [J]. *Discourse Studies*, 5: 147-73. 2003.

Camiciotti, G. D. and E. T. Bonelli (eds.). *Academic Discourse: New Insights into Evaluation* [C]. Bern: Peter Lang, 2004.

Candlin, C. N. and K. Hyland (eds.). *Writing: Texts, Processes and Practices* [C]. London: Longman, 1999.

Cecchetto, V. and M. Stroińska. Systems of self-reference and address forms in intellectual discourse [J]. *Language Sciences*, 18: 777-89, 1996.

Chambon, A. and D. Simeoli. Modality in the therapeutic dialogue [A]. In A. Sánchez-Macarro et al. (eds.). 239-64, 1998.

Champion, D. J. and M. F. Morris. A content analysis of book reviews in the AJS, ASR, and Social Forces [J]. *American Sociological Review*, 78: 1256-65, 1973.

Chandrasegaran, A. and K. M. C. Kong. Stance-taking and stance-support in students' online forum discussion [J]. *Linguistics and Education*, 17: 374-90, 2006.

Charles, M. "This mystery..."： A corpus-based study of the use of nouns to construct stance in theses from two contrasting disciplines [J]. *Journal of English for Academic Purposes*, 2: 313-26, 2003.

Charles, M. Phraseological patterns in reporting clauses used in citation: A corpus-based study of theses in two disciplines [J]. *English for Specific Purposes*, 25: 310-31, 2006a.

Charles, M. The construction of stance in reporting clauses: A cross-disciplinary study of theses [J]. *Applied Linguistics*, 27: 492-518, 2006b.

Charles, M. Argument or evidence? Disciplinary variation in the use of the Noun *that* pattern in stance construction [J]. *English for Specific Purposes*, 26: 203-18, 2007.

Christie, F. and J. R. Martin (eds.). *Genre and Institutions: Social Processes in the Workplace and School* [C]. London: Cassell, 1997.

Christie, F. and J. R. Martin (eds.). *Language, Knowledge and Pedagogy. Functional Linguistics and Sociological Perspectives* [C]. London: Continuum, 2007.

Clayman, S. Speaking on behalf of the public in broadcast news interviews [A]. In E. Holt *et al.* (eds.). 221-43, 2007.

Coates, J. The role of epistemic modality in women's talk [A]. In R. Facchinetti *et al.* (eds.). 331-48, 2003.

Conrad, S. and D. Biber. Adverbial marking of stance in speech and writing [A]. In S. Hunston *et al.* (eds.). 57-73, 2000.

Cornelis, L. Ajax is the agent: Subject versus passive agent as an indicator of the journalist's perspective in soccer reports [A]. In T. Ensink *et al.* (eds.). 171-89, 2003.

Cook, G. *The Discourse of Advertising* [M]. London: Routledge, 1992.

Cortazzi, M. and L. Jin. Evaluating evaluation in narrative [A]. In S. Hunston *et al.* (eds.). 103-20, 2000.

Crismore, A. *Talking with Readers: Metadiscourse as Rhetorical Act* [M]. Bern: Peter Lang, 1989.

Crismore, A., R. Markkanen and M. Steffensen. Metadiscourse in persuasive writing: A study of texts written by American and Finnish university students [J]. *Written Communication*, 10: 39-71, 1993.

Crismore, A. and W. Vande Kopple. Hedges and readers: Effects on attitude and learning [A]. In R. Markkanen *et al.* (eds.). 83-114, 1997.

Dafouz-Milne, E. The pragmatic role of textual and interpersonal metadiscourse markers in the construction and attainment of persuasion: A cross-linguistic study of newspaper discourse [J]. *Journal of Pragmatics*, 40: 95-113, 2008.

Dahl, T. Textual metadiscourse in research articles: A marker of national culture or of academic discipline? [J]. *Journal of Pragmatics*, 36: 1807-25, 2004.

Davies, M. and L. J. Ravelli (eds.). *Advances in Systemic Linguistics: Recent Theory and Practice* [C]. London: Pinter, 1992.

de Oliveira, J. M. and A. S. Pagano. The research article and the science popularization article: A probabilistic functional grammar perspective on direct discourse representation [J]. *Discourse Studies*, 8: 627-46, 2006.

di Luzio, A. Presenting John. J. Gumperz [A]. In S. L. Eerdmans *et al.* (eds.). 1-6, 2002.

Di Pietro, R. J. (ed.). *Linguistics and Professions* [C]. Norwood, NJ: Ablex, 1982.

Diani, G. Evaluation in academic review articles [A]. In A. Partington *et al.* (eds.). 189-203, 2004.

Diessel, H. and M. Tomasello. The acquisition of finite complement clauses in English: A corpus-based analysis [J]. *Cognitive Linguistics*, 12: 97-141, 2001.

Drury, H. The use of systemic linguistics to describe student summaries at university level [A]. In E. Ventola (ed.). 431-56, 1991.

Du Bois, J. W. The stance triangle [A]. In R. Englebretson. (ed.). 137-82, 2007.

DueÑas, P. M. "I/we focus on ... ": A cross-cultural analysis of self-mentions in business management research articles [J]. *Journal of English for Academic Purposes*, 6: 143-62, 2007.

Edge, J. and S. Wharton. Patterns of text in teacher education [A]. In M. Scott *et al.* (eds.). 255-86, 2000.

Eerdmans, S. L., C. L. Prevignano and P. J. Thibault (eds.). *Language and Interaction: Discussion with John J. Gumperz* [C]. Amsterdam: Benjamins, 2002.

Eggins, S. *An Introduction to Systemic Functional Linguistics* (2nd Ed.) [M]. London: Continuum, 2004.

Eggins, S. and J. R. Martin. Genres and registers of discourse [A]. In T. A. van Dijk (ed.). 230-56, 1997.

Eggins, S. and D. Slade. *Analysing Casual Conversation* [M]. London: Cassell, 1997.

Englebretson, R. (ed.). *Stancetaking in Discourse: Subjectivity, Evaluation, Interaction* [C]. Amsterdam: Benjamins, 2007.

Ensink, T. and C. Sauer (eds.). *Framing and Perspectivising in Discourse* [C]. Amsterdam: Benjamins, 2003.

Facchinetti, R., M. Krug and F. Palmer (eds.). *Modality in Contemporary English* [C]. Berlin: de Gruyter, 2003.

Facchinetti, R. and F. Palmer. Introduction [A]. In R. Facchinetti *et al.* (eds.). vii-xv, 2004.

Facchinetti, R. and F. Palmer (eds.). *English Modality in Perspective: Genre Analysis and Contrastive Studies* [C]. Bern: Peter Lang, 2004.

Fairclough, N. *Discourse and Social Change* [M]. Cambridge: Cambridge University Press, 1992.

Fairclough, N. *Media Discourse* [M]. London: Arnold, 1995.

Fant, L. Discourse perspectives on modalisation: The case of accounts in semi-structured interviews [A]. In A. Klinger *et al.* (eds.). 103-21, 2005.

Fetzer, A. "And I think that is a very straightforward way of dealing with it": The communicative function of cognitive verbs on political discourse [J]. *Journal of Language and Social Psychology*, 27: 384-96, 2008a.

Fetzer, A. Theme zones in English media discourse: Forms and functions [J]. *Journal of Pragmatics*, 40: 1543-68, 2008b.

Field, M. The role of factive predicates in the indexicalization of stance: A discourse perspective [J]. *Journal of Pragmatics*, 27: 799-814, 1997.

Fitzmaurice, S. Subjectivity, intersubjectivity and the historical construction of interlocutor stance: From stance markers to discourse markers [J]. *Discourse Studies*, 6: 427-48, 2004.

Flowerdew, J. Pragmatic modifications on the "representative" speech act of defining [J]. *Journal of Pragmatics*, 15: 253-64, 1991.

Flowerdew, J. (ed.). *Academic Discourse* [C]. London: Longman, 2002a.

Flowerdew, J. Introduction: Approaches to the analysis of academic discourse in English [A]. In J. Flowerdew (ed.). 1-18, 2002b.

Flowerdew, J. Ethnographically inspired approaches to the study of academic discourse [A]. In J. Flowerdew (ed.). 235-52, 2002c.

Flowerdew, J. and T. Dudley-evans. Genre analysis of editorial letters to international journal contributors [J]. *Applied Linguistics*, 23: 463-89, 2002.

Flowerdew, L. Interpersonal strategies: Investigating interlanguage corpora [J]. *RELC Journal*, 28: 72-88, 1997.

Flowerdew, L. An integration of corpus-based and genre-based approaches to text analysis in EAP/ESP: Countering criticisms against corpus-based methodologies [J]. *English for Specific Purposes*, 24: 321-32, 2005.

Fortanet, I. (ed.). *Genre Studies in English for Academic Purposes* [C]. Castelló de la Plana: Universitat Jaume, 1998.

Francis, G., S. Hunston and E. Manning. *Collins COBUILD Grammar Patterns 1: Verbs* [Z]. London: Harpercollins, 1996.

Francis, G., S. Hunston and E. Manning. *Collins COBUILD Grammar Patterns 2: Nouns and Adjectives* [Z]. London: Harpercollins, 1998.

Freddi, M. Arguing linguistics: Corpus investigation of one functional variety of academic discourse [J]. *Journal of English for Academic Purposes*, 4: 5-26, 2005.

Freedman, A. and P. Medway (eds.). *Genre and the New Rhetoric* [C]. London: Taylor & Francis, 1994.

Fries, P. H. Themes, methods of development, and texts [A]. In R. Hasan *et al.* (eds.). 317-59, 1995.

Fries, P. H., M. Cummings, D. Lockwood and W. Spruiell (eds.). *Relations and Functions within and around Language* [C]. London: Continuum,

2002.

Garcés-Conejos, P. and A. Sánchez-Macarro. Scientific discourse as interaction: Scientific articles vs. popularizations [A]. In A. Sánchez-Macarro et al. (eds.). 173-90, 1998.

Garner, M. *Language: An Ecological View* [M]. Bern: Peter Lang, 2004.

Gavins, J. *Text World Theory: An Introduction* [M]. Edinburgh: Edinburgh University Press, 2007.

Ghadessy, M. (ed.). *Register Analysis: Theory and Practice* [C]. London: Pinter, 1993.

Ghadessy, M. On the nature of written business communication [A]. In M. Ghadessy (ed.). 149-64, 1993.

Ghadessy, M. (ed.). *Thematic Development in English Texts* [C]. London: Pinter, 1995.

Ghadessy, M. (ed.). *Text and Context in Functional Linguistics* [C]. Amsterdam: Benjamins, 1998.

Giannoni, D. S. Acknowledgement texts in English & Italian research articles [J]. *Applied Linguistics*, 23: 1-31, 2002.

Givón, T. *Functionalism and Grammar* [M]. Amsterdam: Benjamins, 1995.

Goddard, C. Who are *we*? The natural semantics of pronouns [J]. *Language Science*, 17: 99-121, 1995.

Goffman, E. *Interaction Ritual* [M]. Garden City, New York: Doubleday, 1976.

Gofffman, E. *Forms of Talk* [M]. Oxford: Blackwell, 1981.

Gómez-González, M. A. *The Theme-Topic Interface: Evidence from English* [M]. Amsterdam: Benjamins, 2001.

Gragson, G. and J. Selzer. Fictionalizing the readers of scholarly articles in biology [J]. *Written Communication*, 7: 25-58, 1990.

Green, K. (ed.). *New Essays on Deixis: Discourse, Narrative, Literature* [C]. Amsterdam: Rodopi, 1995.

Groom, N. Pattern and meaning across genres and disciplines: An exploratory study [J]. *Journal of English for Academic Purposes*, 4: 257-77, 2005.

Gumperz, J. J. The linguistic and cultural relativity of conversational inference

[A]. In J. J. Gumperz et al. (eds.). 374-437, 1996.

Gumperz, J. J. and S. C. Levinson (eds.). *Rethinking Linguistic Relativity* [C]. Cambridge: Cambridge University Press, 1996.

Haddington, P. Positioning and alignment as activities of stancetaking in news interviews [A]. In R. Englebretson (ed.). 283-317, 2007.

Halliday, M. A. K. Functional diversity in language, as seen from a consideration of modality and mood in English [J]. *Foundations of Language: International Journal of Language and Philosophy*, 6: 322-61, 1970. Republished in *Collected Works of M. A. K. Halliday: Vol. 7: Studies in English language* [C]. 164-204. London: Continuum/Beijing: Peking University Press, 2005/2007.

Halliday, M. A. K. *Language as Social Semiotic: The Social Interpretation of Language and Meaning* [M]. London: Arnold/Beijing: Foreign Language Teaching and Research Press, 1978/2001.

Halliday, M. A. K. Modes of meaning and modes of expression: Types of grammatical structure, and their determination by different semantic functions [A]. In D. J. Allerton, E. Carney and D. Holdcroft (eds.). *Function and Context in Linguistic Analysis: Essays Offers to William Haas* [C]. 57-79. Cambridge: Cambridge University Press, 1979. Republished in *Collected Works of M. A. K. Halliday: Vol. 1: On Grammar* [C]. 196-218. London: Continuum/Beijing: Peking University Press, 2002/2007.

Halliday, M. A. K. The de-automatization of grammar: From Priestley's *An Inspector Calls* [A]. In J. M. Anderson (ed.). *Language Form and Linguistic Variation: Papers Dedicated to Angus McIntosh (Current Issues in Linguistic Theory* 15) [C]. 129-159. Amsterdam: Benjamins, 1982. Republished in *Collected Works of M. A. K. Halliday: Vol. 2: Linguistic Studies of Text and Discourse* [C]. 126-148. London: Continuum/Beijing: Peking University Press, 2002/2007.

Halliday, M. A. K. *An Introduction to Functional Grammar* [M]. London: Arnold, 1985.

Halliday, M. A. K. Some grammatical problems in scientific English [J]. *Australian Review of Applied Linguistics Series*, S6: 13-37, 1990.

Halliday, M. A. K. *An Introduction to Functional Grammar* (2nd Ed.) [M]. London: Arnold, 1994.

Halliday, M. A. K. *Complementarities in Language* [M]. Beijing: The Commercial Press, 2008.

Halliday, M. A. K. and R. Hasan. *Language, Context and Text: Aspects of Language in a Social-Semiotic Perspective* [M]. Victoria: Deacon University Press, 1985.

Halliday, M. A. K. and C. Matthiessen. *Construing Experience through Meaning: A Language-Based Approach to Cognition* [M]. London: Cassell, 1999.

Halliday, M. A. K. and C. Matthiessen. *An Introduction to Functional Grammar* (3rd Ed.) [M]. London: Arnold, 2004.

Hanks, W. F. Exorcism and the description of participant roles [A]. In M. Silverstein *et al.* (eds.). 160-200, 1996.

Hartnett, C. G. The pit after the Theme [A]. In M. Ghadessy (ed.). 198-212, 1995.

Harvey, A. Interaction in public reports [J]. *English for Specific Purposes*, 14: 189-200, 1995.

Harwood, N. 'Nowhere has anyone attempted … In this article I aim to do just that': A corpus-based study of self-promotional *I* and *we* in academic writing across four disciplines [J]. *Journal of Pragmatics*, 37: 1207-31, 2005.

Harwood, N. Political scientists on the functions of personal pronouns in their writing: An interview-based study of "I" and "we" [J]. *Text & Talk*, 27: 27-54, 2009.

Harwood, N. An interview-based study of the functions of citations in academic writing across two disciplines [J]. *Journal of Pragmatics*, 41: 497-518, 2009.

Hasan, R. The nursery tale as a genre [A]. *Nottingham Linguistic Circular*, 13: 71-102, 1984. Reprinted in R. Hasan. 51-72, 1996.

Hasan, R. *Ways of Saying; Ways of Meaning: Selected Papers of Ruqaiya Hasan* [C]. C. Cloran, D. Butt and G. Williams (eds.). London: Cassell, 1996.

Hasan, R., C. Cloran and D. Butt (eds.). *Functional Descriptions: Theories in Practice* [C]. Amsterdam: Benjamins, 1996.

Hasan, R. , C. Matthiessen and J. Webster (eds.). *Continuing Discourse on Language: A Functional Perspective Vol. 2* [C]. London: Equinox, 2007.

Hasan, R. and P. H. Fries (eds.). *On Subject and Theme: From the Perspective of Functions in Discourse* [C]. Amsterdam: Benjamins, 1995.

Haviland, J. B. Projections, transpositions, and relativity [A]. In J. J. Gumperz et al. (eds.). 271-323, 1996.

Hemais, B. The discourse of research and practice in marketing journals [J]. *English for Specific Purposes*, 20: 39-59, 2001.

Henderson, W. , T. Dudley-Evans and R. Backhouse (eds.). *Economics and Language* [C]. London: Routledge, 1993.

Henry, A. and R. Roseberry. An investigation of the functions, strategies and linguistic features of the introductions and conclusions of essays [J]. *System*, 25: 479-95, 1997.

Heritage, J. *Carfinkel and Ethnomethodology* [M]. Cambridge: Polity Press, 1984.

Herriman, J. The functions of extraposition in English texts [J]. *Functions of Language*, 7: 203-30, 2000.

Hewings, A. and C. Coffin. Writing in multi-party computer conferences and single authored assignments: Exploring the role of writer as thinker [J]. *Journal of English for Academic Purposes*, 6: 126-42, 2007.

Hewings, M. and A. Hewings. "It is interesting to note that..." : A comparative study of anticipatory "it" in student and published writing [J]. *English for Specific Purposes*, 21: 367-83, 2002.

Heyvaert, L. *A Cognitive-Functional Approach to Nominalization in English* [M]. Berlin: de Gruyter, 2003.

Hoey, M. Persuasive rhetoric in linguistics: A stylistic study of some features of the language of Noam Chomsky [A]. In S. Hunston et al. (eds.). 29-37, 2000.

Holmes, J. Modifying illocutionary force [J]. *Journal of Pragmatics*, 8: 345-65, 1984.

Holmgreen, L. -L. and T. Vestergaard. Evaluation and audience acceptance in biotech news texts [J]. *Journal of Pragmatics*, 41: 586-601, 2009.

Holt, E. and R. Clift (eds.). *Reporting Talk: Reported Speech in Interaction* [C]. Cambridge: Cambridge University Press, 2007.

Hood, S. The persuasive power of prosodies: Radiating values in academic writing [J]. *Journal of English for Academic Purposes*, 5: 37-49, 2006.

Huang, G. W. *Enhanced Theme in English: Its Structures and Functions* [M]. Taiyuan: Shanxi Education Press, 2003.

Hübler, A. *Understatements and Hedges in English* [M]. Amsterdam: Benjamins, 1983.

Hudson, R. A. *English Complex Sentences: An Introduction to Systemic Grammar* [M]. Amsterdam: North-Holland, 1972.

Hunston, S. Professional conflict: Disagreement in academic discourse [A]. In M. Baker *et al.* (eds.). 115-34, 1993.

Hunston, S. Evaluation and the planes of discourse: Status and value in persuasive texts [A]. In S. Hunston *et al.* (eds.). 177-207, 2000.

Hunston, S. and G. Francis. *Pattern Grammar: A Corpus-Driven Approach to the Lexical Grammar of English* [M]. Amsterdam: Benjamins, 1999.

Hunston, S. and J. Sinclair. A local grammar of evaluation [A]. In S. Hunston *et al.* (eds.). 75-101, 2000.

Hunston, S. and G. Thompson (eds.). *Evaluation in Text: Authorial Stance and the Construction of Discourse* [C]. Oxford: Oxford University Press, 2000.

Hyland, K. Persuasion and context: The pragmatics of academic metadiscourse [J]. *Journal of Pragmatics*, 30: 437-55, 1998.

Hyland, K. Disciplinary discourse: Writer stance in research articles [A]. In C. Candlin *et al.* (eds.). 99-121, 1999.

Hyland, K. *Disciplinary Discourse: Social Interaction in Academic Writing* [M]. London: Longman, 2000.

Hyland, K. Directives: Argument and engagement in academic writing [J]. *Applied Linguistics*, 23: 215-39, 2002a.

Hyland, K. Activity and evaluation: Reporting practices in academic writing [A]. In J. Flowerdew (ed.). 115-30, 2002b.

Hyland, K. Authority and invisibility: Authorial identity in academic writing [J]. *Journal of Pragmatics*, 34: 1091-1112, 2002c.

Hyland, K. Engagement and disciplinarity: The other side of evaluation [A]. In G. Camiciotti *et al.* (eds.). 13-30, 2004a.

Hyland, K. Patterns of engagement: Dialogic features and L2 undergraduate writing [A]. In L. J. Ravelli *et al.* (eds.). 5-23, 2004b.

Hyland, K. *Metadiscourse* [M]. London: Continuum, 2005a.

Hyland, K. Stance and engagement: A model of interaction in academic discourse [J]. *Discourse Studies*, 7: 173-92, 2005b.

Hyland, K. As can be seen: Lexical bundles and disciplinary variation [J]. *English for Specific Purposes*, 27: 4-21, 2008.

Hyland, K. and P. Tse. Metadiscourse in academic writing: A reappraisal [J]. *Applied Linguistics*, 25: 156-77, 2004.

Hyland, K. and P. Tse. Hooking the reader: A corpus study of evaluative *that* in abstracts [J]. *English for Specific Purposes*, 24: 123-39, 2005.

Ifantidou, E. The semantics and pragmatics of metadiscourse [J]. *Journal of Pragmatics*, 37: 1325-53, 2005.

Ilie, C. Cliché-based metadiscursive argumentation in the House of Parliament [J]. *International Journal of Applied Linguistics*, 10: 65-84, 2000.

Irvine, J. T. Shadow conversation: The indeterminacy of participant roles [A]. In M. Silverstein *et al.* (eds.). 131-59, 1996.

Jacobs, G. Self-reference in press releases [J]. *Journal of Pragmatics*, 31: 219-242, 1999.

Jary, M. The relevance of complement choice: A corpus study of "believe" [J]. *Lingua*, 118: 1-18, 2008.

Jespersen, O. *Essentials of English Grammar* [M]. London: George Allen & Unwin, 1933.

Johansson, M. Constructing objects of discourse in the broadcast political interview [J]. *Journal of Pragmatics*, 38: 216-29, 2006.

Jones, P. Philosophical and theoretical issues in the study of deixis: A critique of the standard account [A]. In K. Green (ed.). 27-48, 1995.

Kärkkäinen, E. The role of *I guess* in conversational stancetaking [A]. In R. Englebretson (ed.). 183-219, 2007.

Katriel, T. and M. Dascal. Speakers of commitment and involvement in discourse

[A]. In Y. Tobin (ed.). 275-95, 1989.

Kies, D. The use of passivity: Suppressing agency in *Nineteen eighty-Four* [A]. In M. Davies *et al.* (eds.). 229-50, 1992.

Klinger, A. and H. H. Müller (eds.). *Modality: Studies in Form and Function* [C]. London: Equinox, 2005.

Koenig, J. (ed.). *Discourse and Cognition: Bridging the Gap* [C]. California: CSLI, 1998.

Koutsantoni, D. Attitude, certainty and allusions to common knowledge in scientific research articles [J]. *Journal of English for Academic Purposes*, 3: 163-82, 2004.

Kress, G. *Learning to Write* [M]. London: Routledge, 1994.

Kreutz, H. Some observations on hedging phenomena and modifying devices as regional markers in the speech of young East Germans [A]. In R. Markkanen *et al.* (eds.). 208-31, 1997.

Kuo, C. The use of personal pronouns: Role relationships in scientific journal articles [J]. *English for Specific Purposes*, 18: 121-38, 1999.

Kuo, S. Involvement vs. detachment: Gender differences in the use of personal pronouns in televised sports in Taiwan [J]. *Discourse Studies*, 5: 479-94, 2003.

Lakoff, G. Metaphor and war: The metaphor system used to justify war in the Gulf [A]. In M. Pütz (ed.). 463-81, 1992.

Land, V. and C. Kitzinger. Some uses of third-person reference forms in speaker self-reference [J]. *Discourse Studies*, 9: 493-525, 2007.

Langacker, R. *Foundations of Cognitive Grammar Volume II Descriptive Application* [M]. Stanford: Stanford University Press/Beijing: Peking University Press, 1991/2004.

Lassen, I. Imperative readings of grammatical metaphor: A study of congruency in the imperatives [A]. In A. Simon-Vandenbergen *et al.* (eds.). 279-308, 2003.

Lemke, J. L. Interpersonal meaning in discourse: Value orientation [A]. In M. Davies *et al.* (eds.). 82-104, 1992.

Lemke, J. L. Resources for attitudinal meaning: Evaluative orientations in text semantics [J]. *Functions of Language*, 5: 33-56, 1998.

Lemke, J. L. Ideology, intertextuality and the communication of science [A]. In P. H. Fries *et al.* (eds.). 32-55, 2002.

Lerner, G. H. and C. Kitzinger. Extraction and aggression in the repair of individual and collective self-reference [J]. *Discourse Studies*, 9: 526-57, 2007.

Liebert, W., G. Redeker and L. Waugh (eds.). *Discourse and Perspective in Cognitive Linguistics* [C]. Amsterdam: Benjamins, 1997.

Lindholm-Romantschuk, Y. *Scholarly Book Reviewing in the Social Sciences and Humanities: The Flow of Ideas within and among Disciplines* [M]. Westport, Connecticut: Greenwood Press, 1998.

Lombardo, L. *That*-clause and reporting verbs as evaluation in TV news [A]. In A. Partington *et al.* (eds.). 221-28, 2004.

Low, G. Positioning and metaphor in academic book reviews [Z]. University of Augsburg: International Conference on Evaluation and Text Types, June, 2005.

Lucy, J. A. (ed.). *Reflexive Language: Reported Speech and Metapragmatics* [C]. Cambridge: Cambridge University Press, 1993.

Lunsford, R. and B. Bridges. *The Longwood Guide to Writing* [M]. London: Longman, 2002.

Luukka, M. Social and interpersonal perspectives on scientific discourse [A]. In C. Barron *et al.* (eds.). 221-37, 2002.

Lyons, J. *Semantics* (Vol. 1 and Vol. 2) [M]. Cambridge: Cambridge University Press, 1977.

McCabe, A. Mood and modality in Spanish and English history textbooks: The construction of authority [J]. *Text & Talk*, 24: 1-29, 2004.

McEnery, T. and N. A. Kifle. Epistemic modality in argumentative essays of second-language writers [A]. In J. Flowerdew (ed.). 182-95, 2002.

McLaren, Y. 'We expect to report on significant progress in our product pipeline in the coming year': Hedging forward-looking statements in corporate press releases [J]. *Discourse Studies*, 10: 635-54, 2008.

McEnery, T. and A. Wilson. *Corpus Linguistics. An Introduction* [M].

Edinburgh: Edinburgh University Press, 1996/ 2001.

Markkanen, R. and H. Schröder (eds.). *Hedging and Discourse* [C]. Berlin: de Gruyter, 1997.

Markkanen, R. and H. Schröder. Introduction: Hedging: A challenge for pragmatics and discourse analysis [A]. In R. Markkanen *et al.* (eds.). 1-18, 1997.

Martin, J. R. Process and text: Two aspects of semiosis [A]. In J. D. Benson *et al.* (eds.). 248-74, 1985.

Martin, J. R. *English Text: System and Structure* [M]. Amsterdam: Benjamins/ Beijing: Peking University Press, 1992/2004.

Martin, J. R., C. Matthiessen and C. Painter. *Working with Functional Grammar* [M]. London: Arnold, 1997.

Martin, J. R. and D. Rose. *Working with Discourse: Meaning beyond the Clause* [M]. London: Continuum, 2003.

Martin, J. R. and P. White. *The Language of Evaluation: Appraisal in English* [M]. New York: Macmillan, 2005.

Maschler, Y. and R. Estlein. Stance-taking in Hebrew casual conversation via be'emet ("really, actually, indeed", lit. "in truth") [J]. *Discourse Studies*, 10: 283-316, 2008.

Matoesian, G. Intertextual authority in reported speech: Production media in the Kennedy Smith rape trial [J]. *Journal of Pragmatics*, 32: 879-914, 2000.

Matthiessen, C. Interpreting the textual metafunction [A]. In M. Davies *et al.* (eds.). 37-81, 1992.

Matthiessen, C. Descriptive motifs and generalizations [A]. In A. Caffarel *et al.* (eds.). 537-673, 2004.

Melrose, R. 'Having things both ways': Grammatical metaphor in a systemic-functional model of language [A]. In A. Simon-Vandenbergen *et al.* (eds.). 417-42, 2003.

Meyer, P. G. Hedging strategies in written academic discourse: Strengthening the argument by weakening the claim [A]. In R. Markkanen *et al.* (eds.). 21-41, 1997.

Moreno, A. I. Matching theoretical descriptions of discourse and practical applications to teaching: The case of causal metatext [J]. *English for Specific Purposes*, 22: 265-95, 2003.

Moreno, A. I. and L. Suárez. A study of critical attitude across English and Spanish academic book reviews [J]. *Journal of English for Academic Purposes*, 7: 15-26, 2008.

Morley, D. *Syntax in Functional Grammar: An Introduction to Lexicogrammar in Systemic Linguistics* [M]. London: Continuum, 2000.

Morley, J. The sting in the tail: Persuasion in English editorial discourse [A]. In A. Partington *et al.* (eds.). 239-55, 2004.

Motta-Roth, D. Discourse analysis and academic book reviews: A study of text and disciplinary cultures [A]. In I. Fortanet (ed.). 29-58, 1998.

Moya Guijarro, A. J. The continuity of topics in journal and travel texts: A discourse functional perspective [J]. *Functions of Language*, 13: 37-76, 2006.

Murphy, A. C. A hidden or unobserved presence? Impersonal evaluative structures in English and Italian and their wake [A]. In A. Partington *et al.* (eds.). 205-20, 2004.

Myers, G. The pragmatics of politeness in scientific articles [J]. *Applied Linguistics*, 10: 1-35, 1989.

Namsaraev, V. Hedging in Russian academic writing in sociological texts [A]. In R. Markkanen *et al.* (eds.). 64-82, 1997.

Nattinger, J. R. and J. S. DeCarrico. *Lexical Phrases and Language Teaching* [M]. Oxford: Oxford University Press, 1992.

Neff, J., F. Ballesteros, E. Dafouz, F. Martinez, J. P. Rica, M. Diez and R. Prieto. The expressions of writer stance in native and non-native argumentative texts [A]. In R. Facchinetti *et al.* (eds.). 141-62, 2004.

Nicolaisen, J. Book review [J]. *Journal of the American Society for Information Science and Technology*, 57: 1194-1207, 2006.

Northey, M. and J. Mckibbin. *Making Sense: A Student's Guide to Research and Writing* [M]. Oxford: Oxford University Press, 2005.

Nuyts, J. *Epistemic Modality, Language, and Conceptualization* [M]. Amsterdam: Benjamins, 2000.

Nuyts, J. and E. Pederson (eds.). *Language and Conceptualization* [C]. Cambridge: Cambridge University Press, 1997.

Overstreet, M. and G. Yule. The metapragmatics of *and everything* [J]. *Journal of Pragmatics*, 34: 785-94, 2002.

Palmer, F. R. *Mood and Modality* (2nd Ed.) [M]. Cambridge: Cambridge University Press, 2001.

Paltridge, B. Writing up research: A Systemic Functional perspective [J]. *System*, 21: 175-92, 1993.

Paltridge, B. Working with genre: A pragmatic perspective [J]. *Journal of Pragmatics*, 24: 395-406, 1995.

Paltridge, B. The exegesis as a genre: An ethnographic examination [A]. In L. J. Ravelli et al. (eds.). 84-103, 2004.

Partington, A., J. Morley and L. Haarman (eds.). *Corpora and Discourse* [C]. Bern: Peter Lang, 2004.

Pho, P. D. Research article abstracts in applied linguistics and educational technology: A study of linguistic realizations of rhetorical structure and authorial stance [J]. *Discourse Studies*, 10: 231-50, 2008.

Prince, E., J. Frader and C. Bosk. On hedging in physician-physician discourse [A]. In R. J. Di Pietro (ed.). 83-97, 1982.

Pütz, M. (ed.). *Thirty Years of Linguistic Evolution. Studies in Honour of René Dirven on the Occasion of His Sixtieth Birthday* [C]. Amsterdam: Benjamins, 1992.

Quirk, R. and S. Greenbaum. *A University Grammar of English* [Z]. London: Longman, 1973.

Quirk, R., S. Greenbaum, G. Leech and J. Svartvik. *A Grammar of Contemporary English* [Z]. London: Longman, 1972.

Quirk, R., S. Greenbaum, G. Leech and J. Svartvik. *A Comprehensive Grammar of the English Language* [Z]. London: Longman, 1985.

Ravelli, L. J. Renewal of connection: Integrating theory and practice in an understanding of grammatical metaphor [A]. In A. Simon-Vandenbergen et al. (eds.). 37-64, 2003.

Ravelli, L. J. and R. A. Ellis (eds.). *Analysing Academic Writing*:

Contextualized Frameworks [C]. London: Continuum, 2004.

Reid, S. *Purpose and Process: A Reader for Writers* [M]. New Jersey: Prentice-Hall, 1997.

Reilly, J., A. Zamora and R. F. McGivern. Acquiring perspective in English: The development of stance [J]. *Journal of Pragmatics*, 37: 185-208, 2005.

Rezzano, N. S. Modality and modal responsibility in research articles in English [A]. In R. Facchinetti *et al.* (eds.). 101-18, 2004.

Rodman, L. Anticipatory IT in scientific discourse [J]. *Journal of Technical Writing and Communication*, 21: 17-27, 1991.

Römer, U. Evaluation everywhere! An attempt to identify and classify evaluative language in a corpus of book reviews [Z]. International Conference on Evaluation and Text Types, University of Augsburg, June, 2005.

Rose, D. Pitjantjatjara processes: An Australian experiential grammar [A]. In R. Hasan *et al.* (eds.). 287-323, 1996.

Rowley-Jolivet, E. and S. Carter-Thomas. Genre awareness and rhetorical appropriacy: Manipulation of information structure by NS and NNS scientists in the international conference setting [J]. *English for Specific Purposes*, 24: 41-64, 2005.

Rumsey, A. Language, desire, and the ontogenesis of intersubjectivity [J]. *Language & Communication*, 23: 169-87, 2003.

Rundblad, G. Impersonal, general, and social: The use of metonymy versus passive voice in medical discourse [J]. *Written Communication*, 24: 250-77, 2007.

Samraj, B. An exploration of a genre set: Research article abstracts and introductions in two disciplines [J]. *English for Specific Purposes*, 24: 141-56, 2005.

Samraj, B. A discourse analysis of master's theses across disciplines with a focus on introductions [J]. *Journal of English for Academic Purposes*, 7: 55-67, 2008.

Samson, C. Interaction in written economics lectures: The meta-discursive role of person markers [A]. In K. Aijmer *et al.* (eds.). 199-216, 2004.

Sánchez-Macarro, A. and R. Carter (eds.). *Linguistic Choice across Genres:*

Variation in Spoken and Written English [C]. Amsterdam: Benjamins, 1998.

Sanders, J. and W. Spooren. Perspective, subjectivity, and modality from a cognitive linguistic point of view [A]. In W. Liebert *et al.* (eds.). 85-112, 1997.

Sapir, E. *Language: An Introduction to the Study of Speech* [M]. New York: Harcourt, Brace Jovanovich/Beijing: Foreign Languages Teaching and Research Press, 1921/2001.

Scheibman, J. Subjective and intersubjective uses of generalizations in English conversations [A]. In R. Englebretson (ed.). 111-38, 2007.

Schiffrin, D. *Discourse Marker* [M]. Cambridge: Cambridge University Press, 1987.

Schilperoord, J. and A. Verhagen. Conceptual dependency and the clausal structure of discourse [A]. In J. Koenig (ed.). 141-63, 1998.

Schröder, H. and D. Zimmer. Hedging research in pragmatics: A bibliographical research guide to hedging [A]. In R. Markkanen *et al.* (eds.). 249-72, 1997.

Scott, M. and G. Thompson (eds.). *Patterns of Text: In Honour of Michael Hoey* [C]. Amsterdam: Benjamins, 2000.

Shaw, P. How do we recognize implicit evaluation in academic book reviews? [A]. In G. D. Camiciotti *et al.* (eds.). 121-40, 2004.

Shore, S. Process types in Finnish: Implicate order, covert categories, and prototypes [A]. In R. Hasan *et al.* (eds.). 237-63, 1996.

Siepmann, D. *Discourse Markers across Languages* [M]. London: Routledge, 2005.

Silver, M. The stance of stance: A critical look at ways stance is expressed and modeled in academic discourse [J]. *Journal of English for Academic Purposes*, 2: 359-74, 2003.

Silverstein, M. and G. Urban. The natural history of discourse [A]. In M. Silverstein *et al.* (eds.). 1-17, 1996.

Silverstein, M. and G. Urban (eds.). *Natural Histories of Discourse* [C]. Chicago: The University of Chicago Press, 1996.

Simon-Vandenbergen, A. The function of *I think* in political discourse [J]. *International Journal of Applied Linguistics*, 10: 41-63, 2000.

Simon-Vandenbergen, A. , M. Taverniers and L. J. Ravelli (eds.). *Grammatical Metaphor: Views from Systemic Functional Linguistics* [C]. Amsterdam: Benjamins, 2003.

Simons, M. Observations on embedding verbs, evidentiality, and presupposition [J]. *Lingua*, 117: 1034-56, 2007.

Sinclair, J. M. *Corpus, Concordance, Collocation* [M]. Oxford: Oxfod University Press, 1991.

Sinclair, J. M. *Collins COBUILD English Language Dictionary* [Z]. London: Collins, 1995.

Skelton, J. How to tell the truth in The British Medical Journal: Patterns of judgment in the 19th and 20th centuries [A]. In R. Markkanen *et al.* (eds.). 42-63, 1997.

Speas, M. Evidentiality, logophoricity and the syntactic representation of pragmatic features [J]. *Lingua*, 114: 255-76, 2004.

Stamenov, M. I. (ed.). *Language Structure, Discourse and the Access to Consciousness* [C]. Amsterdam: Benjamins, 1997.

Stamenov, M. I. Grammar, meaning and consciousness: What sentence structure can tell us about the structure of consciousness [A]. In M. I. Stamenov (ed.). 277-342, 1997.

Stanford, J. *Guidelines for Writers: Rhetoric, Reader, Handbook* [M]. New York: Mcgraw-Hill, 1993.

Strong, W. *Writer's Choice: Grammar and Composition* [M]. New York: McGraw-Hlll, 1996.

Stubbs, M. *Discourse Analysis: The Sociolinguistic Analysis of Natural Language* [M]. Oxford: Blackwell, 1983.

Stubbs, M. A matter of prolonged fieldwork: Towards a modal grammar of English [J]. *Applied Linguistics*, 7: 1-25, 1986.

Swales, J. M. *Genre Analysis: English in Academic and Research Settings* [M]. Cambridge: Cambridge University Press, 1990.

Swales, J. M. Integrated and fragmented worlds: EAP materials and corpus linguistics [A]. In J. Flowerdew (ed.). 150-64, 2002.

Swan, T. and O. Jansen (eds.). *Modality in Germanic Languages: Historical and Comparative Perspectives* [C]. Berlin: de Gruyter, 1997.

Tang, R. and S. John. The 'I' in identity: Exploring writer identity in student academic writing through the first person pronoun [J]. *English for Specific Purposes*, 18: 23-39, 1999.

Tarverniers, M. Grammatical metaphor in SFL: A historiography of the introduction and initial study of the concept [A]. In A. Simon-Vandenbergen *et al.* (eds.). 5-33, 2003.

Tejerina, L. S. Evaluation in academic book reviews: The interplay between the ideational, the interpersonal and the textual planes of language [Z]. International Conference on Evaluation and Text Types, University of Augsburg, June, 2005.

Thetela, P. Entities and parameters in academic research articles [J]. *English for Specific Purposes*, 16: 101-18, 1997.

Thibault, P. J. Using language to think interpersonally: Experiential meaning and the cryptogrammar of subjectivity and agency in English [J]. *Language as Cultural Dynamic: Cultural Dynamics*, 6: 131-86, 1993.

Thibault, P. J. Interpersonal meaning and the discursive construction of action, attitudes and values: The global modal program of one text [A]. In P. H. Fries *et al.* (eds.). 56-116, 2002a.

Thibault, P. J. Contextualization and social meaning-making practices [A]. In S. L. Eerdmans *et al.* (eds.). 41-61, 2002b.

Thibault, P. J. *Agency and Consciousness in Discourse* [M]. London: Continuum, 2004.

Thompson, G. Acting the part: Lexico-grammatical choices and contextual factors [A]. In M. Ghadessy (ed.). 101-24, 1998.

Thompson, G. Interaction in academic writing: Learning to argue with the reader [J]. *Applied Linguistics*, 22: 58-78, 2001.

Thompson, G. The elided participant: Presenting an uncommonsense view of the researcher's role [A]. In A. Simon-Vandenbergen *et al.* (eds.). 257-78, 2003.

Thompson, G. *Introducing Functional Grammar* (2nd Ed.) [M]. London: Arnold, 2004.

Thompson, G. But me some buts: A multidimensional view of conjunction [J]. *Text*, 25: 763-91, 2005.

Thompson, G. Unfolding theme: The development of clausal and textual perspectives on theme [A]. In R. Hasan *et al.* (eds.). 671-96, 2007.

Thompson, G. and S. Hunston. Evaluation: An introduction [A]. In S. Hunston *et al.* (eds.). 1-27, 2000.

Thompson, G. and Y. Ye. Evaluation in reporting verbs used in academic papers [J]. *Applied Linguistics*, 12: 365-82, 1991.

Thompson, G. and J. Zhou. Evaluation and organization in text [A]. In S. Hunston *et al.* (eds.). 122-41, 2000.

Thompson, P. Points of focus and position: Intertextual reference in PhD theses [J]. *Journal of English for Academic Purposes*, 4: 307-23, 2005.

Thompson, S. A. "Object complements" and conversation: Towards a realistic account [J]. *Studies in Language*, 26: 125-64, 2002.

Thompson, S. A. and A. Mulac. The discourse conditions for the use of the complementizer "that" in conversational English [J]. *Journal of Pragmatics*, 15: 237-51, 1991.

Tobin, Y. (ed.). *From Sign to Text: A Semiotic View of Communication* [C]. Amsterdam: Benjamins, 1989.

Tolchinsky, L. and E. Rosado. The effect of literacy, text type, and modality on the use of grammatical means for agency alternation in Spanish [J]. *Journal of Pragmatics*, 37: 209-37, 2005.

Toolan, M. 1988. Compromising positions: Systemic linguistics and the locally managed semiotics of dialogue [A]. In D. Birth *et al.* (eds.). 249-60, 1988.

Traugott, E. C. Revisiting subjectification and intersubjectification [A]. In C. Hubert *et al.* (eds.). *Subjectification, Intersubjectification and Grammaticalization* [C]. Berlin: de Gruyter, 2010.

Tse, P. and K. Hyland. "So what is the problem this book addresses?": Interactions in academic book reviews [J]. *Text & Talk*, 26: 767-90, 2006.

van Dijk, T. A. (ed.). *Discourse as Structure and Process. Discourse Studies: A Multidisciplinary Introduction Vol.* 1 [C]. London: SAGE, 1997.

van Hell, J. G., L. Verhoeven, M. Tak, and M. van Oosterhout. To take a stance: A developmental study of the use of pronouns and passives in spoken and written narrative and expository texts in Dutch [J]. *Journal of Pragmatics*, 37: 239-73, 2005.

van Leeuwen, T. The representation of social actors [A]. In C. Caldas-Coulthard et al. (eds.). 32-70, 1996.

Vande Kopple, W. Some exploratory discourse on metadiscourse [J]. *College Composition and Communication*, 36: 82-93, 1985.

Vandelanotte, L. From representational to scopal 'distancing indirect speech or thought': A cline of subjectification [J]. *Text*, 24: 547-85, 2004.

Vassileva, I. Who am I/who are we in academic writing?: A contrastive analysis of authorial presence in English, German, French, Russian and Bulgarian [J]. *International Journal of Applied Linguistics*, 8: 163-90, 1998.

Vassileva, I. Commitment and detachment in English and Bulgarian academic writing [J]. *English for Specific Purposes*, 20: 83-102, 2001.

Ventola, E. *The Structure of Social Interaction: A Systemic Approach to the Semiotics of Service Encounters* [M]. London: Pinter, 1987.

Ventola, E. (ed.). *Functional and Systemic Linguistics: Approaches and Uses* [C]. Berlin: de Gruyter, 1991.

Vergaro, C. Discourse strategies of Italian and English sales promotion letters [J]. *English for Specific Purposes*, 23: 181-207, 2004.

Verhagen, A. *Constructions of Intersubjectivity: Discourse, Syntax, and Cognition* [M]. Oxford: Oxford University Press, 2005.

Verstraete, J. Subjective and objective modality: Interpersonal and ideational functions in the English modal auxiliary system [J]. *Journal of Pragmatics*, 33: 1505-28, 2001.

Visconti, J. From "textual" to "interpersonal": On the diachrony of the Italian particle *mica* [J]. *Journal of Pragmatics*, 41: 937-50, 2009.

Vološinov, V. N. *Marxism and the Philosophy of Language* [M]. Cambridge, MA: Harvard University Press, 2000.

Wang, Y. *A Functional Study of the Evaluative Enhanced Theme Construction in English* [M]. London: Longman, 2008.

Werth, P. Remote worlds: The conceptual representation of linguistic *would* [A]. In J. Nuyts *et al.* (eds.). 84-115, 1999a.

Werth, P. *Text Worlds: Representing Conceptual Space in Discourse* [M]. London: Longman, 1999b.

White, H. D. Citation analysis and discourse analysis revisited [J]. *Applied Linguistics*, 25: 89-116, 2004.

Whittaker, R. Theme, processes and the realization of meanings in academic articles [A]. In M. Ghadessy (ed.). 105-28, 1995.

Whorf, B. L. *Language, Thought and Reality: Selected Writings of Benjamin Lee Whorf* [C]. J. B. Caroll (ed.). Cambridge, MA: MIT Press, 1956.

Wilss, W. Hedging in expert-language reviews [A]. In R. Markkanen *et al.* (eds.). 134-50, 1997.

Yamamoto, M. *Agency and Impersonality: Their Linguistic and Cultural Manifestations* [M]. Amsterdam: Benjamins, 2006.

Yankova, D. Review of *World of Written Discourse: A Genre-based View* (Bhatia, 2004) [J]. *English for Specific Purposes*, 25: 123-29, 2006.

胡壮麟(Hu, Z. L.). 语篇的评价系统 [Z]. 第十一届中国话语分析研讨会, 厦门大学, 2008 (18-22/08).

黄国文(Huang, G. W.). 英语语言问题研究 [M]. 广州: 中山大学出版社, 1999.

黄国文(Huang, G. W.). 语篇分析的理论与实践 [M]. 上海: 上海外语教育出版社, 2001.

黄国文(Huang, G. W.), M. Ghadessy. 功能语篇分析 [M]. 上海: 上海外语教育出版社, 2006.

刘世生(Liu, S. S.). 西方文体学论纲 [M]. 济南: 山东教育出版社, 1998.

杨信彰(Yang, X. Z.). 语篇中的评价性手段 [J]. 外语与外语教学, 2003, (1): 11-14.

杨信彰(Yang, X. Z.). 英语的情态手段与语篇类型 [J]. 外语与外语教学, 2006, (1): 1-4.

杨信彰(Yang, X. Z.). 元话语与语言功能 [J]. 外语与外语教学, 2007, (12):

1-3.

张德禄(Zhang, D. L.). 语言的功能与文体 [M]. 北京：高等教育出版社,
    2005.

朱永生(Zhu, Y. S.), 严世清(Yan, S. Q.). 系统功能语言学多维思考 [M].
    上海：上海外语教育出版社, 2001.

Appendix 1

Data sources

The corpus of ELBR

Applied Linguistics 1-3
Discourse & Communication 32-34
Discourse & Society 4 6 8 9 49-55 56-58
Discourse Studies 27 79-88
English for Specific Purposes 15 31 60-68
First Language 41-45
Functions of Language 59
Human studies 23
Journal of English for Academic Purposes 10 24 25 30
Journal of English Linguistics 22
Journal of Historical Pragmatics 7
Journal of Language and Social Psychology 35-39
Journal of Pragmatics 12 17 18 28 29 47 69-78
Journal of Sociolinguistics 19-21 89-99
Language in Society 5
Lingua 14 16 46 100

Metaphor and Symbol 26
Studies in Language 40 48
System 11 13

The corpus of ELJE

Assessing Writing 14-23
Discourse & Society 83-89
Discourse Studies 91-96
English for Specific Purposes 24-33
First Language 97-100
Journal of English for Academic Purposes 34-45
Journal of Language and Social Psychology 6-8
Journal of Neurolinguistics 9-13
Journal of Pragmatics 60-82
Journal of Second Language Writing 1
Language Science 2-4
Lingua 46-59
Transactions of the American Philosophical Association 5

Appendix 2

Data samples

1 Data samples of ELBR

(1) In the same way that *I would like to* see studies of advertising discourse in general, and of multilingualism in advertising in particular, underpinned by social and economic theory, *I also feel that* some kind of moral—or critical—stance towards these practices is necessary for work in the field to be productive. For instance, in the section on Irish, the author speaks appreciatively of an Irish children's program on TV that has been able to attract advertising for global children's brands... [R19]

(2) *It seems to me that* the problem here is not so much whether implicatures may contribute to truth-evaluable content, but what exactly is focused upon as subject to evaluation in terms of truth and falsity and why. *There would be nothing odd* in considering certain implicatures of an utterance when discussing its truth or falsity, if the truth/falsity assessment were (as in Austin, 1962: 142-145) a matter of global correctness of the speech act with respect to the relevant portion of the world. And *it might not be impossible to* explain why certain alleged

implicatures contribute to determining the truth/falsity of complex sentences, in terms of the speech acts to be assessed. But if truth and falsity are the semantic values of thoughts, i.e., that which it is the whole point of a thought to determine, then of course implicatures cannot have any bearing on them. [R29]

(3) Clearly, nobody can read everything, and multimodality is, *as Baldry and Thibault acknowledge*, a discipline that is as young as it is vast. But surely *one could have reasonably expected them to* have familiarized themselves first-hand with at least some important work done by experts on other modes and media than the ones they themselves are specialists in—even if, or precisely because of the fact that, these experts do not work in a Hallidayan framework. For the reasons outlined above, *I therefore believe that* Baldry and Thibault's is not the best book to steer students across the vast ocean of multimodal discourse. [R72]

2 Data samples of ELJE

(1) On the one hand, both as outside expert and as teacher, *I am amazed that* the field can be so opaque. *I flatter myself (and you, dear readers) that* there is a kind of humility in this. On some level, *I think we are convinced that* if we understand this stuff, surely anyone else can. We simply forget how far into the forest we have walked, and how difficult a time we had finding a pathway when we started our hike. Yet *it is important that* we remember. [E21]

(2) *We hope that* this joint effort will be an important contribution to L2 writing theory and research. *We also hope that* the initiative

taken here to put FL writing in the limelight is followed by future studies and edited collections so that we start redressing the traditional SL-bias of L2 writing scholarship. [E1]

(3) *As should be evident* from these four contributions, the formal examination of bilingual code-switching is centrally implicated in the continued advancement of linguistic theory. In addition, the findings afforded by code-switching studies can offer novel insights into language representation and processing. *It is hoped that* the efforts of the authors included here will inspire readers to further pursue such endeavors. [E48]

Appendix 3

A list of some IPCs in ELBR and ELJE

ELBR

(A) *I*-IPCs

I want to, I mean to, I believe, I think, and I hope, dare I say, I am hoping, I disagree that, But I do not think, I wonder, But I doubted, I wished, I cannot see that, I suspect, I was disappointed, I regret, I felt that, I found, I wish, I would prefer to, I would like to, I would have liked to, I would have preferred to, I find, I feel, I would have expected, as I have in fact argued myself that, I figured, I should note, I suggest, I expect, I an aware that, I would say, if I say, if I propose, I am not convinced that

(B) *we*-IPCs

we can note how, we understand that, we can see how, we could wonder whether, we learn again how, we may assume that, we may say that, we could understand that, one wonders, one might expect that, one argues that, one might hope, one could say, one might have wished, one can anticipate, one must admit, some will feel that, *let's say*

(C) No-interactant IPCs

it is unclear, *it is to be hope*, *it is suggested*, *it might be argued*, *it is a pity*, *it is not*, *it would have been helpful*, *it can not be ignored*, *it emerges*, *it has frequently been found*, *it should not be forgotten*, *it is unfortunate*, *it seems unlikely*, *it is worth noting*, *what is undeniable is*, *the problem is*, *a strength of the book is*, *one point of particular interest is*, *there can be no doubt*, *there would be nothing odd*, *there is no obvious reason*

(D) Non-interactant IPCs

as she notes, *as he rightly points out*, *as the author hopes*, *as she puts it*, *as van Dijk says in the preface*, *as Foucault (1984) has said*, *as the author acknowledges*, *as Popper has taught us*, *as the author points out*, *as the author argues and clearly demonstrates*, *as post-process movement theorists argue*, *as the authors concede*, *as these comments indicate*, *as they say*, *as Carston admits*, *as MP claims*

ELJE

(A) *I*-IPCs

I assume, *I think*, *I must hope*, *I believe*, *I hope to*, *I have suggested*, *I wish*, *I would like to*, *I will here argue*, *I have to wonder*, *I can see that*, *I am amazed that*, *I have been very fortunate*

(B) *we*-IPCs

we hope, *as we know*, *we think*, *we believe*, *we propose*, *we suggest, we argue, we would like to, we are pleased to, we are fortunate to, we should remember, we could say, we expect to, we invite you to, we have been delightful to, we anticipate, we are hopeful, we are keen to, we assume, one expects, as one would hope, one is likely to find, one would like to think, one is tempted to quote, one might perhaps think, some readers seem to, all readers accept*

(C) No-interactant IPCs

it is widely acknowledged, it is hard to deny, it must be recalled, it is useful, it is not surprising, it is predicted, it seems worth stressing, it is probably the case, it is fairly clear, it has been argued, one perception is, what is particularly of note is, one hypothesis would be, the hope is, the main problem being, there is a normative expectation, there seems to, there is strong evidence, there is a general agreement, there is a growing consensus, there is no reason

(D) Non-interactant IPCs

as Schegloff (this issue) observes, as argued by Rogoff (2003), as Aristotle notes, as Candit points out, as they point out, as the authors point out, as should be evident from these four contributions, as Chomsky emphasized, as Casanave (2002) has observed, as Love (this issue) explains, as indicated by Tucker, as the authors suggest, as Mey has recently put it nicely, as Fairclough (1995) assumes, as the author says

Appendix 4

Concordance of IPCs (part) in ELBR and ELJE

ELBR

... aggressively so, *I would say.* Chapter 7, "The Joke as Gloss," is truly...

actual building (144). *I would like to* have seen this topic explored in greater depth...

... Nonetheless, *I would like to* mention two tiny shortcomings. First, in the ...

... Relationships. *I would have liked to* know more about how the author...

... of key topics. *I would have liked to* see more attention given to the kinds...

... However, *I would have preferred to* see Bhatia's definition of...

... Personally, *I would have preferred to* see more in Part I and less in Part...

... corpus compilation, *I would have expected* the compilers to discuss the...

... general conclusion, *I would like to* comment on the general organization of...

... rather wisely *I would say*—to find a solution, but adheres to a consistent...

ELJE

... Fantasy. *We would like to* argue that such familiarity is conductive not only...

... *We would like to* thank the external referee for his insightful comments...

... and *we would like to* think that they also point to solutions (consider the...

... *We would like to* thank those who reviewed so professional papers...

... Finally, *we would like to* welcome our newly added Editorial board member...

... *We would like to* end this introduction by thanking those who made...

... *We would like to* announce a forthcoming special issue of the journal...

... and *we would like to* draw the reader's attention to the extent to which the...

... *We would like to* finish with a word of gratitude. Naturally, we first...

... *We would also like to* take this opportunity to thank the many additional...